CASES IN COLLECTIVE BARGAINING
AND INDUSTRIAL RELATIONS:
A DECISIONAL APPROACH

Cases in
Collective Bargaining
and
Industrial Relations

A Decisional Approach

STERLING H. SCHOEN, Ph.D.
Professor of Management

RAYMOND L. HILGERT, D.B.A.
Professor of Management

Both of the Graduate School of Business Administration
Washington University, St. Louis, Missouri

1974 • REVISED EDITION
RICHARD D. IRWIN, INC. Homewood, Illinois 60430
IRWIN-DORSEY INTERNATIONAL London, England WC2H 9NJ
IRWIN-DORSEY LIMITED Georgetown, Ontario L7G 4B3

Revised Edition

First Printing, January 1974

ISBN 0-256-01516-3
Library of Congress Catalog Card No. 73–85665

Printed in the United States of America

Preface

In this new edition, the authors provide a convenient but relatively extensive set of cases in a variety of union-management problem situations that can be used as a supplementary book in basic courses in collective bargaining and labor relations. The collection of cases is of sufficient magnitude that the book also would be suitable for advanced courses or case courses in the field of industrial relations and collective bargaining.

A major objective is to provide a means by which students may apply the principles and concepts that they have learned to realistic decision situations and confrontations between labor and management. We have used the cases in our classes, and found them challenging and fascinating learning instruments.

The cases represent the types of problems that students are most likely to encounter as managers in situations involving labor unions. They test analytical ability in dealing with complex human relations and union-management situations in a way useful even for students who do not have a management career in mind.

In order to reflect the impact of recent trends and issues, we have collected representative cases dealing with various problems that include current contemporary issues. Of the 57 cases in this revised edition, 29 (or about 50 percent) are new to this collection. We have retained 28 cases from the first edition in order to provide continuity and balance and because these cases are "timeless" in evaluation of union-management confrontations.

The first section of the book is a collection of actual cases heard by the National Labor Relations Board, and restructured from published reports of NLRB and court decisions. Our intent has been to describe the situation from the perspective of impartial writers trying to get at the facts of the case. In order to highlight significant problem areas, the case format has been developed as follows: (a) the background information of the case is first presented, including relevant legal issues involved; (b) the position of the union is stated; and (c) the position of the management or company is stated. A brief discussion of and excerpts from the Labor-Management Relations Act of 1947 (as amended) are included at the outset of this section to enable students to recognize which provisions of the act are at issue in the various case situations.

We believe that the area of legal responsibilities of unions and management as outlined by the Labor-Management Relations Act continues to be one of the most dynamic and important areas confronting collective bargaining today. Although the student may not come to understand all of the provisions and applications of the act, case studies such as are provided in the first section will enable the student to appreciate the nature of this act, its application in numerous union-management situations and, most importantly, the duties and obligations of management and union representatives to bargain in good faith.

The second section of this book consists of cases adapted from labor arbitration decisions. We are grateful to the Bureau of National Affairs, Inc., Mr. John D. Stewart, president, for permission to adapt certain published cases from *Labor Arbitration Reports.* Here, too, the approach has been to restructure actual arbitration cases in a convenient format for the use of the student of industrial relations. The approach has been to restate the highlights and relevant issues of each case by first providing relevant background information, after which the principal arguments of both the union and management sides are presented. Cases in this section represent some of the most controversial areas of labor relations, which are part of the day-to-day relationships between companies and unions.

For both the NLRB and labor arbitration cases—which have not been selected with any intent of presenting "good" or "bad" or "right" or "wrong" union-management practices—the student should ask: "What are the problems or principal issues?" "What is at stake between the parties?" "What is justice or equity in the situation?" "What does the law require?" "What does the contract say on the issue at stake?" "How have previous NLRB decisions or previous labor arbitration decisions handled similar circumstances?" These types of questions urge students toward a depth analysis of issues. Decisions of the NLRB and labor arbitrators for these cases have been included in the Instructor's Manual. It has been the experience of the authors that students usually like to compare their decisions and approaches with those of authorities in the field.

Index and classification tables are included in each section of the book prior to the case materials. These tables briefly cite the major issues in each case, and for the NLRB cases the legal provisions involved are indicated. Brief introductory text material is included in order to introduce the student to the major provisions and applications of the Labor-Management Relations Act and to the principal considerations involved in grievance and arbitration procedures. Selected bibliographies are also provided for more detailed reading in these areas.

Finally, we acknowledge, with many thanks, the cooperation of Dean Karl Hill of the Graduate School of Business Administration of Washington University in helping us to develop our manuscript and providing us with the services of Mrs. Ruth Scheetz of the Washington University staff, who typed the manuscript and who endured patiently changes, corrections, and delays.

December 1973

Sterling H. Schoen
Raymond L. Hilgert

Table of Contents

PART II. Problems in Union-Management Relations:
Cases from Labor Arbitration

CASES

Part I

Legal Aspects of Collective Bargaining

NATIONAL LABOR RELATIONS BOARD CASES

Introduction to the Labor–Management Relations Act

Partial Text of the Labor–Management Relations Act

Index to Cases for Part I

THE CASES

Introduction to
THE LABOR-MANAGEMENT RELATIONS
ACT (LMRA)

This introductory section will briefly introduce the principal provisions of the Labor-Management Relations Act of 1947 as amended. A partial text of this act follows this introductory section. For even more analytical understanding of the provisions of the act and its applications, a selected bibliography for reading is included at the end of this introductory section. It also is recommended for the student of collective bargaining and industrial relations to contact a regional or national office of the National Labor Relations Board to obtain various NLRB publications which explain detailed principles and procedures involved in administration of the law. For example, a publication included in the bibliography entitled, "A Layman's Guide to Basic Law Under the National Labor Relations Act," is prepared by the Office of the General Counsel of the NLRB; this booklet is very helpful in understanding many of the day-to-day activities of the Board and some of its most recent thinking.

The Labor-Management Relations Act of 1947, also known as the Taft-Hartley Act in recognition of the principal congressional authors of the law, is the principal labor legislation governing the "rules of the game" of collective bargaining in the United States.[1] The LMRA of 1947 constituted a major amendment and revision of the National Labor Relations (Wagner) Act of 1935. The act since has been amended several times (1951, 1958, 1959), although these later amendments have been rather minor in nature. As it stands today, the act is the fundamental legislative basis for the majority of

---

[1] The Railway Labor Act of 1926 (as amended) governs collective bargaining in the rail and airline industries. Although the Railway Labor Act is not widely applicable and some of its provisions are considerably different than those in LMRA, its premises and procedures were drawn upon by the framers of the National Labor Relations (Wagner) Act of 1935, upon which the act of 1947 subsequently was based. The student is encouraged to study the provisions of the Railway Labor Act, as well as a history of labor laws in the railroad industries, which led to the passage of the Railway Labor Act of 1926.

union-management relationships in the United States.[2] The Labor-Management Relations Act is an extremely complex document in and of itself. Of even greater complexity, however, is the body of administrative laws and decisions which has evolved over the years of its existence in hundreds of thousands of union-management case situations. The act is constantly being tested, evaluated, and reevaluated by the NLRB, the courts, and even by the Congress of the United States, in the light of changing times, new confrontations, and new decisions. It is not the purpose of this section to completely interpret the act nor to present it in its entirety. Rather, selected parts of the act will be discussed to underscore the major elements of the act governing the collective bargaining process. An understanding of these parts of the act should provide sufficient insights on which various aspects of specific union-management cases may be analyzed.

EXCERPTS AND COMMENTS ON THE TEXT OF THE LABOR-MANAGEMENT RELATIONS ACT, 1947, AS AMENDED

Section 1. The Statement of Findings and Policy

The Labor-Management Relations Act begins with a statement to the effect that industrial strife interferes with the normal flow of commerce. The purpose of the act is to promote the full flow of commerce by prescribing and protecting rights of employers and employees and by providing orderly and peaceful procedures for preventing interference by either with the legitimate rights of the other.

Also included in this statement of public policy is that the labor

---

[2] One of the major new developments in labor relations has been at the federal government employee level. Executive Order 10988 originally signed by President Kennedy in 1962 was replaced by Executive Order 11491 issued by President Nixon in 1970. These orders have provided for federal employees union representation and collective bargaining rights. Executive Order 11491 closely parallels the LMRA in many fundamental areas, with most of its provisions strikingly similar to various provisions in LMRA governing union-management relations in the private sector. Of course, federal government employees do not have the right to strike, and a number of key areas remain outside of the scope of bargaining in the federal sector. For example, wages, and certain working conditions are set by Congress, and a number of areas of employee concern are handled under Civil Service regulations. Nevertheless, Executive Order 11491 is a major development in collective bargaining in the United States. The authors have chosen not to include any cases from the federal sector in this part of the text. However, numerous cases have been decided under Executive Order 11491 which have drawn heavily for precedent and policy from decisions of the National Labor Relations Board in the private sector. Included in the bibliography at the end of this introductory section are a number of sources to consult for public sector bargaining law, cases and decisions.

law of the land is designed to regulate both unions and employers in the public interest. The act encourages the right of employees to organize labor unions and to bargain collectively with their employers as a means of balancing bargaining power. At the same time, the act encourages union and employer practices which are fundamental to the friendly adjustment of industrial disputes, with the objective of eliminating some union and employer practices which impair the public interest by contributing to industrial unrest and strikes.

The National Labor Relations Board, which is the federal agency administering the act, has consistently interpreted this section to mean that the public policy of the United States is to promote and encourage the principle of unionism.

Section 2. Definitions

This section of the act defines various terms used in the course of the act, and also outlines the coverage of the act. By its terms, the act does not apply to employees in a business or industry where a labor dispute would not affect interstate commerce. In addition, the act specifically states that it does not apply to the following:

Agricultural laborers, as defined by the Fair Labor Standards Act (Wage-Hour Law).

Domestic servants.

Any individual employed by his parent or spouse.

Government employees, including those of government corporations or the Federal Reserve Bank, or any political subdivision such as a state or school district.

Employees of hospitals operated entirely on a nonprofit basis.

Independent contractors who depend upon profits, rather than commissions or wages, for their income.

A later section (212) also exempts employees and employers who are subject to provisions of the Railway Labor Act.

Supervisors are excluded from the definition of employees covered by the act. Whether or not a person is a supervisor is determined by his authority rather than his title. The authority required to exclude an employee from coverage of the act as a supervisor is defined in Section 2 (11) of the act.

An *employer* is defined in the law as including "any person acting as an agent of employer, directly or indirectly."

The term *"labor organization"* means any organization, agency, or employee representation committee or plan in which employees participate and which exists for the purpose, in whole or in part, of dealing with employers concerning grievances, labor disputes, wages, rate of pay, hours of employment, or conditions of work.

Section 2 (12) defines the meaning of the term "professional employee" for which specific organizational rights are guaranteed in a later section.

Sections 3, 4, 5, 6. The National Labor Relations Board

Section 3 creates the National Labor Relations Board as an independent agency to administer the act. The NLRB consists of five members appointed by the President of the United States.

Section 3 also authorizes the appointment of a General Counsel of the Board, who is given supervisory authority over the Board attorneys and officers and employees in the regional offices of the Board.

Sections 4 and 5 outline certain procedural and administrative authorities granted to the NLRB by the Congress.

However, the key section is Section 6, which gives the Board authority to establish rules an regulations necessary to carry out provisions of the Labor-Management Relations Act. *In effect, this section empowers the National Labor Relations Board to administer and interpret the labor law in whatever manner it deems appropriate to the situations encountered.*

In order to do this, the Board has developed various standards—for the most part, dollar sales or volume standards—by which it determines whether or not a business enterprise is deemed to be in interstate commerce and thus covered under the provisions of the act.[3] The Board has developed detailed rules, policies, and procedures by which it determines appropriate collective bargaining units, holds representational elections, investigates labor disputes, and other such matters. *The National Labor Relations Board by its policies and rulings in effect can and does reshape the act, subject only to review of the federal courts.*

---

[3] For example, the NLRB as of 1973 used a standard of $500,000 total annual volume of business to determine if a retail enterprise was considered interstate. For non-retail businesses the Board uses two tests: (a) direct sales to consumers in other states or indirect sales through others called outflow of at least $50,000 a year; or direct purchases of goods from suppliers from other states or indirect purchases through others called inflow of at least $50,000 a year. In the most recent years, the Board has extended its jurisdiction to include nursing homes operated for profit where the test is $100,000 annual volume, and to private non-profit universities and colleges who have at least $1,000,000 gross annual revenue from all sources. The NLRB has developed numerous other standards depending upon types of business and various conditions involved in developing its jurisdictional standards.

Section 7. Rights of Employees

This section is perhaps one of the most significant in the act. It guarantees employees the right to self-organization; to form, join, or assist labor organizations; to bargain collectively through representatives of their own choosing; and to engage in (or refrain from) certain other concerted activities for the purpose of collective bargaining or other mutual aid or protection.

Examples of employee rights protected by Section 7 are:

Forming or attempting to form a union among the employees of a company.
Joining a union.
Assisting a union to organize the employees of any company.
Going out on strike for the purpose of attempting to obtain improved wages, hours, or other conditions of employment.
Refraining from joining a union in the absence of a valid union shop agreement.

UNFAIR LABOR PRACTICES: EMPLOYERS

Employers are forbidden from engaging in the following types of unfair labor practices:

Section 8 (a) (1). To interfere with, restrain, or coerce employees in the exercise of rights guaranteed by Section 7;

Section 8 (a) (2). To dominate or interfere with the formation or administration of any labor organization or contribute financial or other support to it.

In this regard, the Board distinguishes between "domination" of a labor organization and conduct which amounts to little more than illegal "interference." When a union is found to be "dominated" by an employer, the Board will normally order the organization completely disestablished as a representative of employees. But if the organization is found only to have been supported by employer assistance amounting to less than domination, the Board usually orders the employer to stop such support and to withhold recognition from the organization until it has been certified by the Board as a bona fide representative of employees.

Section 8 (a) (1) constitutes a broad statement against interference by the employer; an employer violates this section whenever he commits any of the unfair labor practices. Thus, a violation of Section 8 (a) (2), (3), (4), or (5) also results in a violation of Section 8 (a) (1).

Various acts of an employer may independently violate Section 8 (a) (1). Examples of such violations are:

Spying on union meetings, or on the activities of the union organizer.

Threatening to terminate credit at the company store or to force employees to move out of company housing if the union wins bargaining rights for employees.

Circulating antiunion petitions among employees.

Improving wages or other conditions of employment deliberately timed to undercut the union's organizing campaign.

Threatening to move the plant out of town or to close it if the union wins bargaining rights in the plant.

An employer violates Section 8 (a) (2) by engaging in activities such as:

Assisting employees in organizing a union or an employee representation plan by providing financial support, legal counsel, or active encouragement.

Conducting a "straw vote" to determine whether employees favor an inside union, as opposed to one affiliated with one of the national unions.

Signing a union security contract with an inside union to forestall an organizing drive by an outside union.

Exerting pressure on employees to join a particular union.

Permitting a union to solicit dues checkoff authorizations from new employees as they go through the hiring process.

Permitting officers of one union to leave their machines to solicit union members while denying officers of a competing union these same privileges.

Section 8 (a) (3). This section prohibits discrimination in hiring or tenure of employment or any term or condition of employment which tends to encourage or discourage membership in any labor organization. This provisions, together with Section 8 (b) (2), prohibits the "closed shop," in which only persons who already hold membership in a labor organization may be hired. It also prohibits discriminatory hiring hall arrangements by which only persons who have "permits" from a union may be hired. However, a proviso of this section permits an employer and labor union to agree to a union shop where employees may be required to join a union after 30 days of employment. Some examples of types of discrimination in employment prohibited by this section would include:

Discharging or demoting an employee because he urged his fellow employees to join or organize a union.

Refusing to reinstate an employee (when a job for which he can qualify is open) because he took part in a lawful strike of a union.

Refusing to hire a qualified applicant for a job because he belongs to a union.

Refusing to hire a qualified applicant for a job because he does not belong to a union or because he belongs to one union rather than to another union.

Section 8 (a) (4). Employers may not discharge or otherwise discriminate against an employee because he has filed charges or given testimony under this act. An example of a violation of this section is:

Discharging or demoting an employee because he testified before the NLRB.

Section 8 (a) (5). It is an unfair labor practice for an employer to refuse to bargain collectively with the representatives of the employees. The meaning of "bargaining collectively" is more specifically outlined in Section 8 (d) of the act. Section 8 (d) has been interpreted in many ways, and it might be considered as the cornerstone for the basic philosophy of the act.

Examples of employer violations of this section are as follows:

Refusing to meet with representatives of a certified union because employees have threatened to go out on strike.

Insisting that the union withdraw its demand for a union shop before the company would enter negotiations over a contract.

Insisting that members of the negotiating committee of the union be composed of employees of the company.

Refusing to discuss an increase in the price of coffee served in the company cafeteria.

Granting a wage increase without consulting the certified union.

Refusing to supply the union negotiators with information concerning the incentive system.

UNFAIR LABOR PRACTICES: LABOR ORGANIZATIONS

The 1947 and 1959 amendments to the act made certain activities of labor unions unfair labor practices.

Section 8 (b) (1) forbids any activity on the part of a labor organization which tends "to restrain or coerce employees in the exercise of the rights guaranteed in Section 7." This includes activities such as the following:

Trailing or waylaying nonstrikers.

Mass picketing in such numbers that nonstrikers are unable to enter or leave the plant.

Threatening nonstrikers with bodily injury, or with loss of their jobs.

Committing or threatening acts of violence against nonstrikers on a picket line.

This section also prohibits a union from restraining or coercing an employer in his selection of a bargaining representative. For example, a union may not:

Demand that the employer hire only supervisors who are members of the union and give them power to negotiate grievances.

Insist that the employer include or exclude certain persons from his negotiating committee.

Section 8 (b) (2).   The only way by which a union may cause an employer to "discriminate" against a union member (or nonunion member) is if such person has failed to "tender" periodic dues and initiation fees uniformly required as a condition of acquiring or retaining membership in the union, where a union shop agreement is in effect.

Section 8 (b) (2) bars a union from causing or attempting to cause an employer to discriminate against an employee in violation of Section 8 (a) (3). It also prohibits the union from attempting to cause an employer to discriminate against an employee to whom the union has denied or terminated membership, except where this action was taken by the union because the employee failed to "tender" the regular initiation fees and/or periodic dues. Examples of violations of this section are:

In the absence of a union security clause, demanding that the employer discharge an employee who is not a member of the union.

Demanding that the employer discharge an employee who was expelled from the union after refusing to pay a fine levied upon him for failure to attend union meetings.

Insisting upon a contractual clause which requires the employer to employ only members of the union or employees "satisfactory" to the union.

Section 8 (b) (3).   A union may not refuse to bargain collectively in good faith with an employer, if the union is the duly authorized representative of the bargaining group. Examples of violations of this section are as follows:

Demanding that the company post a performance bond as a condition for bargaining.

Striking against an employer who has bargained, and who continues to bargain, on a multiemployer basis in an effort to force him to bargain separately.

Insisting upon the inclusion of an illegal clause, such as a "hot cargo" clause, in the contract.

Section 8 (b) (4).   This section forbids secondary boycotts and certain types of strikes and picketing; it is an extremely complicated section. Secondary boycotts; sympathy strikes or boycotts to force recognition of an uncertified union; a strike to substitute another bargaining representative for cne certified by the Board; strikes over so-called union jurisdictional disputes or work assignment disputes; and several other types of unfair acts—all are forbidden under this section. One proviso in Section 8 (b) (4) (D) permits informational picketing in various circumstances, so long as such publicity and informational picketing do not have the effect of inducing any individual employed by any person other than a primary employer to refuse to pick up, deliver or transfer goods or not to perform services at the establishment of the employer involved in the dispute.

The following union activities are considered to be unfair labor practices under this section:

Picketing a company after three of its four partners refused to comply with the union's demand that they become members [8 (b) (4) (A)].

Insisting that where final court action requires employees to handle goods at premises involved in a labor dispute, the employer must pay triple wages for the day or the entire tour of duty [8 (b) (4) (A)].

Picketing the premises of an employer to compel him to cease doing business with another employer who has refused to recognize the union [8 (b) (4) (B)].

Threatening an employer by telling him that his business will be picketed if he continues to do business with another employer whom the union has designated as "unfair" [8 (b) (4) (B)].

A union's directing its members not to pick up and deliver products from a plant where the drivers had voted to be represented by a different union which had received certification from the NLRB [8 (b) (4) (C)].

A union's engaging in a strike to attempt to force the employer to assign to it the job of installing metal doors, when the employer had assigned the work to the members of another union [8 (b) (4) (D)].

Section 8 (b) (5). A union may not require employees under a union shop agreement to pay an initiation fee which the Board finds excessive or discriminatory. The section states that the Board shall consider in determination of these types of fees the practices and customs of labor organizations in the particular industry and the wages currently paid to employees affected.

For example, a union violated this section when it took the following action with respect to its initiation fees:

A union raised its initiation fee from $50 to $500 when other locals of the same union charged from $10 to $200 and the starting rate for the job was $90 per week.

Section 8 (b) (6). This section prohibits what is commonly known as "featherbedding." Unions may not force an employer to pay or deliver or to agree to pay or deliver, any money or thing of value for services which are not performed or not to be performed. This section has been narrowly interpreted by the Board and does not include situations in which the work is performed, although it may be "unnecessary."

Section 8 (b) (7) is a complex provision prohibiting a union which has not been certified as the bargaining agent from picketing or threatening to picket an employer for the purpose of obtaining recognition by that employer or acceptance by his workers as their bargaining representative. Both recognitional and organizational picketing constitute unfair labor practices when: (*a*) the employer has recognized a certified union and a new representation election would be barred under the act; (*b*) an NLRB election has been conducted during the previous 12 months; or (*c*) a representation petition has not been filed with the Board "within a reasonable period of time not to exceed thirty days from the commencement of such picketing."

However, this section does not prohibit picketing for the purpose of truthfully advising the public (including consumers) that the company does not employ union members, nor have a contract with a union, unless the effect of the picketing is to interfere with deliveries, pickups, and other services required by the picketed employer.

Section 8 (e). This complicated provision forbids both labor organizations and employers to enter into agreements commonly known as "hot cargo" agreements. These are defined as agreements where the employer will not handle, use, sell, transport, or deal in any of the products of another employer as required or forced by the labor organization.

The act excepts both the construction and garment industries from the conditions of this section. In the construction industry the parties may agree to a clause which restricts the contracting or subcontracting of work to be performed at the construction site. Typically, the union and the employer agree that subcontracted work will go to an employer who has a contract with the union. A union may strike, picket, or engage in any other lawful activity in order to obtain such an agreement with the employer. A labor organization in the garment industry may not only strike, picket, or engage in other lawful activity to obtain such an agreement, but it may also engage in such activities in order to enforce it.

Section 8 (f) provides that a union and employer in the construction industry may enter into an agreement whereby employees must join the union not later than 7 days after the date of hire, rather than 30 days, as provided in Section 8 (a) (3) for all other employers. The parties may enter into such an agreement without having first established the majority status of the union, as required in Section 9.

FREE SPEECH

Section 8 (c) of the act provides that the expression of any views, argument, or opinion shall not constitute or be evidence of an unfair labor practice "if such expression contains no threat of reprisal or force or promise of benefit." Examples of situations which this provision does not protect, and which would be ruled as unfair labor practices, are:

Where an employer has made an implied threat that the organization of a union would result in the loss of certain benefits for employees.

If an employer would threaten to close down a plant to move to another location, in the event of a union's winning an election.

A statement by a management official to an employee that the employee will lose his job if the union wins a majority in the plant.

THE MEANING OF COLLECTIVE BARGAINING

Section 8 (d) defines the meaning of collective bargaining as required from both parties by the act. This definition imposes a mutual obligation upon the employer and the representative of the employees "to meet at reasonable times and confer in good faith with respect to wages, hours, and other terms and conditions of employment or the negotiation of an agreement or any question arising thereunder and the execution of a written contract incorporating any agreement reached if requested by either party, but such obligation does not compel either party to agree to a proposal or require the making of a concession."

Section 8 (d) also requires that the parties to a collective agreement follow certain steps in terminating or modifying the agreement. The NLRB has interpreted this section to mean that employees who go on strike without following the prescribed steps for terminating or modifying the contract lose the protection of the law. They may not appeal to the Board if the employer disciplines or discharges them.

REPRESENTATIVES AND ELECTIONS

Section 9 of the act is a lengthy section which governs the procedural and legal requirements for the designation of representatives and election of union representatives.

Section 9 (a) provides that the union representative designated by a majority of employees appropriate for collective bargaining becomes the exclusive representative of the employees in bargaining.

When a union majority representative has been chosen, it becomes illegal for an employer to bargain with anyone else. This section of the act provides three types of elections among employees:[4]

1. *Representation elections* to determine the employees' choice of a collective bargaining agent. These are held upon petition of an employer, employees, or a labor organization. Typically the NLRB will not hold an election unless the labor organization can show that at least 30 percent of the employees involved have indicated their support for the union.

2. *Decertification elections* to determine whether or not the employees wish to withdraw the bargaining authority of the union. These, too, are held upon the petition of the employees of the labor organization.

3. *Deauthorization polls* to determine whether or not the employees wish to revoke the authority of their union to enter into a union shop contract.

Section 9 (b) outlines in general terms the rules of the game for holding of NLRB elections. Included in the section is the designation for the Board to determine what group of employees constitutes an appropriate unit for bargaining. The appropriate bargaining unit may extend to one or more employers, to one or more plants of the same employer, or it may be a subdivision of a plantwide unit such as a unit of skilled craftsmen. It is up to the Board to consider similarities of skills, wages, working conditions; the history of collective bargaining in the company; the wishes of the employees; and any other factors which the Board may consider important in determination of the appropriate unit. In short, employees who possess common employment interests concerning wages, hours, and conditions of employment usually are grouped together in a bargaining unit.

The act specifically limits the Board in its determination of a bargaining unit in several ways. It may not include professional and nonprofessional employees in the same unit, unless a majority of the professional employees votes to be included in the unit. It also prohibits the Board from including plant guards in the same unit with other employees, and from certifying a union of guards if it also includes members who are not guards. The Board also may not use "the extent to which employees have organized" as the controlling factor in deciding the appropriate bargain unit.

---

[4] The Board also conducts "expedited elections" in connection with Section 8 (b) (7) (C) and employer last-offer election in connection with Section 209 of the act.

Thus, Section 9 is one of the key sections which constantly confronts both unions and management in collective bargaining relationships, particularly in the formulative stages of a labor union in a company or plant.

PREVENTION OF UNFAIR LABOR PRACTICES

Section 10 is very important in that it outlines the procedural requirements and limitations which are placed upon the Board and interested parties in processing unfair labor practice cases. The Labor-Management Relations Act is not a criminal statute. The NLRB's actions are designed to stop unfair labor practices and to restore situations to their "original states" which prevailed before the violations occurred, insofar as possible. The orders of the Board serve basically to remedy the situation, not to punish persons who may have violated its provisions.

Sections 10 (a), 10 (b), 10 (c), and 10 (d) of the act outline the general procedures by which the National Labor Relations Board and its regional offices investigate, attempt to prevent, and/or remedy unfair labor practices. Generally, a complaint of an unfair labor practice must be filed with a office of the NLRB within six months of the date of the occurrence of the alleged unfair labor practice. As of 1973, some 42 regional and other field offices of the NLRB were located in major cities in various sections of the country. When a complaint is received in the office of the Board, an agent (*formerly called a trial examiner but more recently designated as an administrative law judge*) typically will investigate the validity of the complaint. If the complaint warrants a full hearing, the administrative law judge will conduct such a hearing to take testimony and examine the evidence. If the opinion of the administrative law judge representing the Board is that the evidence presented is not sufficient to justify a finding that an unfair labor practice has been committed, the office of the Board will issue an order dismissing the complaint. However, if the administrative law judge is of the opinion that an unfair labor practice(s) has occurred, he will make an appropriate recommendation and the Board, through its office, will issue an order accordingly. This order usually will require the person, union or company involved to cease and desist from the unfair labor practice(s) and to take affirmative action designed to remedy the effects of the unfair labor practice(s). Since the Labor-Management Relations Act is not aimed at designating criminal penalties, these orders will be designed to restore equity to the situation on the assumption that such equity is necessary to guarantee rights protected under the act. Examples of affirmative actions required of employers are:

Disestablish a union dominated by the employer.

Reopen a plant closed in a attempt to thwart the employees' attempts at self-organization.

Offer to hire employees denied employment because of their prounion attitudes or activities.

Offer to reemploy workers who were discharged for union activity; reimburse the employees for all lost wages, including interest; restore full seniority and all other rights, including promotions, pay increases, pension privileges, and vacation rights, that would have been received had the discriminatory discharges not occurred.

Examples of affirmative actions required of unions are:

Notification to the employee and the employer that the union does not object to the reinstatement or employment of certain persons who were discharged or denied employment as a result of certain discriminatory actions by the union.

Order the union to refund dues and fees illegally collected, including interest.

Sign an agreement which had been negotiated with employer.

Sections 10 (e) and 10 (f) provide the machinery for the legal enforcement of Board orders and for appeal for relief from Board orders by an employer or union who believes that an order has been issued in error. Normally, the first appeal from an order of the administrative law judge and the regional office of the Board will go to the full five-member NLRB itself in Washington, D.C. Further appeal, if any, can take the route of the federal judicial system, that is, to a federal district court, next to a federal appeals court, and ultimately to the United States Supreme Court. The large majority of cases, however, are not appealed to the federal courts, but are decided at Board regional office and/or national NLRB levels.

Section 10 (j) provides for special injunction procedures designed to stop quickly certain union strikes and boycotts which may result in "irreparable harm" to the employer.

Section 10 (k) provides for special procedures for hearing and adjudicating jurisdictional disputes.

MISCELLANEOUS PROVISIONS

The remainder of the Labor-Management Relations Act, although quite extensive in length, is not nearly so important to the duty to bargain collectively as are the provisions discussed to this point. Only brief mention will be made of the more salient miscellaneous provisions covered in the remaining sections.

Sections 11 and 12—Investigatory Powers and Penalties. As the name suggests, Section 11 outlines the legal powers of investigation given the NLRB by the Congress. Section 12 provides for penalties under the act.

Sections 13 to 18—Limitations.   Sections 13 through 18 state a series of limitations which the act is not to be construed as interfering with or diminishing in any way. Section 13 guarantees that the right to strike is still a right not limited by the Labor-Management Relations Act. Section 14 (a) permits supervisors to be members of a labor organization, but states that employers are not required to bargain with supervisors as part of labor organizations. Section 14 (b) permits so-called right-to-work laws in states where these laws are enacted. Specifically, Section 14 (b) allows states to ban union shop contracts if they so choose. (As of 1973, 19 states had right-to-work laws on their statute books. Organized labor is seeking to have Section 14 (b) repealed, which in effect would make these state laws banning the union shop illegal.)

Sections 201 through 205 create and outline the functions of the Federal Mediation and Conciliation Service and create a National Labor Relations Panel to advise the President on problems of industrial relations. The National Labor Relations Panel, consisting of representatives of management, labor, and the public, has not been active in recent years.

Sections 206 through 210 outline the National Emergency Strike provisions, giving the President power to intervene in those types of disputes which he deems to be national emergencies.

Section 301 provides that suits for violation of contracts between an employer and a union may be brought into the federal district courts. Unions are made responsible for the acts of their agents; however, money judgments assessed against a labor organization in a district court are only enforceable against the organization as an entity and not against individual members per se.

Section 303 makes strikes and boycotts enumerated in Section 8 (b) (4) illegal, as well as their being unfair labor practices. Employers may sue to collect damages for injury resulting from such strikes.

SUMMARY

The remaining provisions of the act are minor in nature but should be studied by the student of industrial relations. Certainly, the complexity of the Labor-Management Relations Act is one which the student recognizes from both study and application in case situations. Only by extensive analysis of labor-management cases can the student come to understand and appreciate the intent and effectiveness of the act and its purpose to govern the duty to bargain collectively.

SELECTED BIBLIOGRAPHY

A Layman's Guide to Basic Law Under the National Labor Relations Act. Washington, D.C.: Office of the General Counsel of the NLRB, U.S. Govt. Printing Office, 1971.

Abner, Willoughby. "The FMCS and Dispute Mediation in the Federal Government," *Monthly Labor Review* (May 1969), 27–29.

Barbash, Jack. *American Unions: Structure, Government and Politics.* New York: Random House, 1967.

Beal, Edwin F., Edward D. Wickersham, and Philip Kienast. *The Practice of Collective Bargaining.* 4th ed., Homewood, Ill.: Richard D. Irwin, Inc., 1972.

Bloom, Gordon F. and Herbert R. Northrup. *Economics of Labor Relations.* 7th ed., Homewood, Ill.: Richard D. Irwin, Inc., 1973.

Bok, Derek C. and John T. Dunlop. *Labor and the American Community.* New York: Simon and Schuster, 1970.

Chamberlain, Neil W. and James W. Kuhn. *Collective Bargaining.* 2d ed., New York: McGraw-Hill, 1965.

Chamberlain, Neil W. and John Dunlop. (eds.) *Frontiers of Collective Bargaining.* New York: Harper and Row, 1967.

Cohen, Sanford. *Labor Law.* Columbus, Ohio: Charles E. Merrill Publishing Co., 1964.

Cohen, Sanford. *Labor in the United States.* 3d ed., Columbus, Ohio: Charles E. Merrill Publishing Co., 1970.

Cullen, Donald E. *Negotiating Labor-Management Contracts* (Bulletin # 56). Ithaca, N.Y.: New York State School of Industrial and Labor Relations at Cornell University, 1970.

Falcone, Nicholas S. *Labor Law.* New York: John Wiley & Sons, Inc., 1962.

Fritz, Richard J. *Management Electioneering Guide.* Detroit, Michigan: Management Labor Relations Service, Inc., 1969.

Major Labor-Law Principles Established by the NLRB and the Courts (December 1964–February 1971). Washington D.C.: The Bureau of National Affairs, Inc., 1971.

Mansour, M. A. *The Legal Rights of Federal Employees to Unionize, Bargain Collectively, and Strike.* University Microfilms, Inc., 1970.

McGuinsess, Kenneth C. *Silverberg's How to Take a Case Before the National Labor Relations Board.* 3d ed., Washington, D.C.: The Bureau of National Affairs, 1967.

Millis, Harry A., and Emily Clark Brown. *From the Wagner Act to Taft-Hartley: A Study of National Labor Policy and Labor Relations.* Chicago: University of Chicago Press, 1950.

Morris, Charles (ed.). *The Developing Labor Law.* Washington, D.C.: The Bureau of National Affairs, 1971.

Neufeld, Maurice F. *A Representative Bibliography of American Labor History.* Ithaca, N.Y.: New York State School of Industrial and Labor Relations, Cornell University, 1964.

Powell, Lyman B. *How to Handle a Union Organizing Drive: A Supervisor's Handbook.* Los Angeles: Libby's Lithograph Company, 1968.

Randle, C. Wilson and Max S. Wortman. *Collective Bargaining: Principles and Practices.* 2d ed., Boston: Houghton Mifflin Co., 1966.

Schlossberg, Stephen I. *Organizing and the Law.* Washington, D.C.: The Bureau of National Affairs, 1967.

Seidman, Joel. *Democracy in the Labor Movement.* 2d ed., Ithaca, N.Y.: New York State School of Industrial and Labor Relations, Cornell University, ILR Bulletin #39, 1969.

Selekman, Benjamin M., et al. *Problems in Labor Relations.* 3d ed., New York: McGraw-Hill Book Company, 1964.

Simkin, William E. *Mediation and the Dynamics of Collective Bargaining.* Washington, D.C.: The Bureau of National Affairs, 1971.

Sloane, Arthur A., and Fred Witney. *Labor Relations.* 2d ed., Englewood Cliffs, N.J.: Prentice-Hall, 1972.

Stern, James L. "Alternative Dispute Settlement Procedures," *Wisconsin Law Review,* 1968, pp. 1100-1112.

The Labor Board and the Collective Bargaining Process. Washington D.C.: The Bureau of National Affairs, Inc., 1971.

Partial Text of

THE LABOR-MANAGEMENT RELATIONS ACT, 1947*

(as amended by the Labor-Management Reporting and Disclosure Act of 1959)†

[Public Law 101—80th Congress]
[Chapter 120—1st Session]
[H.R. 3020]

AN ACT

To amend the National Labor Relations Act, to provide additional facilities for the mediation of labor disputes affecting commerce, to equalize legal responsibilities of labor organizations and employers, and for other purposes.

Be it enacted by the Senate and House of Representatives of the United States of America in Congress assembled,

Short Title and Declaration of Policy

Section 1.   (a) This Act may be cited as the "Labor-Management Relations Act, 1947."

(b) Industrial strife which interferes with the normal flow of commerce and with the full production of articles and commodities for commerce, can be avoided or substantially minimized if employers, employees, and labor organizations each recognize under law one another's legitimate rights in their relations with each other, and above all recognize under law that neither party has any right in its relations with any other to engage in acts or practices which jeopardize the public health, safety, or interest.

It is the purpose and policy of this Act, in order to promote the full flow of commerce, to prescribe the legitimate rights of both

---

*Also known as the Taft-Hartley Act.
† Also known as the Landrum-Griffin Act.

employees and employers in their relations affecting commerce, to provide orderly and peaceful procedures for preventing the interference by either with the legitimate rights of the other, to protect the rights of individual employees in their relations with labor organizations whose activities affect commerce, to define and proscribe practices on the part of labor and management which affect commerce and are inimical to the general welfare, and to protect the rights of the public in connection with labor disputes affecting commerce.

TITLE I–AMENDMENT OF
NATIONAL LABOR RELATIONS ACT

Sec. 101. The National Labor Relations Act is hereby amended to read as follows:

Findings and Policies

Section 1. The denial by some employers of the right of employees to organize and the refusal by some employers to accept the procedure of collective bargaining lead to strikes and other forms of industrial strife or unrest, which have the intent or the necessary effect of burdening or obstructing commerce by (a) impairing the efficiency, safety, or operation of the instrumentalities of commerce; (b) occurring in the current of commerce; (c) materially affecting, restraining, or controlling the flow of raw materials or manufactured or processed goods from or into the channels of commerce, or the prices of such materials or goods in commerce; or (d) causing diminution of employment and wages in such volume as substantially to impair or disrupt the market for goods flowing from or into the channels of commerce.

The inequality of bargaining power between employees who do not possess full freedom of association or actual liberty of contract, and employers who are organized in the corporate or other forms of ownership association substantially burdens and affects the flow of commerce, and tends to aggravate recurrent business depressions, by depressing wage rates and the purchasing power of wage earners in industry and by preventing the stabilization of competitive wage rates and working conditions within and between industries.

Experience has proved that protection by law of the right of employees to organize and bargain collectively safeguards commerce from injury, impairment, or interruption, and promotes the flow of commerce by removing certain recognized sources of industrial strife and unrest, by encouraging practices fundamental to the friendly adjustment of industrial disputes arising out of differences as to wages, hours, or other working conditions, and by restoring equality of bargaining power between employers and employees.

Experience has further demonstrated that certain practices by some labor organizations, their officers, and members have the intent or the necessary effect of burdening or obstructing commerce by preventing the free flow of goods in such commerce through strikes and other forms of industrial unrest or through concerted activities which impair the interest of the public in the free flow of such commerce. The elimination of such practices is a necessary condition to the assurance of the rights herein guaranteed.

It is hereby declared to be the policy of the United States to eliminate the causes of certain substantial obstructions to the free flow of commerce and to mitigate and eliminate these obstructions when they have occurred by encouraging the practice and procedure of collective bargaining and by protecting the exercise by workers of full freedom of association, self-organization, and designation of representatives of their own choosing, for the purpose of negotiating the terms and conditions of their employment or other mutual aid or protection.

Definitions

Sec. 2.   When used in this Act—

(1) The term "person" includes one or more individuals, labor organizations, partnerships, associations, corporations, legal representatives, trustees, trustees in bankruptcy, or receivers.

(2) The term "employer" includes any person acting as an agent of an employer, directly or indirectly, but shall not include the United States or any wholly owned Government corporation, or any Federal Reserve Bank, or any State or political subdivision thereof, or any corporation or association operating a hospital, if no part of the net earnings inures to the benefit of any private shareholder or individual, or any person subject to the Railway Labor Act, as amended from time to time, or any labor organization (other than when acting as an employer), or anyone acting in the capacity of officer or agent of such labor organization.

(3) The term "employee" shall include any employee, and shall not be limited to the employees of a particular employer, unless the Act explicitly states otherwise, and shall include any individual

whose work has ceased as a consequence of, or in connection with, any current labor dispute or because of any unfair labor practice, and who has not obtained any other regular and substantially equivalent employment, but shall not include any individual employed as an agricultural laborer, or in the domestic service of any family or person at his home, or any individual employed by his parent or spouse, or any individual having the status of an independent contractor, or any individual employed as a supervisor, or any individual employed by an employer subject to the Railway Labor Act, as amended from time to time, or by any other person who is not an employer as herein defined.

(4) The term "representatives" includes any individual or labor organization.

(5) The term "labor organization" means any organization of any kind, or any agency or employee representation committee or plan, in which employees participate and which exists for the purpose, in whole or in part, of dealing with employers concerning grievances, labor disputes, wages, rates of pay, hours of employment, or conditions of work.

(6) The term "commerce" means trade, traffic, commerce, transportation, or communication among the several States, or between the District of Columbia or any Territory of the United States and any State or other Territory, or between any foreign country and any State, Territory, or the District of Columbia, or within the District of Columbia or any Territory, or between points in the same State but through any other State or any Territory or the District of Columbia or any foreign country.

(7) The term "affecting commerce" means in commerce, or burdening or obstructing commerce or the free flow of commerce, or having led or tending to lead to a labor dispute burdening or obstructing commerce or the free flow of commerce.

(8) The term "unfair labor practice" means any unfair labor practice listed in section 8.

(9) The term "labor dispute" includes any controversy concerning terms, tenure or conditions of employment, or concerning the association or representation of persons in negotiating, fixing, maintaining, changing, or seeking to arrange terms or conditions of employment, regardless of whether the disputants stand in the proximate relation of employer and employee.

(10) The term "National Labor Relations Board" means the National Labor Relations Board provided for in section 3 of this Act.

(11) The term "supervisor" means any individual having authority, in the interest of the employer, to hire, transfer, suspend, lay off, recall, promote, discharge, assign, reward, or discipline other employees, or responsibly to direct them, or to adjust their grievances, or effectively to recommend such action, if in connection with the foregoing the exercise of such authority is not of a merely routine or clerical nature, but requires the use of independent judgment.

(12) The term "professional employee" means—

(a) any employee engaged in work (i) predominately intellectual and varied in character as opposed to routine mental, manual, mechanical, or physical work; (ii) involving the consistent exercise of discretion and judgment in its performance; (iii) of such a character that the output produced or the result accomplished cannot be standardized in relation to a given period of time; (iv) requiring knowledge of an advanced type in a field of science or learning customarily acquired by a prolonged course of specialized intellectual instruction and study in an institution of higher learning or a hospital, as distinguished from a general academic education or from an apprenticeship or from training in the performance of routine mental, manual, or physical processes; or

(b) any employee, who (i) has completed the courses of specialized intellectual instruction and study described in clause (iv) of paragraph (a), and (ii) is performing related work under the supervision of a professional person to qualify himself to become a professional employee as defined in paragraph (a).

(13) In determining whether any person is acting as an "agent" of another person so as to make such other person responsible for his acts, the question of whether the specific acts performed were actually authorized or subsequently ratified shall not be controlling.

National Labor Relations Board

Sec. 3. (a) The National Labor Relations Board . . . shall consist of five . . . members, appointed by the President by and with the advice and consent of the Senate . . . for terms of five years each. . . . The President shall designate one member to serve as Chairman of the Board. Any member of the Board may be removed by the President, upon notice and hearing, for neglect of duty or malfeasance in office, but for no other cause.

(b) The Board is authorized to delegate to any group of three or more members any or all of the powers which it may itself exercise. The Board is also authorized to delegate to its regional directors its powers under section 9 to determine the unit appropriate for the purpose of collective bargaining, to investigate and provide for hearings, and determine whether a question of representation exists, and to direct an election or take a secret ballot under subsection (c) or (e) of section 9 and certify the results thereof, except that upon the filing of a request therefor with the Board by any interested person, the Board may review any action of a regional director delegated to him under this paragraph, but such a review shall not, unless specifically ordered by the Board, operate as a stay of any action taken by the regional director. A vacancy in the Board shall not impair the right of the remaining members to exercise all of the powers of the Board, and three members of the Board shall, at all times constitute a quorum of the Board, except that two members shall constitute a quorum of any group designated pursuant to the first sentence hereof. The Board shall have an official seal which shall be judically noticed.

. . . .

[Omitted: Section 3 (c)–Board reports to Congress.]

(d) There shall be a General Counsel of the Board who shall be appointed by the President, by and with the advice and consent of the Senate, for a term of four years. The General Counsel shall exercise general supervision over all attorneys employed by the Board (other than trial examiners and legal assistants to Board members) and over the officers and employees in the regional offices. He shall have final authority, on behalf of the Board, in respect of the investigation of charges and issuance of complaints under section 10, and in respect of the prosecution of such complaints before the Board and shall have such other duties as the Board may prescribe or may be provided by law. In case of a vacancy in the office of the General Counsel the President is authorized to designate the officer or employee who shall act as General Counsel during such vacancy, but no person or persons so designated shall so act (1) for more than forty days when the Congress is in session unless a nomination to fill such vacancy shall have been submitted to the Senate, or (2) after the adjournment sine die of the session of the Senate in which such nomination was submitted.

. . . .

[Omitted: Sections 4 and 5–Compensation and offices of the NLRB.]

Sec. 6.   The Board shall have authority from time to time to make, amend, and rescind, in the manner prescribed by the Administrative Procedure Act, such rules and regulations as may be necessary to carry out the provisions of this Act.

Rights of Employees

Sec. 7.   Employees shall have the right to self-organization, to form, join, or assist labor organizations, to bargain collectively through representatives of their own choosing, and to engage in other concerted activities for the purpose of collective bargaining or other mutual aid or protection, and shall also have the right to refrain from any or all of such activities except to the extent that such right may be affected by an agreement requiring membership in a labor organization as a condition of employment as authorized in section 8 (a) (3).

Unfair Labor Practices

Sec. 8.   (a) It shall be an unfair labor practice for an employer—

(1) to interfere with, restrain, or coerce employees in the exercise of the rights guaranteed in section 7;

(2) to dominate or interfere with the formation or administration of any labor organization or contribute financial or other support to it: Provided, That subject to rules and regulations made and published by the Board pursuant to section 6, an employer shall not be prohibited from permitting employees to confer with him during working hours without loss of time or pay;

(3) by discrimination in regard to hire or tenure of employment or any term or condition of employment to encourage or discourage membership in any labor organization: Provided, That nothing in this Act, or in any other statute of the United States, shall preclude an employer from making an agreement with a labor organization (not established, maintained, or assisted by any action defined in section 8 (a) of this Act as an unfair labor practice) to require as a condition of employment membership therein on or after the thirtieth day following the the beginning of such employment or the effective date of such agreement, whichever is the later, (i) if such labor organization is the representative of the employees as provided in section 9 (a), in the appropriate collective-bargaining unit covered by such agreement when made; and (ii) unless following an election held as provided in section 9 (e) within one year preceding the effective date of such agreement, the Board shall have certified that at least a majority of the employees eligible to vote in such election have voted to rescind the authority of such labor organization to make such an agreement: Provided further, That no employer shall justify any dis-

crimination against an employee for nonmembership in a labor organization (A) if he has reasonable grounds for believing that such membership was not available to the employee on the same terms and conditions generally applicable to other members, or (B) if he has reasonable grounds for believing that membership was denied or terminated for reasons other than the failure of the employee to tender the periodic dues and the initiation fees uniformly required as a condition of acquiring or retaining membership;

(4) to discharge or otherwise discriminate against an employee because he has filed charges or given testimony under this Act;

(5) to refuse to bargain collectively with the representatives of his employees, subject to the provisions of section 9 (a).

(b) It shall be an unfair labor practice for a labor organization or its agents—

(1) to restrain or coerce (A) employees in the exercise of the rights guaranteed in section 7: Provided, That this paragraph shall not impair the right of a labor organization to prescribe its own rules with respect to the acquisition or retention of membership therein; or (B) an employer in the selection of his representatives for the purposes of collective bargaining or the adjustment of grievances;

(2) to cause or attempt to cause an employer to discriminate against an employee in violation of subsection (a) (3) or to discriminate against an employee with respect to whom membership in such organization has been denied or terminated on some ground other than his failure to tender the periodic dues and the initiation fees uniformly required as a condition of acquiring or retaining membership;

(3) to refuse to bargain collectively with an employer, provided it is the representative of his employees subject to the provisions of section 9 (a);

(4) (i) to engage in, or to induce or encourage any individual employed by any person engaged in commerce or in an industry affecting commerce to engage in, a strike or a refusal in the course of his employment to use, manufacture, process, transport, or otherwise handle or work on any goods, articles, materials, or commodities or to perform any services; or (ii) to threaten, coerce, or restrain any person engaged in commerce or in an industry affecting commerce, where in either case an object thereof is:

(A) forcing or requiring any employer or self-employed person to join any labor or employer organization or to enter into any agreement which is prohibited by section 8 (e);

(B) forcing or requiring any person to cease using, selling, handling, transporting, or otherwise dealing in the products of any other producer, processor, or manufacturer, or to cease doing business with any other person, or forcing or requiring any other employer to recognize or bargain with a labor organization as the representative of his employees unless such labor organization has been certified as the representative of such employees under the provisions of section 9: Provided, That nothing contained in this clause (B) shall be construed to make unlawful, where not otherwise unlawful, any primary strike or primary picketing;

(C) forcing or requiring any employer to recognize or bargain with a particular labor organization as the representative of his employees if another labor organization has been certified as the representative of such employees under the provisions of section 9;

(D) forcing or requiring any employer to assign particular work to employees in a particular labor organization or in a particular trade, craft, or class rather than to employees in another labor organization or in another trade, craft, or class, unless such employer is failing to conform to an order or certification of the Board determining the bargaining representative for employees performing such work: Provided, That nothing contained in this subsection (b) shall be construed to make unlawful a refusal by any person to enter upon the premises of any employer (other than his own employer), if the employees of such employer are engaged in a strike ratified or approved by a representative of such employees whom such employer is required to recognize under this Act: Provided further, That for the purposes of this paragraph (4) only, nothing contained in such paragraph shall be construed to prohibit publicity, other than picketing, for the purpose of truthfully advising the public, including consumers and members of a labor organization, that a product or products are produced by an employer with whom the labor organization has a primary dispute and are distributed by another employer, as long as such publicity does not have an effect of inducing any individual employed by any person other than the primary employer in the course of his employment to refuse to pick up, deliver, or transport any goods, or not to perform any services, at the establishment of the employer engaged in such distribution.

(5) to require of employees covered by an agreement authorized under subsection (a) (3) the payment, as a condition precedent to becoming a member of such organization, of a fee in an amount which the Board finds excessive or discriminatory under all the cir-

cumstances. In making such a finding, the Board shall consider, among other relevant factors, the practices and customs of labor organizations in the particular industry, and the wages currently paid to the employees affected;

(6) to cause or attempt to cause an employer to pay or deliver or agree to pay or deliver any money or other thing of value, in the nature of an exaction, for services which are not performed or not to be performed; and

(7) to picket or cause to be picketed, or threaten to picket or cause to be picketed, any employer where an object thereof is forcing or requiring an employer to recognize or bargain with a labor organization as the representative of his employees, or forcing or requiring the employees of an employer to accept or select such labor organization as their collective bargaining representative, unless such labor organization is currently certified as the representative of such employees:

(A) where the employer has lawfully recognized in accordance with this Act any other labor organization and a question concerning representation may not appropriately be raised under section 9 (c) of this Act.

(B) where within the preceding twelve months a valid election under section 9 (c) of this Act has been conducted, or

(C) where such picketing has been conducted without a petition under section 9 (c) being filed within a reasonable period of time not to exceed thirty days from the commencement of such picketing: Provided, That when such a petition has been filed the Board shall forthwith, without regard to the provisions of section 9 (c) (1) or the absence of a showing of a substantial interest on the part of the labor organization, direct an election in such unit as the Board finds to be appropriate and shall certify the results thereof: Provided further, That nothing in this subparagraph (C) shall be construed to prohibit any picketing or other publicity for the purpose of truthfully advising the public (including consumers) that an employer does not employ members of, or have a contract with, a labor organization unless an effect of such picketing is to induce any individual employed to any other person in the course of his employment, not to pick up, deliver or transport any goods or not to perform any services.

Nothing in this paragraph (7) shall be construed to permit any act which would otherwise be an unfair labor practice under this section (8) (b).

(c) The expressing of any views, argument, or opinion, or the dissemination thereof, whether in written, printed, graphic, or visual form, shall not constitute or be evidence of an unfair labor practice under any of the provisions of this Act, if such expression contains no threat of reprisal or force or promise of benefit.

(d) For the purposes of this section, to bargain collectively is the performance of the mutual obligation of the employer and the representative of the employees to meet at reasonable times and confer in good faith with respect to wages, hours, and other terms and conditions of employment, or the negotiation of an agreement, or any question arising thereunder, and the execution of a written contract incorporating any agreement reached if requested by either party, but such obligation does not compel either party to agree to a proposal or require the making of a concession: Provided, That where there is in effect a collective-bargaining contract covering employees in an industry affecting commerce, the duty to bargain collectively shall also mean that no party to such contract shall terminate or modify such contract, unless the party desiring such termination or modification—

(1) serves a written notice upon the other party to the contract of the proposed termination or modification sixty days prior to the expiration date thereof, or in the event such contract contains no expiration date, sixty days prior to the time it is proposed to make such termination or modification;

(2) offers to meet and confer with the other party for the purpose of negotiating a new contract or a contract containing the proposed modifications;

(3) notifies the Federal Mediation and Conciliation Service within thirty days after such notice of the existence of a dispute, and simultaneously therewith notifies any State or Territorial agency established to mediate and conciliate disputes within the State or Territory where the dispute occurred, provided no agreement has been reached by that time; and

(4) continues in full force and effect, without resorting to strike or lockout, all the terms and conditions of the existing contract for a period of sixty days after such notice is given or until the expiration date of such contract, whichever occurs later:

The duties imposed upon employers, employees, and labor organizations by paragraphs (2), (3), and (4) shall become inapplicable upon an intervening certification of the Board, under which the labor organization or individual, which is a party to the contract, has been superseded as or ceased to be the representative of the employees subject to the provisions of section 9 (a), and the duties so imposed shall not be construed as requiring either party to discuss or agree to any modification of the terms and conditions contained in a contract for a fixed period, if such modification is to become effective before such terms and conditions can be reopened under the provisions of the contract. Any employee who engages in a strike within the sixty-day period specified in this subsection shall lose his status as an employee of the employer engaged in the particular labor dispute, for the purposes of sections 8, 9, and 10 of this Act, as amended, but such loss of status for such employee shall terminate if and when he is reemployed by such employer.

(e) It shall be an unfair labor practice for any labor organization and any employer to enter into any contract or agreement, express or implied, whereby such employer ceases or refrains or agrees to cease or refrain from handling, using, selling, transporting or otherwise dealing in any of the products of any other employer, or to cease doing business with any other person, and any contract or agreement entered into heretofore or hereafter containing such an agreement shall be to such extent unenforceable and void: Provided, That nothing in this subsection (e) shall apply to an agreement between a labor organization and an employer in the construction industry relating to the contracting or subcontracting of work to be done at the site of the construction, alteration, painting, or repair of a building, structure, or other work: Provided further, That for the purposes of this subsection (e) and section 8 (b) (4) (B) the terms "any employer," "any person engaged in commerce or an industry affecting commerce," and "any person" when used in relation to the terms "any other producer, processor, or manufacturer," "any other employer," or "any other person" shall not include persons in the relation of a jobber, manufacturer, contractor, or subcontractor working on the goods or premises of the jobber or manufacturer or performing parts of an integrated process of production in the apparel and clothing industry: Provided further, That nothing in this Act shall prohibit the enforcement of any agreement which is within the foregoing exception.

(f) It shall not be an unfair labor practice under subsections (a) and (b) of this section for an employer engaged primarily in the building and construction industry to make an agreement covering employees engaged (or who, upon their employment, will be engaged) in the building and construction industry with a labor organization of which building and construction employees are members (not established, maintained, or assisted by any action defined in section 8 (a) of this Act as an unfair labor practice) because (1) the majority status of such labor organization has not been established under the provisions of section 9 of this Act prior to the making of such agreement, or (2) such agreement requires as a condition of employment, membership in such labor organization after the seventh day following the beginning of such employment or the effective date of the agreement, whichever is later, or (3) such agreement requires the employer to notify such labor organization of opportunities for employment with such employer, or gives such labor organization an opportunity to refer qualified applicants for such employment, or (4) such agreement specifies minimum training or experience qualifications for employment or provides for priority in opportunities for employment based upon length of service with such employer, in the industry or in the particular geographical area; Provided, That nothing in this subsection shall set aside the final proviso to section 8 (a) (3) of this Act: Provided further, That any agreement which would be invalid but for clause (1) of this subsection, shall not be a bar to a petition filed pursuant to section 9 (c) or 9 (e).

Representatives and Elections

Sec. 9.   (a) Representatives designated or selected for the purposes of collective bargaining by the majority of the employees in a unit appropriate for such purposes, shall be the exclusive representatives of all the employees in such unit for the purposes of collective bargaining in respect to rates of pay, wages, hours of employment, or other conditions of employment: Provided, That any individual employee or a group of employees shall have the right at any time to present grievances to their employer and to have such grievances adjusted, without the intervention of the bargaining representative, as long as the adjustment is not inconsistent with the terms of a collective-bargaining contract or agreement then in effect: Provided further, That the bargaining representative has been given opportunity to be present at such adjustment.

(b) The Board shall decide in each case whether, in order to assure to employees the fullest freedom in exercising the rights guaranteed by this Act, the unit appropriate for the purposes of collective bargaining shall be the employer unit, craft unit, plant unit, or subdivision thereof: Provided, That the Board shall not (1) decide that any unit is appropriate for such purposes if such unit includes both professional employees and employees who are not professional employees unless a majority of such professional employees vote for inclusion in such unit; or (2) decide that any craft unit is inappropriate for such purposes on the ground that a different unit has been established by a prior Board determination, unless a majority of the employees in the proposed craft unit vote against separate representation or (3) decide that any unit is appropriate for such purposes if it includes, together with other employees, any individual employed as a guard to enforce against employees and other persons rules to protect property of the employer or to protect the safety of persons on the employer's premises; but no labor organization shall be certified as the representative of employees in a bargaining unit of guards if such organization admits to membership, or is affiliated directly or indirectly with an organization which admits to membership, employees other than guards.

(c) (1) Whenever a petition shall have been filed, in accordance with such regulations as may be prescribed by the Board—

(A) by an employee or group of employees or any individual or labor organization acting in their behalf alleging that a substantial number of employees (i) wish to be represented for collective bargaining and that their employer declines to recognize their representative as the representative defined in section 9 (a), or (ii) assert that the individual or labor organization, which has been certified or is being currently recognized by their employer as the bargaining representative, is no longer a representative as defined in section 9 (a); or

(B) by an employer, alleging that one or more individuals or labor organizations have presented to him a claim to be recognized as the representative defined in section 9 (a);

the Board shall investigate such petition and if it has reasonable cause to believe that a question of representation affecting commerce exists shall provide for an appropriate hearing upon due notice. Such hearing may be conducted by an officer or employee of the regional office, who shall not make any recommendations with respect thereto. If the Board finds upon the record of such hearing that such a question of representation exists, it shall direct an election by secret ballot and shall certify the results thereof.

(2) In determining whether or not a question of representation affecting commerce exists, the same regulations and rules of decision shall apply irrespective of the identity of the persons filing the petition or the kind of relief sought and in no case shall the Board deny a

labor organization a place on the ballot by reason of an order with respect to such labor organization or its predecessor not issued in conformity with section 10 (c).

(3) No election shall be directed in any bargaining unit or any subdivision within which, in the preceding twelve-month period, a valid election shall have been held. Employees engaged in an economic strike who are not entitled to reinstatement shall be eligible to vote under such regulations as the Board shall find are consistent with the purposes and provisions of this Act in any election conducted within twelve months after the commencement of the strike. In any election where none of the choices on the ballot receives a majority, a run-off shall be conducted, the ballot providing for a selection between the two choices receiving the largest and second largest number of valid votes cast in the election.

(4) Nothing in this section shall be construed to prohibit the waiving of hearings by stipulation for the purpose of a consent election in conformity with regulations and rules of decision of the Board.

(5) In determining whether a unit is appropriate for the purposes specified in subsection (b) the extent to which the employees have organized shall not be controlling.

(d) Whenever an order of the Board made pursuant to section 10 (c) is based in whole or in part upon facts certified following an investigation pursuant to subsection (c) of this section and there is a petition for the enforcement or review of such order, such certification and the record of such investigation shall be included in the transcript of the entire record required to be filed under section 10 (e) or 10 (f), and thereupon the decree of the court enforcing, modifying, or setting aside in whole or in part the order of the Board shall be made and entered upon the pleadings, testimony, and proceedings set forth in such transcript.

(e) (1) Upon the filing with the Board, by 30 per centum or more of the employees in a bargaining unit covered by an agreement between their employer and a labor organization made pursuant to section 8 (a) (3), of a petition alleging they desire that such authority be rescinded, the Board shall take a secret ballot of the employees in such unit and certify the results thereof to such labor organization and to the employer.

(2) No election shall be conducted pursuant to this subsection in any bargaining unit or any subdivision within which, in the preceding twelve-month period, a valid election shall have been held.

Prevention of Unfair Labor Practices

Sec. 10. (a) The Board is empowered, as hereinafter provided, to prevent any person from engaging in any unfair labor practice (listed in section 8) affecting commerce. This power shall not be affected by any other means of adjustment or prevention that has been or may be established by agreement, law, or otherwise: Provided, That the Board is empowered by agreement with any agency of any State or Territory to cede to such agency jurisdiction over any cases in any industry (other than mining, manufacturing, communications, and transportation except where predominantly local in character) even though such cases may involve labor disputes affecting commerce, unless the provision of the State or Territorial statute applicable to the determination of such cases by such agency is inconsistent with the corresponding provision of this Act or has received a construction inconsistent therewith.

(b) Whenever it is charged that any person has engaged in or is engaging in any such unfair labor practice, the Board, or any agent or agency designated by the Board for such purposes, shall have power to issue and cause to be served upon such person a complaint stating the charges in that respect, and containing a notice of hearing before the Board or a member thereof, or before a designated agent or agency, at a place therein fixed, not less than five days after the serving of said complaint: Provided, That no complaint shall issue based upon any unfair labor practice occurring more than six months prior to the filing of the charge with the Board and the service of a copy thereof upon the person against whom such charge is made, unless the person aggrieved thereby was prevented from filing such charge by reason of service in the armed forces, in which event the six-month period shall be computed from the day of his discharge. Any such complaint may be amended by the member, agent, or agency conducting the hearing or the Board in its discretion at any time prior to the issuance of an order based thereon. The person so complained of shall have the right to file an answer to the original or amended complaint and to appear in person or otherwise and give testimony at the place and time fixed in the complaint. In the discretion of the member, agent, or agency conducting the hearing or the Board, any other person may be allowed to intervene in the said proceeding and to present testimony. Any such proceeding shall, so far as practicable, be conducted in accordance with the rules of evidence applicable in the district courts of the United States under the rules of civil procedure for the district courts of the United States, adopted by the Supreme Court of the United States pursuant to the Act of June 19, 1934 (U.S.C., title 28, secs. 723-B, 723-C).

(c) The testimony taken by such member, agent, or agency or the Board shall be reduced to writing and filed with the Board. Thereafter, in its discretion, the Board upon notice may take further testimony or hear argument. If upon the preponderance of the testimony taken the Board shall be of the opinion that any person named in the complaint has engaged in or is engaging in any such unfair labor practice, then the Board shall state its findings of fact and shall issue and cause to be served on such person an order requiring such person to cease and desist from such unfair labor practice, and to take such affirmative action including reinstatement of employees with or without back pay, as will effectuate the policies of this Act: Provided, That where an order directs reinstatement of an employee, back pay may be required of the employer or labor organization, as the case may be, responsible for the discrimination suffered by him: And provided further, That in determining whether a complaint shall issue alleging a violation of section 8 (a) (1) or section 8 (a) (2), and in deciding such cases, the same regulations and rules of decision shall apply irrespective of whether or not the labor organization affected is affiliated with a labor organization national or international in scope. Such order may further require such person to make reports from time to time showing the extent to which it has complied with the order. If upon the preponderance of the testimony taken the Board shall not be of the opinion that the person named in the complaint has engaged in or is engaging in any such unfair labor practice, then the Board shall state its findings of fact and shall issue an order dismissing the said complaint. No order of the Board shall require the reinstatement of any individual as an employee who has been suspended or discharged, or the payment to him of any back pay, if such individual was suspended or discharged for cause. In case the evidence is presented before a member of the Board, or before an examiner or examiners thereof, such member, or such examiner or examiners, as the case may be, shall issue and cause to be served on the parties to the proceeding a proposed report, together with a recommended order, which shall be filed with the Board, and if no exceptions are filed within twenty days after service thereof upon such parties, or within such further period as the Board may authorize, such recommended order shall become the order of the Board and become effective as therein prescribed.

(d) Until the record in a case shall have been filed in a court, as hereinafter provided, the Board may at any time, upon reasonable notice and in such manner as it shall deem proper, modify or set aside, in whole or in part, any finding or order made or issued by it.

(e) The Board shall have power to petition any court of appeals of the United States, or if all the courts of appeals to which application may be made are in vacation, any district court of the United States, within any circuit or district, respectively, wherein the unfair labor practice in question occurred or wherein such person resides or transacts business, for the enforcement of such order and for appropriate temporary relief or restraining order, and shall file in the court the record in the proceedings, as provided in section 2112 of title 28, United States Code. Upon the filing of such petition, the court shall cause notice thereof to be served upon such person, and thereupon shall have jurisdiction of the proceeding and of the question determined therein, and shall have power to grant such temporary relief or restraining order as it deems just and proper, and to make and enter a decree enforcing, modifying, and enforcing as so modified, or setting aside in whole or in part the order of the Board. No objection that has not been urged before the Board, its member, agent, or agency, shall be considered by the court, unless the failure or neglect to urge such objection shall be excused because of extraordinary circumstances. The findings of the Board with respect to questions of fact if supported by substantial evidence on the record considered as a whole shall be conclusive. If either party shall apply to the court for leave to adduce additional evidence and shall show to the satisfaction of the court that such additional evidence is material and that there were reasonable grounds for the failure to adduce such evidence in the hearing before the Board, its member, agent, or agency, the court may order such additional evidence to be taken before the Board, its member, agent, or agency, and to be made a part of the record. The Board may modify its findings as to the facts, or make new findings, by reason of additional evidence so taken and filed, and it shall file such modified or new findings, which findings with respect to questions of fact if supported by substantial evidence on the record considered as a whole shall be conclusive, and shall file its recommendations, if any, for the modification or setting aside of its original order. Upon the filing of the record with it the jurisdiction of the court shall be exclusive and its judgment and decree shall be final, except that the same shall be subject to review by the appropriate

United States court of appeals if application was made to the district court as hereinabove provided, and by the Supreme Court of the United States upon writ of certiorari or certification as provided in section 1254 of title 28.

(f) Any person aggrieved by a final order of the Board granting or denying in whole or in part the relief sought may obtain a review of such order in any circuit court of appeals of the United States in the circuit wherein the unfair labor practice in question was alleged to have been engaged in or wherein such person resides or transacts business, or in the United States Court of Appeals for the District of Columbia, by filing in such court a written petition praying that the order of the Board be modified or set aside. A copy of such petition shall be forthwith transmitted by the clerk of the court to the Board, and thereupon the aggrieved party shall file in the court the record in the proceeding, certified by the Board, as provided in section 2112 of title 28, United States Code. Upon the filing of such petition, the court shall proceed in the same manner as in the case of an application by the Board under subsection (e) of this section, and shall have the same jurisdiction to grant to the Board such temporary relief or restraining order as it deems just and proper, and in like manner to make and enter a decree enforcing, modifying, and enforcing as so modified, or setting aside in whole or in part the order of the Board; the findings of the Board with respect to questions of fact if supported by substantial evidence on the record considered as a whole shall in like manner be conclusive.

(g) The commencement of proceedings under subsection (e) or (f) of this section shall not, unless specifically ordered by the court, operate as a stay of the Board's order.

(h) When granting appropriate temporary relief or a restraining order, or making and entering a decree enforcing, modifying, and enforcing as so modified, or setting aside in whole or in part an order of the Board, as provided in this section, the jurisdiction of courts sitting in equity shall not be limited by the Act entitled "An Act to amend the Judicial Code and to define and limit the jurisdiction of courts sitting in equity, and for other purposes," approved March 23, 1932 (U.S.C., Supp. VII, title 29, secs. 101–115).

(i) Petitions filed under this Act shall be heard expeditiously, and if possible within ten days after they have been docketed.

(j) The Board shall have power, upon issuance of a complaint as provided in subsection (b) charging that any person has engaged in or is engaging in an unfair labor practice, to petition any district court of the United States (including the District Court of the United States for the District of Columbia), within any district wherein the unfair labor practice in question is alleged to have occurred or wherein such person resides or transacts business, for appropriate temporary relief or restraining order. Upon the filing of any such petition the court shall cause notice thereof to be served upon such person, and thereupon shall have jurisdiction to grant to the Board such temporary relief or restraining order as it deems just and proper.

(k) Whenever it is charged that any person has engaged in an unfair labor practice within the meaning of paragraph (4) (D) of section 8 (b), the Board is empowered and directed to hear and determine the dispute out of which such unfair labor practice shall have arisen, unless, within ten days after notice that such charge has been filed, the parties to such dispute submit to the Board satisfactory evidence that they have adjusted, or agreed upon methods for the voluntary adjustment of, the dispute. Upon compliance by the parties to the dispute with the decision of the Board or upon such voluntary adjustment of the dispute, such charge shall be dismissed.

(1) Whenever it is charged that any person has engaged in an unfair labor practice within the meaning of paragraph (4) (A), (B), or (C) of section 8 (b) or section 8 (e) or section 8 (b) (7), the preliminary investigation of such charge shall be made forthwith and given priority over all other cases except cases of like character in the office where it is filed or to which it is referred. If, after such investigation, the officer or regional attorney to whom the matter may be referred has reasonable cause to believe such charge is true and that a complaint should issue, he shall, on behalf of the Board, petition any district court of the United States ... for appropriate injunctive relief pending the final adjudication of the Board with respect to the matter. Upon the filing of any such petition the district court shall have jurisdiction to grant such injunctive relief or temporary restraining order as it deems just and proper, not withstanding any other provision of law: Provided further, That no temporary restraining order shall be issued without notice unless a petition alleges that substantial and irreparable injury to the charging party will be unavoidable and such temporary restraining order shall be effective for no longer than five days and will become void at the expiration of such period: Provided further, That such officer or regional attorney shall not apply for any restraining order under section 8 (b) (7) if a

charge against the employer under 8 (a) (2) has been filed and after the preliminary investigation, he has reasonable cause to believe that such charge is true and that a complaint should issue.

(m) Whenever it is charged that any person has engaged in an unfair labor practice within the meaning of subsection (a) (3) or (b) (2) of section 8, such charge shall be given priority over all other cases except cases of like character in the office where it is filed or to which it is referred and cases given priority under subsection (1).

. . . .

[Omitted: Sections 11 and 12—Investigatory powers of the NLRB.]

Limitations

Sec. 13.   Nothing in this Act, except as specifically provided for herein, shall be construed so as either to interfere with or impede or diminish in any way the right to strike, or to affect the limitations or qualifications on that right.

Sec. 14.   (a) Nothing herein shall prohibit any individual employed as a supervisor from becoming or remaining a member of a labor organization, but no employer subject to this Act shall be compelled to deem individuals defined herein as supervisors as employees for the purpose of any law, either national or local, relating to collective bargaining.

(b) Nothing in this Act shall be construed as authorizing the execution or application of agreements requiring membership in a labor organization as a condition of employment in any State or Territory in which such execution or application is prohibited by State or Territorial law.

(c) (1) The Board, in its discretion, may, by rule of decision or by published rules adopted pursuant to the Administrative Procedure Act, decline to assert jurisdiction over any labor dispute involving any class or category or employers, where, in the opinion of the Board, the effect of such labor dispute on commerce is not sufficiently substantial to warrant the exercise of its jurisdiction: Provided, That the Board shall not decline to assert jurisdiction over any labor dispute over which it would assert jurisdiction under the standards prevailing upon August 1, 1959.

. . . .

[Omitted: Sections 15, 16, 17, 18, 102, 103, 104, relating to limitations and effective date of certain changes.]

TITLE II–CONCILIATION OF LABOR DISPUTES
IN INDUSTRIES AFFECTING COMMERCE;
NATIONAL EMERGENCIES

Sec. 201.   That it is the policy of the United States that—

(a) sound and stable industrial peace and the advancement of the general welfare, health, and safety of the Nation and of the best interest of employers and employees can most satisfactorily be secured by the settlement of issues between employers and employees through the processes of conference and collective bargaining between employers and the representatives of their employees;

(b) the settlement of issues between employers and employees through collective bargaining may be advanced by making available full and adequate governmental facilities for conciliation, mediation, and voluntary arbitration to aid and encourage employers and the representatives of their employees to reach and maintain agreements concerning rates of pay, hours, and working conditions, and to make all reasonable efforts to settle their differences by mutual agreement reached through conferences and collective bargaining or by such methods as may be provided for in any applicable agreement for the settlement of disputes; and

(c) certain controversies which arise between parties to collective-bargaining agreements may be avoided or minimized by making available full and adequate governmental facilities for furnishing assistance to employers and the representatives of their employees in formulating for inclusion within such agreements provision for adequate notice of any proposed changes in the terms of such agreements, for the final adjustment of grievances or questions regarding the application or interpretation of such agreements, and other provisions designed to prevent the subsequent arising of such controversies.

. . . .

[Omitted: Section 202, which creates the Federal Mediation and Conciliation Service and its offices.]

Functions of the Service

Sec. 203.   (a) It shall be the duty of the Service, in order to prevent or minimize interruptions of the free flow of commerce growing out of labor disputes, to assist parties to labor disputes in industries affecting commerce to settle such disputes through conciliation and mediation.

(b) The Service may proffer its services in any labor dispute in any industry affecting commerce, either upon its own motion or upon the request of one or more of the parties to the dispute, whenever in its judgment such dispute threatens to cause a substantial interruption of commerce. The Director and the Service are directed to avoid attempting to mediate disputes which would have only a minor effect on interstate commerce if State or other conciliation services are available to the parties. Whenever the Service does proffer its services in any dispute, it shall be the duty of the Service promptly to put itself in communication with the parties and to use its best efforts, by mediation and conciliation, to bring them to agreement.

(c) If the Director is not able to bring the parties to agreement by conciliation within a reasonable time, he shall seek to induce the parties voluntarily to seek other means of settling the dispute without resort to strike, lock-out, or other coercion, including submission to the employees in the bargaining unit of the employer's last offer of settlement for approval or rejection in a secret ballot. The failure or refusal of either party to agree to any procedure suggested by the Director shall not be deemed a violation of any duty or obligation imposed by this Act.

(d) Final adjustment by a method agreed upon by the parties is hereby declared to be the desirable method for settlement of grievance disputes arising over the application or interpretation of an existing collective-bargaining agreement. The Service is directed to make its conciliation and mediation services available in the settlement of such grievance disputes only as a last resort and in exceptional cases.

. . . .

[Omitted: Section 204 urges employers and unions to use the FMCS. Section 205 creates a national labor–management panel to advise the director of the FMCS.]

National Emergencies

Sec. 206.   Whenever in the opinion of the President of the United States, a threatened or actual strike or lock-out affecting an entire industry or a substantial part thereof engaged in trade, commerce, transportation, transmission, or communication among the several States or with foreign nations, or engaged in the production of goods for commerce, will, if permitted to occur or to continue, imperil the national health or safety, he may appoint a board of inquiry to inquire into the issues involved in the dispute and to make a written report to him within such time as he shall prescribe. Such report shall include a statement of the facts with respect to the dispute, including each party's statement of its position but shall not contain any recommendations. The President shall file a copy of such report with the Service and shall make its contents available to the public.

Sec. 207. (a) A board of inquiry shall be composed of a chairman and such other members as the President shall determine, and shall have power to sit and act in any place within the United States and to conduct such hearings either in public or in private, as it may deem necessary or proper, to ascertain the facts with respect to the causes and circumstances of the dispute.

. . . .

Sec. 208. (a) Upon receiving a report from a board of inquiry the President may direct the Attorney General to petition any district court of the United States having jurisdiction of the parties to enjoin such strike or lock-out or the continuing thereof, and if the court finds that such threatened or actual strike or lock-out—

(i) affects an entire industry or a substantial part thereof engaged in trade, commerce, transportation, transmission, or communication among the several States or with foreign nations, or engaged in the production of goods for commerce; and

(ii) if permitted to occur or to continue, will imperil the national health or safety, it shall have jurisdiction to enjoin any such strike or lock-out, or the continuing thereof, and to make such other orders as may be appropriate.

. . . .

Sec. 209. (a) Whenever a district court has issued an order under section 208 enjoining acts or practices which imperil or threaten to imperil the national health or safety, it shall be the duty of the parties to the labor dispute giving rise to such order to make every effort to adjust and settle their differences, with the assistance of the Service created by this Act. Neither party shall be under any duty to accept, in whole or in part, any proposal of settlement made by the Service.

(b) Upon the issuance of such order, the President shall reconvene the board of inquiry which has previously reported with respect to the dispute. At the end of a sixty-day period (unless the dispute has been settled by that time), the board of inquiry shall report to the President the current position of the parties and the efforts which have been made for settlement, and shall include a statement by each party of its position and a statement of the employer's last offer of settlement. The President shall make such report available to the public. The National Labor Relations Board, within the succeeding fifteen days, shall take a secret ballot of the employees of each employer involved in the dispute on the question of whether they wish to accept the final offer of settlement made by their employer as stated by him and shall certify the results thereof to the Attorney General within five days thereafter.

Sec. 210.   Upon the certification of the results of such ballot or upon a settlement being reached, whichever happens sooner, the Attorney General shall move the court to discharge the injunction, which motion shall then be granted and the injunction discharged. When such motion is granted, the President shall submit to the Congress a full and comprehensive report of the proceedings, including the findings of the board of inquiry and the ballot taken by the National Labor Relations Board, together with such recommendations as he may see fit to make for consideration and appropriate action.

. . . .

[Omitted: Section 211 covers authorization for collection and dissemination of collective bargaining information by federal agencies. Section 212 exempts persons covered by provisions of the Railway Labor Act from the provisions of the LMRA.]

TITLE III

Suits by and against Labor Organizations

Sec. 301.   (a) Suits for violation of contracts between an employer and a labor organization representing employees in an industry affecting commerce as defined in this Act, or between any such labor organizations, may be brought in any district court of the United States having jurisdiction of the parties, without respect to the amount in controversy or without regard to the citizenship of the parties.

(b) Any labor organization which represents employees in an industry affecting commerce as defined in this Act and any employer whose activities affect commerce as defined in this Act shall be bound by the acts of its agents. Any such labor organization may sue or be sued as an entity and in behalf of the employees whom it represents in the courts of the United States. Any money judgment against a labor organization in a district court of the United States shall be enforceable only against the organization as an entity and against its assets, and shall not be enforceable against any individual member or his assets.

. . . .

[Omitted: Section 302—Restrictions on payments to employee representatives.]

Boycotts and Other Unlawful Combinations

Sec. 303.   (a) It shall be unlawful, for the purpose of this section only, in an industry or activity affecting commerce, for any labor organization to engage in any activity or conduct defined as an unfair labor practice in section 8 (b) (4) of the National Labor Relations Act, as amended.

(b) Whoever shall be injured in his business or property by reason of any violation of subsection (a) may sue therefor in any district court of the United States subject to the limitations and provisions of Section 301 hereof without respect to the amount of the controversy, or in any other court having jurisdiction of the parties, and shall recover the damages sustained by him and the cost of the suit.

. . . .

[Omitted are the following concluding sections: Section 304 — Restriction on political contributions. Section 305—Strikes by government employees are prohibited. Title IV—Creation of joint committee to study and report on basic problems affecting labor relations and productivity. Title V—Definitions.]

Index to Cases for Part I

46

1. AN ISSUE OF BARGAINING IN GOOD FAITH

COMPANY: Fibreboard Paper Products Corporation

UNION: East Bay Union of Machinists, Local 1304, United Steelworkers of America, AFL-CIO

BACKGROUND

The Fibreboard Corporation operates 20 plants in the states of California, Nevada, Oregon, and Colorado. It manufactures, sells, and distributes paints, industrial insulation, roofing materials, floor-covering materials, and related products. The plant involved in this case is located at Emeryville, California.

Local 1304 of the United Steelworkers has been the exclusive bargaining agent for certain maintenance employees in the Emeryville plant since 1937.[1] In September 1958, the union and the company entered a collective bargaining agreement which was to expire on July 31, 1959. The agreement provided for automatic renewal for an additonal year unless one of the contracting parties gave 60 days' notice of a desire to modify or terminate the contract.[2]

On May 26, the union wrote the company as follows:

Pursuant to the provisions of the Labor-Management Relations Act, 1947, you are hereby notified that the Union desires to modify as of August 1, 1959, the collective bargaining contract dated July 31, 1958, now in effect between the Company and the Union.

The Union offers to meet with the Company at such early time and suitable place as may be mutually convenient, for the purpose of negotiating a new contract.

On June 2, Mr. R. C. Thurmann, director of industrial relations and chief negotiator with the union for 10 years, replied:

---

[1] Job classifications included within the bargaining unit were: maintenance mechanics, electricians and helpers, working foremen, firemen and engineers employed in the power-house, and the storekeeper in the central storeroom.

[2] See appendix following this case for relevant provisions of the collective agreement.

This will acknowledge your letter of May 26, 1959, requesting a meeting to discuss the modifications of the current agreement between the Emeryville Plant of Fibreboard Paper Products Corporation and the United Steelworkers of America on behalf of the East Bay Union of Machinists, Local 1304.

We will contact you at a later date regarding a meeting for this purpose.

The union wrote a letter on June 15 requesting a meeting to discuss the following proposals:

Section I. Wage Scales. We would like to arrive at a basis to eliminate the unfair wage discrepancy between the machinists and the other crafts in the plant.

Section IV. Seniority. Paragraph b—Change ninety (90) days to thirty (30) days.

Section V. Hours of Work and Overtime. We request a 35 hour week—schedule of shifts to be worked out.

Section XII. Holidays. (1) Add, one additional paid holiday. (2) Delete worked the day before and the day after, for qualifying.

Section XIII. Night Differentials. (a) Change to ten (10) percent, and fifteen (15) percent.

Section XV. Vacations. We request three weeks vacation after five years of service, and four weeks vacation after fifteen years of service.

Section XVII. Welfare Plan. The plant to pay full cost of Health and Welfare. The plant also to extend the coverage to retired employees under the pension plan.

Section XXI. Adjustment of Complaints. Add new section between (a) and (b) as follows: Such meetings between an executive of the Plant and a representative of the Machinists Union no later than five working days after referral to the above representatives of the parties. Failure of either party to be available shall constitute concession of the grievance to the other party. The time limit may be extended by mutual agreement.

New. We request five cents per hour to be placed into a fund to provide for supplementary unemployment benefits for employees laid off in a reduction of force. To provide at least sixty-five percent of the employee's normal weekly wage, including unemployment benefits.

Qualifications to be those of the State of California Department of Employment.

On June 26, Mr. Lloyd Ferber, the business agent of Local 1304 for over seven years, telephoned Thurmann. During the conversation Ferber requested a meeting; Thurmann replied that he would telephone during the week of July 12 to arrange such a meeting.

Ferber telephoned Thurmann again during the week of July 12. Thurmann was not in his office; however, he conveyed a message through his secretary to Ferber saying that he would endeavor to call Ferber before the end of that week to fix a time for a meeting.

On July 27, company representatives notified the union of a decision which management had reached. This decision was to contract out to an independent contractor the maintenance work in the plant which currently was being performed by men represented by the Steelworkers union. Upon receipt of this notice, Mr. Ferber requested an immediate meeting with the company. A meeting was agreed to be held at 5:30 p.m. the same day.

The Meeting

William F. Stumpf, international representative for the United Steelworkers of America, and Lloyd Ferber, business agent for Local 1304, met with R. C. Thurmann, director of industrial relations of the Emeryville plant of the Fibreboard Paper Products Corporation, at 5:30 p.m., July 27, 1959, to discuss a decision made that morning by the company to contract out the work which was currently being performed by the men covered by the Steelworkers contract.

Ferber opened the discussion by announcing that Thurmann would receive in a few days a communication from the union's Central Labor Council informing him that Ferber had "asked for strike action against the plant." Thurmann thereupon handed both Ferber and Stumpf copies of letters, dated July 27, which read as follows:

Mr. William F. Stumpf, Representative
United Steelworkers of America
610 Sixteenth Street, Rooms 219–220
Oakland, California
Subject: Emeryville Plant Agreement

Under date of May 26, 1959, Mr. Stumpf, you notified us of your desire to modify our collective bargaining agreement with your Union dated September 24, 1958, relative to maintenance employees at our Emeryville plant, and of your desire to meet for the purpose of negotiating a new contract to be effective August 1, 1959. Under date of June 15, 1959, you forwarded your contract proposals.

For some time we have been seriously considering the question of letting out our Emeryville maintenance work to an independent contractor, and have now reached a definite decision to do so effective August 1, 1959.

In these circumstances, we are sure that you will realize that negotiation of a new contract would be pointless. However, if you have any questions, we will be glad to discuss them with you.

(S)   R. C. Thurmann
Director of Industrial Relations

After Mr. Ferber and Mr. Stumpf had read the letter which Mr. Thurmann had handed them, considerable discussion ensued regarding the company's legal right to enter into a contract with a third party to perform the work which was being done by members of Local 1304. When Ferber mentioned that a picket line would be established at the plant if the company entered into such a contract, Thurmann stated that such a picket line would be directed against the contractor in order to force him to hire Local 1304 members. Thurmann stated that the company would give each person laid off all the termination pay and other monetary and similar benefits due under the collective bargaining agreement. In addition, even though the agreement did not require it, the company would grant the laid-off men vacation pay on a pro rata basis.

When Mr. Ferber asked the name of the contractor who was to do the maintenance work, Mr. Thurmann replied that the company had two contractors under consideration. He said that he would notify Ferber as soon as the company decided between them. The meeting concluded with the understanding that the parties would meet again the following Thursday, July 30.

The following day, July 28, Thurmann telephoned Ferber to inform him that the contract had been let to Fluor Maintenance, Incorporated.

The company received the following letter on July 30:

Fibreboard Paper Products Corporation
P.O. Box 4317
Oakland, California

(Attention: Mr. R. C. Thurmann, Director of Industrial Relations)

Gentlemen:

Reference is made to your letter of July 27, 1959.

We interpret your letter to mean that you are attempting to cancel your present agreement with us. If that is your intention, you are too late. We direct you to the provision of the agreement which requires that you should have given us at least sixty (60) days notice of cancellation prior to the July 31, 1959 expiration date.

In the absence of such notice, the contract has been automatically renewed for another year, subject, of course, to your obligation to meet with us at once to discuss the modifications which we sent you, following our notice of May 26 for modification of the existing agreement.

We trust that you will not lock out the employees covered by our agreement, and that you will not consummate the plan outlined in your letter of July 27. We call upon you to meet with us at once.

> Very truly yours,
> United Steelworkers of America, AFL–CIO
>
> By William F. Stumpf,
> *Wm. F. Stumpf, Representative*
> By Lloyd Ferber,
> *Lloyd Ferber, Business Representative*
> *Local 1304*

On the afternoon of July 30, Thurmann and four other company representatives met with Stumpf, Ferber, and the union negotiating committee. At the opening of the meeting, Thurmann handed copies of the following letter signed by him to Stumpf and Ferber:

Messrs. Wm. F. Stumpf, Representative, and
 Lloyd H. Ferber, Business Representative, Local 1304
United Steelworkers of America
610 Sixteenth Street, Room 219–220
Oakland, California
Gentlemen:

The following is in reply to your letter of July 29, 1959.

1. The introductory provisions of our agreement with your Union provide in pertinent part:

> This agreement shall continue in full force and effect to and including July 31, 1959, and shall be considered to be renewed from year to year thereafter between the respective parties unless either party hereto shall give written notice to the other of its desire to change, modify, or cancel the same at least sixty (60) days prior to expiration.

Under date of May 26, 1959, you notified us of your desire to modify the agreement and to meet with us for the purpose of negotiating a new agreement to be effective August 1, 1959. Under the provision quoted above, our agreement therefore will expire at midnight July 31, 1959, and will not be automatically renewed. See *American Woolen Company*, 57 NLRB 647. Our letter of July 27, 1959, was not an attempt to cancel the agreement but was written in contemplation of the fact that it will, by its terms, expire at midnight, July 31, as set forth above.

2. Aside from the foregoing, the agreement does not prohibit us from letting work to an independent contractor, and we have the right to do so. See *Amalgamated Association, etc., v. Greyhound Corporation*, 231 F(ed) 585.

3. While it will be necessary for us to lay off or terminate employees heretofore performing the work to be taken over by the contractor, we do not contemplate any lockout.

4. As we have stated in our letter of July 27, it appears that since we will have no employees in the bargaining unit covered by our present agreement, negotiations of a new or renewed agreement would appear to us to be pointless. However, we repeat that we will be glad to discuss with you at your convenience any questions that you may have.

After everyone had read the letter, Mr. Stumpf stated that the union committee was ready to negotiate a new contract; he also inquired as to whether or not the company had any counterproposals to submit. Thurmann replied that it would be pointless for management to proceed with any suggested modifications of the current agreement since, as of midnight July 31, 1959, the contract would have been terminated by its own language. Since the union had opened the contract, and since at the same time the Fluor Maintenance Corporation was taking over the maintenance work of the plant, Thurmann stated that to negotiate any modifications of an agreement being terminated by its own language "would be pointless." Stumpf argued that the agreement had not terminated, nor would it terminate at midnight, July 31, because of the automatic renewal clause.

Mr. Dan Arca, a member of the union negotiating committee, indicated concern over the shortness of the advance notice given employees and the union. He also wanted to know why the company decided to contract out its maintenance work.

Thurmann stated that the company first reached a definite decision to contract out the work to an independent contractor on July 27; he then had notified the union immediately.

Thurmann also stated that during the bargaining sessions in previous years, he had endeavored by the use of statistical data and various visual aids to point out "just how expensive and costly our maintenance work was and how it was creating quite a burden upon the Emeryville plant." He indicated that certain other unions representing the company's employees "had joined hands with management, thereby bringing about an economical and efficient operation." However, in his opinion, the Steelworkers had refused to cooperate in attempting to reduce maintenance costs.

Thurmann further commented that if the employees or the Steelworkers should desire to discuss the maintenance work contract at some later date, they should say so and he would give the request due consideration. Thurmann informed the union representatives that the men about to be terminated should apply to Fluor for jobs; he had already told Fluor's employment manager that some of the employees about to be terminated were very capable maintenance men. Fluor's employment manager had indicated that he "would be most happy to interview them and to consider them for employment."

Stumpf requested that the company modify the current labor agreement to require that all maintenance work to be performed under the Fluor contract should be given to members of Local 1304. Thurmann refused, saying, "We entered into this contracting of maintenance work for economy and efficiency of operation, and for us to tie the contractor's hands in any fashion, shape, or form would be senseless."

On July 30, the company distributed the following memorandum to all employees:

Nearly every month the cost of manufacturing the products of American industry shoots up another couple of percentage points. In most industries, and Fibreboard is no exception, stiff competition makes it impossible to pass on these higher costs through increased prices. This "cost-price" squeeze has forced many companies, and again Fibreboard is no exception, to face the economic facts of life and control costs efficiently all along the line.

This cost control is vital to us at Fibreboard because it is one of the few ways to assure the company and its more than 6,000 employees a future of greater prosperity through more efficient service to its customers.

Here at Emeryville, the cost of doing maintenance work has grown steadily. Studies during the past two years have shown that maintenance of our facilities by an outside crew instead of by our own employees would produce savings that would reduce the cost of our Emeryville products and make them more competitive.

Each of us is acutely aware of the implications of a decision to take this action. We have reached this decision only after long and careful study of all the facts.

We are confident that maintenance employees affected by this action—who are members of highly skilled and specialized trades—will have little difficulty in finding new jobs in time of great demand for skilled labor.

Fortunately, some of the employees affected will be able to share immediately in retirement benefits, which will provide them right away with some continuing income.

Additionally, we have prepared a program of termination allowances which would be distributed on a basis of length of service. For those who will share in retirement benefits, this termination allowance would be an added contribution to their income.

> J. P. Cornell, *Manager*
> Emeryville Floor Covering Plant
>
> E. W. Torbohn, *Manager*
> Emeryville Insulation Plant
>
> W. L. Maffey, *Works Engineer*
> Emeryville Utilities Group
>
> E. J. Vaught, *Manager*
> Emeryville Paint Plant
>
> S. F. Fridell, *Manager*
> Emeryville Roofing Plant & Felt Mill

On July 31, each of 73 terminated employees, about 50 of whom were members of Local 1304, was handed the following notice:

Inasmuch as we have contracted out all powerhouse and maintenance work, we will no longer need your services. Here is the paycheck due today and you will receive through the mails a termination allowance as shown on the personnel statement memo.

Your paycheck for this week will either be given to you at the close of the shift today or put in the mail tonight.

About 6 p.m. on July 31, the Steelworkers established a picket line around the Emeryville plant.

The employees of Fluor Maintenance, Incorporated, started performing the maintenance work at midnight, July 31.

Subsequently, the union filed unfair labor practice charges against the company, claiming that the company's actions were discriminatory in nature against the union, and were a refusal to bargain in good faith.

POSITION OF THE UNION

The union argued that the company entered into a hasty agreement with the Fluor company for the purpose of destroying the duly elected bargaining representative of the maintenance workers. This violated Section 8 (a) (3) of the Labor-Management Relations Act.

As evidence of this charge, the union noted that the company had announced its decision only four days prior to the expiration date of the contract. In support of its charge of discrimination, the union pointed to such things as: (*a*) the sequence of events; (*b*) the accelerated manner in which the maintenance contract had been executed;

(*c*) the delay in fixing a date for a bargaining conference; and (*d*) the company's refusal to bargain with respect to the Fluor contract or termination pay.

Further, the union claimed that the company did not give adequate notice of termination of the current collective agreement. The agreement required 60 days' advance notice, but the company notified the union only 4 days prior to the expiration date.

But most importantly of all, the company refused to bargain in good faith with the union over a significant change in the terms of employment. Under Sections 8 (a) (5) and 8 (d) of the Labor-Management Relations Act, the company had both a moral and legal obligation to negotiate the issue of contracting out the maintenance work at the Emeryville plant. By its actions, the union claimed that the company was guilty of unfair labor practices.

POSITION OF THE COMPANY

The company's argument proceeded as follows:

In 1954 the company became very concerned over the high cost of maintenance work at the Emeryville plant. The company initiated a two-year study in order to analyze reasons for the high costs and to explore the feasibility of effecting economies by contracting out the work. The study indicated that contracting out the work would result in substantial savings. Other pressing problems in the plant caused the company to drop the matter of contracting out the maintenance work until 1958.

In 1958, Mr. Thurmann informed Mr. George Burgess, the new vice president of manufacturing about the 1954–56 study; Mr. Burgess suggested that the data be brought up to date. The new data revealed that maintenance costs amounted to $750,000 per year.

The company then contacted four maintenance contractors, including Fluor. On July 27, the company received a written report which indicated that maintenance savings might run as high as $225,000. Fluor was selected over the other contractors principally because of its experience, reputation, and size.

The two-year contract with Fluor was on a cost-plus-fixed-fee basis; the company would pay Fluor the cost of operation plus a fixed fee of $2,250 per month. The contract provided that Fluor would:

Furnish all labor supervision and office help required for the performance of maintenance work ... at the Emeryville plant of Owner as Owner shall from time to time assign to Contractor during the period of this contract; and shall also furnish such tools, supplies and equipment in connection therewith as Owner shall order from Contractor, it being understood however, that Owner shall ordinarily do its own purchasing of tools, supplies and equipment.

The contract could be terminated by the company at any time on 60 days' notice.

Fluor had assured the company that maintenance costs could be curtailed by reducing the work force, decreasing fringe benefits and overtime payments, and by preplanning and scheduling the services to be performed.

The company maintained that it was not motivated by any desire to destroy the union. The company maintained good relations with the Steelworkers and other unions which represented its employees. The decision to contract out work simply represented the result of a five-year study of comparative costs. The company had repeatedly attempted to obtain the cooperation of the Steelworkers in reducing maintenance costs.

The very short notice given both employees and the union was caused by the need to obtain bids from maintenance contractors. The company did not engage in any form of delaying tactics. Both the company and the union had followed a bargaining pattern that was well established. For example, in 1957 the first bargaining meeting was not held until July 23; in 1958 the first meeting was held on July 13 and the contract was not signed until September 24.

In summary, the company claimed: (*a*) that its actions were motivated solely by economic reasons and not from any posture of trying to destroy the union, and (*b*) that it was not required under the circumstances of the case to bargain the issue with the union. The unfair labor practice charges should be dropped.

APPENDIX

The pertinent provisions of the current contract read as follows:

This agreement shall continue in full force and effect to and including July 31, 1959, and shall be considered renewed from year to year thereafter between the respective parties unless either party hereto shall give written notice to the other of its desire to change, modify, or cancel the same at least sixty (60) days prior to expiration.

Within fifteen (15) days after notice of reopening is given, the opening party shall submit a complete and full list of all proposed modifications. All other sections shall remain in full force and effect. Negotiations shall commence no later than forty-five (45) days prior to the anniversary date of the Agreement unless otherwise mutually changed.

QUESTIONS

1. Discuss the central issue of this case to both the union and management parties.
2. Is the company obligated under Section 8 (d) of the Labor-Management Relations Act to notify the union and to bargain over the issue of contracting out of maintenance work? Discuss.
3. Was the company's action in contracting out maintenance work and discharging maintenance employees discriminatory against the union as defined by Section 8 (a) (3) of LMRA? Discuss.
4. Are the company's claims that its actions were motivated by economic reasons alone valid in this situation? Should a company be permitted to contract out maintenance work or contract out other types of work where substantial economic advantages can be realized?
5. What are the major precedent implications of this case?

2. WHO IS ELIGIBLE TO VOTE IN A CERTIFICATION ELECTION?

COMPANY: Lock Joint Tube Company

UNION: International Union of Electrical, Radio, and Machine Workers, AFL-CIO

PRINCIPAL ISSUES OF THE CASE

There were three principal issues involved in this case. As a result of a series of incidents related to its organization attempts, the union filed several charges with the NLRB. In these charges, the union claimed that company management had violated the Labor-Management Relations Act by:

(a) Discriminating in violation of Section 8 (a) (3). This charge resulted from three layoff and separation actions, totaling 40 men.

(b) Interference in violation of Section 8 (a) (1). This issue was brought about by activities of the company after the union filed an election petition.

(c) Violation of Section 9 (c). Both the company and the union challenged the eligibility of a number of discharged employees and newly hired replacements to vote in the certification election.

BACKGROUND

Lock Joint Tube Company is an Indiana corporation having its office and place of business in South Bend, Indiana. The company is engaged in the manufacturing and finishing of electrically welded steel and butted tubing. About 40 persons were employed in production by the company in 1958.

The major issues in this case stemmed from self-organizational efforts begun by Lock Joint's employees in September, 1958. The company had been in operation for many years, but employees previously had never been represented by a recognized bargaining agent.

Mr. Joseph Smith,[1] the president of the company, had shown previous opposition towards union organizational attempts. In 1956, when a different union tried to organize the company, Mr. Smith sent a letter addressed to each "employee and wife" in which he said, among other things, "Remember, under protection of the National Labor Board, a union organizer or leader does not have to tell the truth."

Events Leading up to the First Layoff

In 1958, plant employee Jerry Friday assumed leadership in obtaining signatures upon union authorization cards furnished him by Al Keane, a field representative of the International Union of Electrical Workers. Between September 16 and 19, 18 employees signed these cards, and on the latter date Keane notified Mr. Smith by letter that he was filing a petition with the National Labor Relations Board seeking a certification election.

In his written response dated September 22, Mr. Smith said:

In reply to your letter of September 19, 1958, I do not consent to any agreement with your affiliation for any of our employees.

I do not believe that your union represents the majority of our employees and we will request a hearing by the National Relations Board [sic] in the event the matter is brought to our attention by that Board.

Smith then spent a good part of the same day in calling plant employees to his office, individually or in small groups, where he questioned them as to whether or not they had signed union cards. To a number of them he said that they did not have to tell him because he would find out anyway. If a hearing were held, he explained, the union would have to show him the cards. To several he termed the IUE as "Communist"; he further told several employees that "a union like that he would never accept." Two employees were told that he would eliminate another mill if necessary, and Smith warned them that if the employees went on strike they would be "walking out there a long, long time." Smith asked one group of three employees to reveal the names of anyone who had approached them asking them to sign cards.

On the evening of October 6, IUE representative Keane met with all the employees on the night shift, either at the company gate or off company property. Among those present were Jerry Friday and

---

[1] All names disguised.

Leadman William Jubel. The next morning Jubel informed Production Manager Joseph Metzler of this meeting.

Later that day (October 7) Chief Engineer Stibor and Mr. Smith decided to discontinue the plant's double-shift operation.

The Layoff of October 10

With no previous warning, all employees at the plant were notified two days later, on October 9, with the following bulletin signed by Mr. Smith:

TO ALL EMPLOYEES   OCTOBER 9, 1958

Certain business developments and change of conditions beyond the control of the Company require the discontinuance of the night shift effective at the close of such shift Friday night, October 10, 1958.

At such time it will be necessary to lay off the following employees for lack of work:

[11 employees listed by name]

The Company regrets the necessity for taking this action, but within the foreseeable future can see no opportunity of it being able to provide work for this group.

All other night shift employees will report for work on the day shift beginning at 8 a.m. Monday, October 13, 1958.

At least 9 of the 11 employees laid off had indicated their IUE affiliation by wearing union buttons on October 7 or earlier.

Events Leading to the Second Layoff and the Walkout

On October 16, about a week after the layoff, the NLRB regional office conducted a hearing on the petition for a certification election filed by the IUE. At this hearing, IUE representative Keane placed on a table before Smith and his counsel signed union cards, offering them for inspection. Mr. Smith's counsel told Keane that the company would not consider recognizing the IUE as the collective bargaining agency for the employees.

On October 23, Mr. Smith posted a notice announcing the layoff of seven more employees—all of whom were known by management to be IUE adherents, since they had openly been wearing union buttons. The notice listed the layoff at the close of the work shift the next day, October 24.

Among other things the notice said:

The Company regrets the necessity for taking the following action, but within the foreseeable future, can see no opportunity of it being able to provide work for this group.

That night, 22 employees gathered at Keane's home and voted unanimously to strike the next day in protest against the layoffs.

The Strike

About 9:30 a.m. on October 24, 23 workers walked out—only 7 production employees remaining—and proceeded to picket the plant carrying signs bearing legends protesting, among other things, against the "unfair layoffs."

Shortly after the strike began, Mr. Smith made the following statement to union representative Keane in a manner such that the strikers would be able to hear, "Thanks a lot, Keane, for letting me hire a new work force." He also made a statement to his leadman, "Them guys out there are all fired," and "Prepare to break in new help."

However, on November 25, the NLRB issued an order directing that a union certification election be held. The order stated that the critical date for eligibility to vote should be the payroll date immediately preceding issuance of the order, which was November 21. The same order contained the phrase: "ineligible to vote are employees who have, since that period, quit or been discharged for cause and have not been rehired or reinstated before the election date and employees who strike who are not entitled to reinstatement." After receipt of this direction, Mr. Smith sent 22 striking employees letters of discharge on December 4 and omitted their names from the eligibility list.

Each letter of discharge stated that the reason for termination was "misconduct in connection with current strike activities." All letters were of the same text; none cited any specific item of misconduct claimed for individual persons.

The Challenged Ballots

At the election on December 11, 1958, the company challenged the ballots of 27 voters on the ground that they had been strikers in an economic strike and had been replaced. As additional grounds for its challenge of 22 of this number, the company claimed that they had been discharged on December 4 for misconduct.

The company also challenged the ballots of two men on the ground that sometime after November 24 they notified the company that they had quit and obtained employment elsewhere. These two employees were among the 11 laid off on October 10.

At the same election, the IUE challenged the ballots of 12 employees, all of whom had been first hired by the company on November 4 or thereafter. The union claimed that if the company had not illegally created job vacancies, none of these 12 new employees would have been hired.

POSITION OF THE UNION

In substance, the following arguments outline the position of the union in regard to each of the principal issues stated at the outset of this case.

The Discrimination Charge

1) The company had rejected overtures toward union recognition and collective bargaining.
2) Dismissal of 11 employees on October 10 was done as a result of their union organization activities.
3) Layoff of seven more employees on October 24 was again the result of company hostility toward the union's organizing efforts.
4) Discharge of 22 strikers for misconduct was unjustified because:
   a) No specific item of misconduct was charged in the individual letters to the employees.
   b) Employer was engaged in a deliberate campaign to stop union activity among its employees.
   c) All of the above constituted illegal discrimination.

The Interference Charge

1) The company interrogated employees as to whether they had signed union cards.
2) The company requested from employees names of their fellow employees who solicited union cards.
3) The company had stated to employees that it would not accept the union and if they attempted to organize they would be locked out. All of the above constituted illegal interference.

The Election Charge

1) Discharged unfair labor practice strikers and five discriminatorily laid-off employees should have been eligible to vote in the representation election.

2) Two discriminatorily laid-off employees who were permanently employed elsewhere should still be eligible to vote, since they were illegally forced into a position of obtaining other employment.

POSITION OF THE COMPANY

Chief Engineer Stibor, who claimed that he "suggested" the layoffs to Mr. Smith, testified while holding in his hands certain documents which he called "master production schedules": "Had we continued to operate two shifts, mill No. 1 would have been out of the schedule of work on the 17th of the same month, October 1958." He went on to state that the same records showed that for mill No. 2 there were no orders beyond October 15, none for mill No. 3 beyond October 20, and none for mill No. 4 beyond October 15. He further said that such records showed this to be the state of affairs on October 7, 1958.

When asked as to his reasons for deciding to lay off the night shift, Mr. Smith stated, "We had a further reduction in orders." Smith also claimed that his "financial situation" necessitated the layoffs. Further, Smith advanced his financial situation as a reason for interviewing employees on September 22, and claimed that just before this he had received from his accountants a report showing that for the first six months of the year he had had a loss of "approximately $20,000."

In support of its discharging of 22 striking employees for misconduct, management representatives testified as to a series of incidents which had occurred during October and November, 1958. These were as follows:

October 24. Fourteen strikers blocked a driveway at the plant, not permitting a local employer named William Wiese to pass until police arrived.

October 24. A nonstriking employee was told by a striking employee "not to try to come in to work Monday or he would be sorry." This occurred as the nonstriker was driving through the gate.

October 27. Three nonstrikers were stopped by picketing employees for periods of up to 15 minutes as they tried to enter the plant to work.

October 28. Mr. Smith was delayed some 10 minutes by pickets circling the gate to the plant before he could drive through.

November 3. In three separate instances, nonstrikers were delayed by striking employees for periods of 10 to 15 minutes as they tried to enter the plant. One nonstriker, being subjected to profane language, drove home as a result.

November 5. A car window of a newly hired employee was broken as he attempted to enter the plant. Some 100 people were gathered near the gate, including at least 8 strikers.

November 7. Late in the afternoon, when a number of nonstrikers were leaving the plant, a large mob of unidentified people and many police were gathered outside the gate. The mob was unruly and disorderly, and the exit of the cars was impeded for about one half hour. The back window of one car was broken. Among the mass of several hundred people—according to management witnesses—were some nine strikers near the gate. The owner of the car was a newly hired employee, who testified that he saw a striking employee break the car window. [*Note:* The crowds of unidentified people present on both November 5 and November 7 included many people who had appeared at the plant as a result of the company's newspaper advertisement for new employees.]

November 13. As Mr. Stibor was leaving the plant with a number of nonstriking employees in his car, some 13 pickets whom he identified were circling in front of the exit gate. Police were there, opened the way, and Stibor went through.

November 28. On this occasion IUE representative Keane put a hand on the arm of one newly hired employee and told him not to go in. This same employee decided not to go in and accepted Keane's invitation to ride back into town with him. Later that afternoon, as nonstrikers left the plant, they were called names.

In light of all of these incidents, management witnesses claimed that their discharges of the 22 striking employees for misconduct on December 4 were justified. Therefore, these employees were not eligible to participate in a representational election.

The company further challenged the ballots of seven other men who had originally been laid off on October 10. On November 24, the company had offered reinstatement to nine of the laid-off men in view of a "better economic position of the company." Five of these men failed to respond to the company's offer of reinstatement;

therefore, management claimed, they had refused employment with the company. Also, two men who tried to vote in the December 11 election had notified the company in November that they had found employment elsewhere and did not wish reinstatement. Therefore, they, too, no longer were employees of Lock Joint Tube Company and had forfeited their voting eligibility. In support of this position, the company cited the NLRB order of November 25, which specifically stated that employees who had quit or who had been discharged for cause were ineligible to vote in the IUE representational election.

QUESTIONS

1. Did the company violate Section 8 (a) (3) of LMRA in: laying off the 11 night shift employees? in discharging the 22 unfair labor practice strikers? in the layoff of 7 additional employees during the second reduction in force? What evidence must an employer develop if an economic reduction in labor force is to be legal within the provisions of the Labor-Management Relations Act?
2. Did the company violate Section 8 (a) (1) of the act? If so, how and why?
3. Which of the discharged unfair labor practice strikers and laid-off employees, if any, should be ruled eligible to vote in the representation election? Why?
4. What, if any, remedial action should be taken in this case?

3. CAN AN UNFAIR LABOR PRACTICE BE COMMITTED IN A LOCAL CEMETERY?

COMPANY: Inglewood Park Cemetery Association

UNION: Miscellaneous Warehousemen, Drivers, and Helpers, Local 986, International Brotherhood of Teamsters, Chauffeurs, Warehousemen, and Helpers of America

PRINCIPAL ISSUES OF THE CASE

Inglewood Park Cemetery Association was charged with having engaged in certain unfair labor practices in violation of Section 8 (a) (1) and Section 8 (a) (3) of the Labor-Management Relations Act. Management of the cemetery association denied the jurisdiction of the National Labor Relations Board and further denied the commission of the alleged unfair labor practices.

BACKGROUND

Inglewood Park Cemetery Association is a California corporation engaged in the operation of a cemetery located in Inglewood, California. From July 1, 1962, through June 30, 1963, the association received revenue in excess of $500,000 from the sale to the public of services, burial lots, crypt spaces, and related items. In addition, it had purchased goods directly from outside the state of California totaling $3,086.

Miscellaneous Warehousemen, Drivers, and Helpers, Local 986, International Brotherhood of Teamsters, Chauffeurs, Warehousemen, and Helpers of America is the labor organization which filed unfair labor practice charges against the cemetery association on behalf of four employees of the association, John Lavan, Sam Doyle, Hector Lopez, and Willie Zobo.[1]

On June 26, 1963, Lavan, Doyle, and Lopez, after having completed their work for the day, went to the office of the business

---

[1] All names disguised.

representative for the union. They made inquiries concerning how Inglewood Park Cemetery employees might obtain membership in that organization. The union business representative explained the procedures to be followed and gave them a number of authorization cards. On the following day, before and after working hours and during the lunch period, the three employees distributed a number of these cards to their fellow workers.

During the afternoon of June 27, the foreman of the cemetery association ground crews approached Lavan, and asked him if he had passed out union cards. Lavan asked the foreman who had given him such information. The foreman replied that another employee had told him. Lavan requested that he be confronted with the foreman's informant. The foreman did not comply with Lavan's request, but told Lavan that if the superintendent of the cemetery association ever found out that employees were passing out union authorization cards, he would discharge them immediately.

On June 28, all employees were assembled in the cemetery chapel to hear the superintendent, Mr. A. H. Ponder. Mr. Ponder stated that he had heard that employees were trying to form a union, and that he would fight against it. He told them that workers at a nearby cemetery had joined a union and were receiving an hourly wage less than that paid by Inglewood Park. He reminded them that Inglewood Park also gave its employees uniforms and a Christmas basket. Finally, he stated that unionized employees at the other cemetery were dissatisfied with their union, and were waiting for the year to expire so that they could get out of the union.

When the meeting was over, each of the three employee organizers, Lavan, Doyle, and Lopez, plus a fellow worker, Willie Zobo, were summoned to Mr. Ponder's office. The four were ushered into the superintendent's office separately. Each was told that he was discharged and was given his final paycheck. Lavan and Doyle were informed that their discharges were for insufficient productivity and wasting time on the job. Lopez and Zobo, who worked together as marker trimmers, were told that as a team they had done nothing but "fool around" for three years, and therefore they were being discharged. Lopez, who was of Spanish extraction, testified later that he did not understand at the time why he was discharged.

POSITION OF THE UNION

The union charged that the management of the cemetery association engaged in unfair labor practices when: (*a*) the foreman approached Lavan inquiring about his union organizational activities; (*b*) when Superintendent Ponder made coercive statements to the group; and (*c*) when the same superintendent discharged the four employees, not for poor work records, but for union activities of an organizational nature.

The union presented evidence which indicated that each of the four employees had received periodic wage increases during their terms of service, which ranged from 4 to 11 years. Prior to the date of their discharges, the employees claimed that they had never received any warnings to the effect that their work was unsatisfactory, or that they were wasting excessive time. Their discharges were therefore based upon their union activity—including Zobo's discharge, since management felt that both Lopez and Zobo were closely related by the nature of their work.

The union argued that the cemetery association should be required to restore each employee to his former job, including all back wages and seniority rights, and further, that all discriminatory antiunion activity by management should be prohibited.

POSITION OF THE COMPANY

In its answer, Inglewood Park Cemetery Association admitted the foregoing facts of the case with respect to the four employees, but management denied that these facts constituted unfair labor practices. Management contended that Inglewood Park Cemetery was not engaged in interstate commerce; consequently, the association and its employees were not subject to the Labor-Management Relations Act. In support of this, management contended that its dollar purchases of some $3,000 worth of goods outside of California were not sufficient for classifying the association as being engaged in interstate commerce.

Management further claimed that the discharges of the four men were "coincidental" with their union activities. The work of the men had been unsatisfactory for a long period of time, and their union activities were the culmination of management's dissatisfaction with the men as employees.

Management's primary argument, however, rested upon the assertion that a local cemetery was an *intrastate* business and, therefore, Inglewood Park Cemetery Association was not subject to federal labor law.

QUESTIONS

1. What is the central issue upon which any decision in this case rests?
2. Did the company violate Section 8 (a) (3) and Section 8 (a) (1) of the Labor-Management Relations Act? Why?
3. Does the NLRB have jurisdiction in this case? Why? Are the standards used by the NLRB in asserting jurisdiction in this type of situation clear and reasonable?
4. Are remedial actions justified in this case? If so, what remedy should be taken?

4. THE CASE OF THE DISPUTED BAKERY PRODUCTS DELIVERIES

COMPANY: Associated Grocers, Incorporated

UNION: Bakery Salesmen's Local Union No. 227, International Brotherhood of Teamsters, Chauffeurs, Warehousemen, and Helpers of America

PRINCIPAL ISSUE OF THE CASE

Technically, this case focused upon a charge issued by the company that the union violated the secondary boycott provisions of the Labor-Management Relations Act. The fundamental issue involved, however, was what constitutes an illegal secondary boycott as opposed to the limits of a union's legitimate actions in trying to maintain its perceived jurisdictional job rights.

BACKGROUND

Associated Grocers, Inc., of Seattle, Washington, is a cooperative association engaged in supplying (at wholesale) groceries and related products to its members, who operate retail grocery establishments.

The Ruth Ashbrook Bakeries Corporation of Seattle is engaged in the operation of a bakery and in selling bakery products at wholesale.

Bakery Salesmen's Local 227, of the Teamsters Union, is the collective bargaining representative of Ashbrook's office employees, and of those employees engaged in wrapping, shipping, and delivery functions. Since May, 1960, Local 227 had a contract with Ashbrook covering the above-mentioned employees.

Until early 1961, Ashbrook baked sweet rolls, pastries, buns, rolls, and "brown and serve" products. Ashbrook's entire line was sold to other bakeries, who received the baked goods either by delivery by Ashbrook or by pickup at Ashbrook's loading dock. All trucks used for delivery and those used for pickup were manned by members of Local 227.

In September 1960, Ashbrook entered into a contract with Associated Grocers in which it agreed to supply baked goods— including private-label bread—to Associated. Associated was to supply these products to the stores of its members to be sold at retail.

Learning of the newly formed contract, Ross Stokke, an officer of Local 227, telephoned Ashbrook to inquire how delivery would be made to Associated. The president of Ashbrook, Mr. Stiles, answered that pickups would be made at the company's dock by Associated drivers. The union officer was told that in all probability Associated would join the Seattle Bakery Bureau, an organization through which Ashbrook was represented for collective bargaining with Local 227. This would mean that the new delivery jobs would come under Local 227 jurisdiction. Over the next few months, Stokke spoke on a number of occasions to Arthur Laline, manager of the Seattle Bakery Bureau. Mr. Laline suggested that Stokke contact Lewis Turner, a division manager for Associated, in order to inquire how Associated would distribute products supplied to it by Ashbrook and whether Associated would join the Bureau.

On December 29, Stokke met with officials of Associated. The purpose of the meeting was to present the fact that Local 227 desired to be recognized by Associated and to reach agreement with it concerning the distribution of bakery products. A spokesman for Associated stated that Associated already had a contract with another union covering employees who drove Associated's trucks. Stokke then asserted that the delivery of bakery products fell under the jurisdiction of Local 227. He suggested that Local 227, with the cooperation of the union representing the bakers, might stop the delivery of Ashbrook's products to Associated's drivers. Officials of Associated refused to make concessions to Local 227.

On January 2, Stokke sent a telegram to Ashbrook advising that picketing of Ashbrook's premises would begin in order to force Ashbrook "to bargain collectively with us concerning your plan to change your method of distribution."

In the early morning of January 3, an Associated truck appeared and began to load at the dock. At this time, Stokke and other union officials began to picket. Their signs read as follows:

"On Strike. Ruth Ashbrook Bakeries Refused to Bargain Collectively with Local 227." The truck was loaded by supervisory personnel. Union officials told Ashbrook employees not to load any Associated trucks. Beginning on January 5, Ashbrook employees represented by Local 227 went on strike and did not return until the removal of union pickets, which occurred one week later. During the picketing, some of the employees of Ashbrook's other customers refused to cross the picket line. On January 4 and 6, Local 227 sent telegrams to Ashbrook asserting that Ashbrook was changing its method of distribution and refusing to bargain with Local 227 about the change. Union officials informed their Ashbrook members that if Associated drivers would transfer into Local 227, "that would settle everything," and that Associated was refusing to bargain with Local 227.

Associated Grocers, Inc., filed charges with the NLRB that Local 227 was engaging in unfair labor practices in violation of Sections 8 (b) (4) (i) and (ii) (B) of the LMRA.

POSITION OF THE COMPANY

Management representatives claimed that the picketing by Local 227 and the strike, even if nominally characterized as an attempt to force Ashbrook to bargain, was of necessity an attempt to force Ashbrook to change its contractual relations with Associated. The picketing on the first day was designed to affect only the pickups by Associated. Ashbrook and Associated had agreed upon a plan for doing business with each other, and Local 227 by the picketing and strike was seeking to disrupt this arrangement. Local 227 exercised its authority of influence over Ashbrook employees to bring about a strike and posted its pickets to bring about a cessation of business between Ashbrook and Associated because it disapproved of the method of distribution which the contract established.

Associated management argued that these actions of the union were directly in violation of the secondary boycott and strike provisions of the Labor-Management Relations Act.

POSITION OF THE UNION

Local 227 contended that its contract with Ashbrook and the practices and customs of the industry required that no delivery of baked goods from Ashbrook be made, and no pickup at that location be permitted, unless the vehicle was driven by a member of Local 227. Although there was no specific provision in the contract to that effect, all delivery and pickups at Ashbrook's dock prior to the advent of Associated trucks were made by employees represented by Local 227, under the multiemployer contract with the Seattle Bakery Bureau to which Ashbrook was a party. Accordingly, Local 227, as the collective bargaining representative of the employees in the bargaining unit, had a direct interest: to protect the work assignments historically and customarily performed by the employees of Ashbrook in the bargaining unit. This it sought to accomplish. It contacted Ashbrook when it first heard about the proposed arrangement with Associated. Ashbrook refused to negotiate this matter, told Local 227 that it had nothing to worry about since Associated probably was going to join the Bureau, and suggested a meeting with Associated. Associated, in turn, when a meeting was arranged, flatly refused any accommodation because of the collective bargaining agreement it had with another labor organization.

Local 227 asserted that its dispute in reality was with Ruth Ashbrook Bakeries, which derived from Ashbrook's refusal to bargain concerning whose employees were to drive the trucks to deliver products for Associated Grocers. Ashbrook was contractually obligated to bargain this matter with Local 227, but unilaterally chose to enter into a contract with Associated which ceded the jobs to Associated employees.

The actions of Local 227 were necessary in order to protect the jobs and job opportunities of Ashbrook's employees. These actions included a primary strike action against Ashbrook Bakeries, which is not prohibited by the LMRA. The disruptions in Ashbrook's arrangements with Associated Grocers were "incidental" to the union's primary dispute with Ashbrook Bakeries.

Local 227's hope that Associated Grocers would become a member of the Seattle Bakery Bureau and thus have its trucks manned by members of Local 227 was an expectation suggested and encouraged by Ashbrook, and not a primary object of Local 227's strike against Ashbrook.

The unfair labor practice charge filed by Associated should be dismissed.

QUESTIONS

1. Was management justified in filing an unfair labor practice charge against Local 227 of the Teamsters Union? Why?

2. Was the union justified in its actions? Was the union guilty of engaging in unfair labor practices? If so, what remedial actions are necessary?
3. What is the difference between a primary strike action and a secondary strike action? Is this issue clear in this case?
4. Does a union have a right to try to protect jurisdictional job rights for members which it represents? What are the limits of this right? Are these limits easily definable?

5. MUST A UNION BARGAIN OVER SUPERVISORY SENIORITY?

COMPANY: Mobil Oil Company

UNION: Oil, Chemical, and Atomic Workers (OCAW)
International Union, Local Union No. 7-6444, AFL-CIO

On March 8, 1963, Local 7-6444 of the Oil, Chemical, and Atomic Workers International Union filed a charge with the National Labor Relations Board alleging that the Mobil Oil Company at its plant at East St. Louis, Illinois, was violating Section 8 (a) (5) of the Labor-Management Relations Act by insisting upon inclusion of the following supervisory seniority clause in the contract:

> If an employee covered by this Agreement or any previous agreement is or has been promoted to a management position, he will retain all position seniority in the department which he left and will accumulate plant seniority during the period he holds a management position.

BACKGROUND

Mobil Oil Company is engaged in the processing, sale, and distribution of petroleum and allied products at its plant in East St. Louis, Illinois. The OCAW Union is the certified bargaining agent of all production and maintenance employees, excluding office clerical employees, guards, professional employees, and supervisors. At the time of this case, the parties had negotiated 12 collective bargaining agreements, the first in 1944.

On April 1, 1962, negotiations began for a new contract. On April 19, 1962, the union proposed a change in Article IV, Section 26, of the contract, quoted above, which in varying forms had been included in each of the prior 12 contracts. The union wanted to add to that clause a new paragraph providing that any management employee who had retained seniority under the prior contract would forfeit seniority if during a strike he performed work normally assigned to an employee in the bargaining unit. This demand—including the proviso that such a strike be legal—was repeated in negotiation sessions of May 15 and July 9, 1962. The company's position was that supervisory persons had earned their seniority under the terms of the contract and if at any time they were no longer qualified for management positions, or if there were no management positions available, they should be able to return to jobs in the bargaining unit.

On August 27, 1962, OCAW took a new position: that any agreement reached in negotiations must exclude any reference to supervisory seniority. The union adhered to this position at a September 13 meeting. On November 1, union representatives stated that if Mobil insisted on retaining supervisory seniority, the union would file an unfair labor practice charge. However, both sides agreed that this issue should not hold up the signing of a contract.

During the bargaining sessions of December 5 and 6, OCAW proposed two alternatives to the company. The first would have eliminated the disputed clause from the contract. The second would have allowed present employees to retain their seniority for a 60-day probationary period following their promotion to management positions and would also give 30 days to those presently in management positions to decide whether they would return to the bargaining unit with their accumulated seniority. Failure to do so would result in forfeiture of all previously accumulated or retained seniority. On January 12, 1963, a revised version of this plan was submitted by OCAW to the company for its consideration. This modification would have allowed employees to retain their seniority in the bargaining unit for 90 days, instead of 60 days. The company refused to accept any of these plans, and insisted upon retention of the existing supervisory seniority clause in any new contract.

Between January 12 and February 1, 1963, the union agreed to sign a new contract under protest, with the understanding that the union would file an unfair labor practice charge. The parties agreed orally that the disputed clause would be deleted from the contract if it was declared a nonmandatory subject of bargaining by the National Labor Relations Board. But if the Board held the clause to be a mandatory subject of bargaining, it would remain in the contract. On February 1 the company wrote OCAW acknowledging that OCAW signed the contract under protest with the understanding that it would file an unfair labor practice charge. The new contract became effective February 5, 1963, for a term extending to March 10, 1964.

On March 8, 1963, OCAW filed a charge alleging violation of

Section 8 (a) (5). The union claimed that the company was committing an unfair labor practice in insisting upon retaining a supervisory seniority clause in the contract. The union argued that such a clause, since it did not cover employees in the bargaining unit, was not a mandatory subject for collective bargaining.

QUESTIONS

1. Why would the company insist on retaining a supervisory seniority clause in its labor agreement? Is this an important issue to the management and the union? Why?
2. Was the agreement between the company and the union that the union would file an unfair labor practice charge unusual? Did it serve any purpose?
3. Is seniority a mandatory subject for collective bargaining? Is supervisory seniority a mandatory subject for collective bargaining? Why, or why not?
4. Are issues such as these ("either-or" type problems) easy to bargain? How can a subject be bargained which appears to represent a basic policy dispute between the parties?

6. WHO ERECTS THE CONCRETE BEAMS?

COMPANY: Structural Concrete Corporation

UNION: International Association of Bridge, Structural, and Ironworkers, Local 474

BACKGROUND

The Structural Concrete Corporation designs, manufactures, and erects precast and prestressed concrete structural elements, such as beams, blocks, pilings, and slabs, for use in bridges and buildings. These products are designed in the company's plant at Laconia, New Hampshire, and manufactured in another plant at Franklin, New Hampshire. The company transports these products directly to the job site where crews erect these structural parts into place. All work normally is performed by the company's own employees, who since 1962 have been represented by the United Steelworkers of America, AFL–CIO.

Although precast concrete members have been utilized in northern New England since 1947, the use of prestressed concrete members in construction is a relatively new process in the United States. The Structural Concrete Corporation introduced this method of construction into northern New England in 1959.

In this method of construction, the members are fabricated at the company's plant, where iron reinforcing rods inside the members are placed under very high tension by means of hydraulic jacks in accordance with the load factor determined from the job specification. The tensioning process greatly increases the strength of the structural members. The members are shipped to the construction site, where they are erected. The principal erection problems arise out of the fact that these beams, slabs, and pilings are very heavy; they are easily damaged; and they fit together with very close tolerances.

When the company first started in the business of manufacturing and erecting precast and pretensioned structural elements, employees were not highly specialized in their work activities. Those who made up the erection crews actually spent a substantial amount of time in the manufacturing plant at Franklin. As the business expanded and the amount of erection work increased, the erection crews spent more time at the work sites than in the manufacturing plant. By 1960 erection crews were devoting only 5 percent of their time to manufacturing. These crews handle all phases of the erection operation, including the grouting of the structural members after they have been fitted together.[1]

The company includes in all its contracts provisions for the erection, as well as for the fabrication and delivery, of the prestressed concrete members. Except in two instances prior to October, 1962, the company utilized its own crews for all its erection work in the Maine, Vermont, and New Hampshire area where it operates. On these two occasions the company employed members of the Ironworkers union because they threatened a work stoppage at the job site if Ironworkers were not employed.

On October 19, 1962, the Steelworkers union filed a petition for certification of all production and maintenance employees and truckdrivers at the Laconia and Franklin, New Hampshire, plants, excluding office clerical employees, guards, and supervisors. It was determined at the representation hearing that erection work was part of the customary work of Structural.

The National Labor Relations Board certified the Steelworkers as the representative of all the employees indicated above.

The Manchester Incident

In April, 1963, the Structural Concrete Corporation subcontracted the erection of certain structural members from the Harvey Construction Company on a job for the Auclair Transportation Company in Manchester, New Hampshire. Nils Skorve, chief engineer for Structural, received a call from the Harvey Construction Company on the morning of April 15, indicating that trouble was brewing on the job and requesting him to phone Benjamin Roy, president of the Ironworkers. Skorve discussed the situation with Peter Millham, Structural's attorney, who later spoke to Roy on the telephone while Skorve listened to this conversation on the extension. In this conversation, Roy claimed the work of erecting the concrete members on

---

[1] After the concrete beams, slabs, or pavements have been put into place, the joints are grouted, that is, filled with a mortar mixture fluid enough to be poured.

the Auclair job. Roy stated that Ironworkers would be required to take action if the work were not awarded to it. Millham's version of the conversation was that Roy declared, "If you don't put our men on this job, we are going to pull everybody off; we are going to close the job down."

On the same date, Skorve received a call from Bernard Cowette, business agent for the Ironworkers. Cowette repeated the point that employees of Structural could not perform erection work in Manchester and threatened to take action on the job if the crew were not changed. At this point, because of a promise to Mr. Harvey not to have trouble on the job, the Structural company management decided to hire the Ironworkers. Skorve instructed the foreman of the erection crew at the construction site to obtain Ironworkers the next morning.

According to Henry Lessard, construction foreman for the Harvey company, Benjamin Roy came to the Auclair job on the afternoon of April 15. On the following morning, the foreman for the Smith Masonry Company, a mason subcontractor on the job, told him that his men would not go to work until after the dispute about the beams had been settled. The masons did not report to work at their usual 8 a.m. starting hour. The Structural foreman, following instructions from Skorve, hired Ironworkers to complete the job. After he had begun to hire Ironworkers, the masons returned to work.

Benjamin Roy stated that it was his understanding that Ironworkers would be used on the Auclair job. Roy claimed that on April 12, Richard Carrier, a foreman employed by Structural, had told him that he would be called upon to supply Ironworkers for the Auclair job. William J. Welsh, an Ironworker foreman, substantiated Roy's statement. Roy said that when he did not receive the expected call, he visited the site to determine what was happening. He stated that he found that the job had begun without Ironworkers; he became involved in an argument with Carrier; and then he called Mr. Harvey, who told him that he had also thought Structural planned to use Ironworkers on the job. Roy denied that he made any threats to close down the job and also denied inducing any other tradesmen on the job to refrain from doing any work for Harvey or his subcontractors. He admitted that he noticed that the masons were not working on the job on the morning following his first visit. Fred Jada, representative of the Mason Tenders Union, stated that neither Roy nor any of the other Ironworkers representatives requested that he call his men off the job.

POSITION OF THE COMPANY

The Structural Concrete Corporation, following this incident, filed charges under Section 8 (b) (4) (D) of the Labor-Management Relations Act, alleging that the International Association of Bridge, Structural, and Ornamental Ironworkers, Local 474, induced or encouraged employees to cease work in order to force or require Structural to assign the work in dispute to members of Ironworkers.

The company contended that the NLRB certification of the Steelworkers encompassed erection crews as well as production and maintenance employees. Since its assignment of work to the Steelworkers conformed to this certification, the work must be awarded by the Board to employees in this unit.

The company further argued that the skill and experience of its regular crews in performing the work, customary practice of the industry and of the company, and efficiency and economy required that the work be assigned to its own employees, who were represented by the Steelworkers.

POSITION OF THE UNIONS

The Steelworkers union agreed with the company that it should be awarded the work in question.

The Ironworkers union contended that NLRB certification did not cover the Structural employees performing the erection work, since the classification of "erection employee" was not specifically mentioned in the certified unit.

The Ironworkers union further argued that erection work is a task traditionally assigned to members of, or employees represented by, the Ironworkers.

ADDITIONAL BACKGROUND INFORMATION

The members of the Ironworkers union do not customarily grout the pieces after they are put in place, and they cannot work outside of their geographical jurisdictional limits. The Steelworkers, on the other hand, perform the grouting task and follow the company's operations wherever they may be located. At the time of this case, members of the Steelworkers union performed 60 percent of the erection of prestressed concrete members in northern New England.

QUESTIONS

1. Is this situation covered by Section 8 (b) (4) (D) of the Labor-Management Relations Act? Why?
2. Was the fact that the job in the case was subcontracted to a second company germane to the union's claim that another union besides the Steelworkers was entitled to the jurisdictional rights?
3. Should the NLRB rule to prevent similar disputes of this sort in the future? Does it have authority under the LMRA to do so?

7. DOES MANAGEMENT HAVE THE RIGHT TO DECIDE WHICH UNION IS ENTITLED TO PERFORM WORK ON NEW MACHINES?

COMPANIES: Libbey-Owens-Ford Glass Company and Pittsburgh Plate Glass Company

UNIONS: Window Glass Cutters League of America, AFL-CIO, and United Glass and Ceramic Workers of North America, AFL-CIO-CLC

PRINCIPAL ISSUES OF THE CASE

This case arose under Section 10 (k) of the Labor-Management Relations Act, which states:

> Whenever it is charged that any person has engaged in an unfair labor practice within the meaning of paragraph (4) (D) of Section 8 (b), the Board is empowered and directed to hear and determine the dispute out of which such unfair labor practice shall have arisen . . . .

Libbey-Owens-Ford and Pittsburgh Plate Glass jointly filed charges against five locals of the Window Glass Cutters League. The charges alleged that the league had induced its members to strike the companies in order to force the companies to assign work connected with operating of glass-cutting machines to league members, rather than to employees who were members of the Glass and Ceramic Workers union. This strike allegedly violated paragraph 8 (b) (4) (D) of the Labor-Management Relations Act. The regional director of the NLRB examined the facts and provided for a hearing.

The case thus involved a dispute over jurisdictional rights to work claimed by two recognized bargaining units. An added issue concerned the right of management to arbitrarily assign certain work to one of two recognized bargaining units.

BACKGROUND

Libbey-Owens-Ford Glass Company and Pittsburgh Plate Glass Company operate window glass plants at several locations in West Virginia and Ohio. Both companies bargain collectively with locals of the Window Glass Cutters League and with the United Glass and Ceramic Workers (here to be referred to as the Glass Workers union).

The Window Glass Cutters League is a craft union of window glass cutters and inspectors. The league has been recognized by the Libbey-Owens-Ford company as the representative of all its plants with respect to glass cutters and inspectors since 1917. This recognition was received at Pittsburgh Plate Glass in 1928. Both companies have recognized the Glass Workers union as the representative bargaining unit of all remaining production and maintenance workers since 1933.

In 1939, the Glass Workers union obtained proper NLRB certification for all plant workers, excluding the glass cutters and inspectors. The league never received NLRB certification for representation of any segment of the work forces of the companies involved, although in 1948, the league did receive union-shop authorization certificates for its units after an NLRB-conducted election.[1]

Since 1945, both companies have bargained jointly with the league.

Prior to 1933, all glass cutting was done by hand. This manual process requires a high degree of skill; a three-year apprenticeship was provided for the acquisition of these skills. In 1933, both companies introduced automatic cutting machines to replace some manual operations. The period 1933 to 1958 saw an increase in the number of cutting machines and a corresponding decrease in the amount of manual work performed. During this 25-year period, skilled jobs on the cutting machines were carried out by cutters, and the league was the recognized bargaining unit for these jobs. In both the manual cutting operations and the machine operations, the Glass Workers performed only miscellaneous unskilled jobs, such as bringing the glass to the cutting tables and removing it.

During contract negotiations carried out in April, 1958, the companies proposed to transfer all machine glass-cutting jobs to the Glass Workers union. The league objected and further negotiations failed

---

[1] Under 1947 Taft-Hartley amendments to the National Labor Relations Act, union-shop contract provisions were not permitted unless the workers in the bargaining unit voted to approve the union shop in an NLRB-conducted election. This union-shop election requirement was repealed in 1951.

to resolve the disagreement. The parties agreed not to include the question of awarding the machine glass-cutting jobs in the April, 1958, contract. Rather, a supplemental agreement was negotiated, independent of the contract, which stated: [2]

1) That the league and the Glass Workers both claimed jurisdiction over the machine glass-cutting work.
2) That the companies claimed the work of operating the cutting machines belonged to the Glass Workers.
3) That in view of the fact that the parties had failed to reach agreement, the jurisdiction of the NLRB could be invoked to resolve the issue; any decision reached would be final and not subject to appeal.

In May, 1958, several new glass-cutting machines were bought and installed by the Libbey-Owens-Ford company and by Pittsburgh Plate Glass. Notices were posted by each stating that the companies were accepting applications for the jobs involved in operating the new machines. Applications turned in by members of the league were categorically refused by the companies. On May 12, 1958, the companies began to operate these new machines with members of the Glass Workers. The members of the league struck in protest, with the league claiming that these jobs belonged to it. The machines were immediately closed down, and the cutters then returned to their work. The companies' 8 (b) (4) (D) charges were based on that strike action.

Both parties agreed that operation of the new machines was substantially similar to the operation of older installed machines. The major difference was that with the new machines a "management employee" (i.e., foreman), rather than a cutter, would be responsible for setting up the machine and laying out the work in preparation for the cutting to be performed on large panes of glass.

POSITION OF THE UNIONS

1. United Glass and Ceramic Workers of North America.   The Glass Workers union contended that operations performed by the new machines were much more closely integrated into the production process than were operations performed by workers cutting glass manually. Therefore, the jobs properly belonged in the production and maintenance units, because they fell within the 1939 certifications for such jobs.

---

[2] See appendix following this case for full statement.

2. *Window Glass Cutters League of America.*

a) The league claimed that the 25 years of bargaining for the disputed work, with obvious management recognition, had established representation and bargaining rights which constituted a "lawful basis" for its strike activity.

b) The NLRB union-shop certification received in 1948 was sufficient certification within the meaning of paragraph 8 (b) (4) (D), and established the league's right to the disputed work.

c) The similarity in operation of the new machines as compared with the old refuted any logical basis for reassignment of the work to the Glass Workers union.

POSITION OF THE COMPANIES

The companies contended that it was unlawful under Section 8 (b) (4) (D) for the league to strike to secure the disputed work, unless the league had a Board certification, or a Board order, or a current contract entitling it to the work, and that the league had none of these. They contended further that the strike could not be justified on the ground of the past practice and custom with respect to the assignment of the machine cutting jobs, and that even if such past practice and custom were material, there had been no consistent practice in this respect or clear establishment of past contract rights to the work. In support of this primary contention, they pointed to certain cases in which the Board has said that an employer is free to make work assignments without being subject to strike pressure, unless the employer is failing to conform to an order or certification of the Board, or unless the employer is bound by a current agreement to assign the disputed work to the claiming union.

In support of their contention that the league had no current contract right to the disputed work, the companies pointed to the fact that the current contract did not cover the machine cutting jobs, and asserted that the league thereby bargained away any contract right to those jobs.

APPENDIX

The April 25, 1958, Supplemental Agreement provided:

Whereas the Companies are about to put into operation cutting machines for mechanical cutting of window glass;

Whereas the League claims jurisdiction over the occupations of Cutting Machine Operator, Reject Cutter—Machine Cut Glass, and Inspector—Machine Cut Glass (referred to herein as the Cutting Machine Occupations);

Whereas the United Glass and Ceramic Workers of North America, AFL–CIO–CLC, claims jurisdiction over the Cutting Machine Occupation;

Whereas the position of the Companies is that the Cutting Machine Occupations properly belong in the bargaining unit represented by the United Glass and Ceramic Workers of North America, AFL–CIO–CLC;

Whereas the parties have been unable to resolve the foregoing issues by agreement and the jurisdiction of the National Labor Relations Board may be invoked to resolve the jurisdictional issues;

Now, therefore, in the event the jurisdictional issues are decided by the National Labor Relations Board, the parties agree as follows:

1) Any decision of the National Labor Relations Board as to the union which shall have jurisdiction over the Cutting Machine Occupations shall be final and binding and no party hereto shall appeal from such decision.

2) In the event the National Labor Relations Board shall decide that the League has jurisdiction over one or more of the Cutting Machine Occupations the following procedures are agreed to:

   a) Within ten (10) days after the Board's final decision, the parties will meet in joint session and endeavor to reach agreement on the base rate to be paid on any Cutting Machine Occupation within the League's jurisdiction.

   .   .   .   .

   b) The parties recognize that there is at present no procedure in the bargaining unit represented by the League for installing wage incentives on the Cutting Machine Occupations. Accordingly, it is agreed that in the event either Company elects to install wage incentive on any Cutting Machine Occupation within the League's jurisdiction at any window glass plant, such incentive will be installed in accordance with the practice currently being followed at that plant when putting other machine operation on incentives. . . . .

QUESTIONS

1. What are the principal arguments in favor of awarding the work on the new glass-cutting machines to members of the Window Glass Cutters League? To the Glass Workers union?

2. Why was the company anxious to see that the Glass Workers union received jurisdictional rights to the new work? Should management be given free latitude to decide in the case of instituting new work and new work practices?

3. Did the Window Glass Cutters League bargain away its contract right to the jobs by signing the supplemental agreement included in the appendix of the case? Which union should be awarded the work on the new machines? Why?

8. THE CASE OF THE FROZEN ORANGE CROP

COMPANY: Minute Maid Corporation

UNION: International Brotherhood of Teamsters, Chauffeurs, Warehousemen, and Helpers of America, Cannery, Citrus Workers, Drivers, Warehousemen and Allied Employees, Local 444

PRINCIPAL ISSUES OF THE CASE

The union filed charges against Minute Maid Corporation in April, 1958, alleging that Minute Maid had engaged in unfair labor practices by: (*a*) withdrawing recognition of the union pending decertification proceedings; and (*b*) avoiding its duty to bargain collectively in good faith. The union complaint alleged that these actions of Minute Maid violated Sections 8 (a) (1) and 8 (a) (5) of the Labor-Management Relations Act.

BACKGROUND

Minute Maid Corporation is a Florida corporation having offices and a plant located in Auburndale, Florida, and is engaged in the business of processing fruits and juices and other agricultural commodities.

International Brotherhood of Teamsters, Chauffeurs, Warehousemen, and Helpers of America, Cannery, Citrus Workers, Drivers, Warehousemen, and Allied Employees, Local 444, gained representational rights for the company's production and maintenance employees (including warehousemen, checkers, cafeteria employees, leadmen, and peel oil operators) in an NLRB election held in February, 1957. These workers continued to work without a formal contract while Minute Maid and the union engaged in a series of bargaining conferences beginning in April of 1957. A "final" proposal for a contract was submitted by the union in October of that year. Minute

Maid submitted a counterproposal in November, 1957. Both Minute Maid and the union rejected each other's proposals; the union rejection came on December 7, 1957. On the night of December 11 and the morning of December 12, a severe freeze hit the Florida citrus area, inflicting extensive damage on the crops. The following day (December 13, 1957), Minute Maid sent a telegram to the union withdrawing its November contract offer in entirety, assertedly because of the union's rejection of that agreement and "the economic uncertainty created by the freeze."

On December 19, 1957, both parties again met at the bargaining table. In this meeting, Minute Maid representatives stated that further bargaining should be delayed until January, 1958, due to the unsettled economic conditions resulting from the freeze. The plant superintendent stated at this meeting that the company wouldn't engage in a discussion of any proposals until more information on actual crop damage was available. A written memorandum to this effect was given to the union.

Early in January, 1958, the union submitted to Minute Maid another "final" offer; this offer was a modification of its previous offer in October that Minute Maid had rejected. In this proposal, the union agreed to an 8½¢-per-hour pay increase which had been part of the company's rejected offer in November. This union proposal was rejected by the company's director of industrial relations on the grounds that it contained matters that had not previously been agreed upon, and that freeze damage from December and another freeze on January 9, 1958, had not been determined, making cost considerations impossible at the time. Along with its notice of rejection, the company proposed that the parties meet on February 6, 1958; the union agreed to this meeting.

At the February 6 meeting, Minute Maid's director of industrial relations stated that the company couldn't discuss economic issues but "might reach *tentative* agreement on other aspects of the contract." Arguments and name calling on both sides resulted in the meeting's termination with an agreement to meet again on February 13. This meeting on the 13th was a continuation of the deadlocked negotiations of February 6. On the nights of February 14, 18, and 21, further freezes occurred.

On February 21, an employee of Minute Maid filed a decertification petition with the National Labor Relations Board's regional office. Three days following the filing of this petition, the industrial relations director of Minute Maid sent a telegram to the union withdrawing recognition of the union and canceling the next scheduled meeting on the ground that a "large majority" of the employees had signed the petition "repudiating the union and requesting that Minute Maid break off negotiations." Minute Maid stated that since the NLRB's certification year had expired effective February 20, 1958, it would be illegal for the company to continue to recognize and deal with the union until after the decertification matter was settled. For the next two months, the union sought—without success—to continue further contract negotiations with Minute Maid, while Minute Maid sought—also without success—to have the union agree to an election on the decertification issue.

On April 18, 1958, Minute Maid, without prior consultation with the union, announced the granting of a nominal bonus to company employees based upon the amount of company earnings for the 1957–58 season; these bonuses were paid over the next 8 to 10 weeks.

On June 9, 1958, the regional director of the NLRB dismissed the decertification petition. Further attempts at reaching an agreement were attempted by the union, but were rejected by the company.

POSITION OF THE COMPANY

Essentially, Minute Maid contended that in view of the economic uncertainty created by the freezes, it was justified on December 19, 1957, and thereafter, in asking for a *temporary delay* in wage negotiations. The company stated that this uncertainty justified its temporary refusal to discuss wage proposals, even after the union had agreed to company wage terms offered prior to the freezes. Minute Maid claimed that no company should be placed in a position of bargaining over wages when economic conditions facing the company are virtually unknown. Further, since the company had serious doubts as to whether the union actually represented the majority of its employees, the company certainly was justified in refusing to negotiate with the union until after the decertification issue had been settled.

The company cited Section 8 (d) of the LMRA, which states that the obligation to bargain collectively "does not compel either party to agree to a proposal or require the making of a concession." The company claimed that under the uncertain conditions surrounding both the industry and the union itself, a temporary refusal to reach a wage agreement was in accordance with the above provision.

POSITION OF THE UNION

In regard to the decertification petition, the union contended that Minute Maid's unfair and illegal actions in refusing to bargain in good faith brought about the conditions that led to the filing of the petition. The unilateral granting of bonuses to the employees was an attempt by the company to discredit the union in violation of Section 8 (a) (1). The fact that a decertification petition was pending did not justify the company's refusal to continue negotiations with the union in good faith.

The union contended that the company's firm and inflexible refusal to bargain with the union, even under conditions of economic uncertainty, constituted a direct violation of Section 8 (a) (5) of the LMRA as further defined in Section 8 (d): ". . . to bargain collectively is the performance of the mutual obligation of the employer and the representative of the employees to meet at reasonable times and confer in good faith with respect to wages, hours, and other terms and conditions of employment, or the negotiation of an agreement, or any question arising thereunder . . .".

QUESTIONS

1. Was the company guilty of an unfair labor practice in refusing to bargain over economic issues under the circumstances involved? Should any company be placed in a position of bargaining over wages when economic conditions facing a company are virtually unknown?
2. Was the company justified in refusing to bargain with the union on the premise that the company doubted whether the union actually represented the majority of its employees?
3. Should the company be permitted to withdraw recognition of the union and grant the bonuses to the employees?
4. Was the company guilty of unfair labor practices in violation of Section 8 (a) (1) and 8 (a) (5) of the LMRA? Why, or why not? Are remedial actions required in this situation?

9. THE DUTY TO BARGAIN AND THE MANAGEMENT PREROGATIVES CLAUSE

COMPANY: Le Roy Machine Company, Incorporated

UNION: Local 481, International Union, United Automobile, Aerospace, and Agricultural Implement Workers of America (UAW)

PRINCIPAL ISSUES OF THE CASE AND APPLICABLE CONTRACT CLAUSE

Each of the two principal problems of this case involved the legal issue of what constitutes the duty to bargain collectively of Section 8 (a) (5) of the Labor-Management Relations Act. The specific problems were concerned with the following questions: (*a*) Does a demand by management that certain employees take physical examinations have to be opened to collective bargaining with the union? and (*b*) Should the setting of wage rates on new jobs be left to management's discretion, or must they be open to collective bargaining?

Under the contract effective at the time of this case (June 1, 1962 to May 31, 1965), the following "management prerogatives" clause was included as Article IV of the agreement:

The Company retains the sole right to manage its business and direct the working force, including the rights to decide the number and location of plants . . . ; to determine whether and to what extent the work required in its business shall be performed by employees covered by this agreement; . . . including the sole right to discipline, suspend and discharge employees for cause; to hire, lay off, assign, transfer, promote, and determine the qualifications of employees; . . . subject only to such regulations governing the exercise of these rights as are expressly provided in this agreement.

The above rights of management are not all-inclusive, but indicate the type of matters or rights which belong to and are inherent to management. Any of the rights, powers, and authority the Company had prior to entering this collective bargaining are retained by the Company, except as expressly and specifically abridged, delegated, granted, or modified by this agreement.

The interpretation of this clause—and its relationship to Section 8 (a) (5) of LMRA—were key elements in the issues of the case.

The Physical Examinations

In mid-January, 1963, company representatives hand-delivered a letter to 19 of approximately 170 employees in the bargaining unit.[1] Each letter stated that the employee's attendance record indicated an excessive amount of tardiness and absenteeism, and that the company wished to ascertain whether this was occasioned by the employee's physical condition. Each employee was asked to take the letter and an enclosed sheet to a doctor of his choice; at the company's expense, the doctor was to examine the employee and report the result to the company.

On March 1, 1963, the company sent a follow-up letter to four employees who had not complied with the request in the January letter. This March 1 letter included a statement to the effect that failure to arrange for a physical examination by March 15 would result in disciplinary action. The company letter further stated that its purpose in requesting the physical examination was to determine whether the employee's health was such as to necessitate his transfer to another job, to another shift, or perhaps termination.

On March 14, 1963, a committee from the union, together with a UAW International representative, met with the plant manager and personnel manager to discuss the company's request that the 19 employees submit to physical examinations. The union asked if the taking of the examinations was a condition of employment of the 19 men. The company representatives replied that in regard to these 19 employees and any other employees who might later be asked to submit to such examinations, the results of the examination would be a factor in their continued employment with the company. The UAW International representative then asked that the company bargain with the union regarding "the rules and regulations of how, when, why, and what

---

[1] The selection of the 19 employees to receive the letter was on the basis that their individual absentee and tardy rate exceeded 12½ percent.

physical examinations will be required." Under Article IV of the contract, the company refused, taking the position that it was the company's prerogative to require such examinations. At the union's request, the plant manager put in writing his refusal to discuss the subject with the union. Eventually, all 19 employees submitted to the examination, although at the time of the hearing of this case, the company had taken no action concerning these employees.

Rates for New Jobs

In April, 1963, the local union president, chief shop steward, and vice president met with officials of the company. The meeting was requested by the union to protest the company's unilateral fixing of a wage rate on a new job in the plant—a Mack truck job—which the union regarded as lower than the rate being paid for comparable work in the plant. The company's vice president took the position that under the management prerogative clause (Article IV) in the contract, the company was entitled to unilaterally fix any rate it pleased for a new job. No solution satisfactory to the union representatives was reached at this meeting, so a future meeting at which the union's international representative could be present was arranged. At this meeting held early in May, the international representative stated that the company was obligated to bargain with the union regarding the proper rate of pay for new jobs. Company officials again insisted that the management prerogative clause reserved to management the right to fix the rates on new jobs unilaterally, and that it would not bargain with the union on that subject. The meeting concluded on that note.

In the interval between the April and May meetings, as the union sought to bargain the wage rates for new jobs, three grievances were filed protesting the company's actions in this regard. The company declined to process the first grievance because "it presented a policy issue not subject to the grievance procedure provided in the contract." The grievance was then refiled by an individual, and the company refused to process it on the ground that it presented the same issue as the previous one. The third filing was by an individual assigned to the particular job, and the company declined to process it on the ground that the time limitation for such a grievance had expired.

POSITION OF THE UNION

The union filed an unfair labor practice charge with the NLRB, contending that the Le Roy Machine Company had violated Section 8 (a) (1) and (5) of the Labor-Management Relations Act by refusing to bargain with Local 481 concerning: (*a*) the company's demand that certain employees submit to physical examinations, and (*b*) the rates of pay for new jobs.

The union argued that Section 8 (a) (5) of the act imposes upon an employer the obligation to bargain collectively with the representatives of his employees, and Section 8 (d) defines the term "bargain collectively" as imposing the obligation:

... to meet at reasonable times and confer in good faith with respect to wages, hours, and other terms and conditions of employment, or the negotiation of an agreement, or any question arising thereunder ....

The union claimed that the company had assumed a *fixed* position not to bargain concerning either the physical examinations or the new job wage rates. Yet these clearly are "conditions of employment" over which an employer is obligated to bargain under Section 8 (d) of the act.

The union requested that the company be ordered to bargain collectively with Local 481 with respect to the taking of physical examinations by any of the union employees and the fixing of wage rates for new jobs; if an understanding was reached, this was to be included in a signed agreement.

POSITION OF THE COMPANY

Concerning the physical examination issue, the company contended that requiring its employees to submit to a physical examination was not a "term or condition of employment," but rather a "prerequisite of employment." The company noted that it is a well-accepted principle that the establishment of employee qualifications is a basic management decision not subject to collective bargaining. Therefore, an employer from time to time and without consultation with the union should be permitted to require an employee to submit to a physical examination to demonstrate that he still possesses the "underlying prerequisites of employment."

However, even if the Board should hold that the physical examinations were a mandatory subject of collective bargaining, the union had waived its right to bargain about this matter by virtue of the management prerogative clause (Article IV).

Article IV—the management prerogative clause of the collective-bargaining agreement—provides that: "The Company retains the sole right to . . . hire, lay off, assign, transfer, promote, and determine the qualifications of employees; . . . subject only to such regulations governing the exercise of these rights as are expressly provided in this agreement." The language of the contract is clear; it gives management the right to determine the "qualifications of employees," which—the company contended—would certainly include periodic physical examinations. Therefore, by agreement with the union this issue was removed from the scope of collective bargaining during the term of the contract.

In regard to the issue of rates of pay for the new jobs, the company conceded that the appropriate rate of pay for a new job was a bargainable issue, but argued that the company satisfied its bargaining obligation by reason of the current contract negotiated and executed by the parties.

In support of this argument, the company pointed out the following:

(1) For many years the company had unilaterally fixed and posted rates for new jobs; (2) a union grievance on this issue filed in 1958 was withdrawn when the company took the position that fixing rates of pay for new jobs was a matter of management prerogative; (3) during 1959 and 1962 contract negotiations, the matter of wage rates for new jobs was neither raised nor discussed by the union; (4) in the 1962 negotiations, wage rates were agreed upon and incorporated into the contract for new jobs which came into the plant after the 1959 contract; (5) except for the 1958 grievance mentioned above, the company had received no protest concerning its unilateral fixing of wage rates for new jobs; and (6) the management prerogatives clause (Article IV) was made a part of the contract in 1962, reserving to management all authority not "expressly and specifically" surrendered by the contract. From all of this, the company argued, the union had waived its right to require the company to bargain with respect to the issue of wage rates for new jobs.

QUESTIONS

1. What is meant by the duty to bargain in good faith as required under the Labor-Management Relations Act? Must a union and management bargain over any issue?

2. Was the requirement for employees to submit to a physical examination a "condition of employment" or a "prerequisite of employment"? Does this determination have a bearing upon this case?
3. Was the company acting arbitrarily and unjustly in requesting the 19 employees to submit to physical examinations? Was this a bargainable issue?
4. Was the wage rate for the new job in the plant a bargainable issue? Did the company commit an unfair labor practice by not bargaining over this issue? Did the management prerogative clause reserve to management the right to fix rates on new jobs unilaterally?
5. Evaluate the arguments of the company in support of its position concerning the fixing of wage rates on a new job.

10. SHOULD THE UNION BE ALLOWED TO CONDUCT ITS OWN TIME STUDY ON COMPANY PREMISES?

COMPANY: The Fafnir Bearing Company

UNION: The International Union, United Automobile, Aerospace, and Agricultural Implement Workers of America, Local No. 133, UAW

BACKGROUND

Fafnir Bearing Company is a manufacturer and marketer of ball bearings and other related products. It is located in New Britain, Connecticut. Since 1944, the company has engaged in collective bargaining with the UAW.

The agreement in force at the time of this case (1963) contained an incentive wage clause. According to the agreement, the company could establish standard rates of production which were intended to reflect the number of pieces that would be produced by an average employee with normal incentive. Any employee who exceeded this rate was entitled to piecework compensation that was proportionately in excess of his regular hourly rate.

The company's industrial engineers—or ratesetters—are responsible for establishing the standard rates. Their time study procedures follow the generally accepted elemental time study method, which usually is described in production management or industrial management literature.[1]

The ratesetter must observe the employee performing work tasks. As a preliminary step, the ratesetter writes up the conditions and circumstances connected with the operation involved, and under which he intends to conduct the time study. These include the lay-

---

[1] For example, see Raymond R. Mayer, *Production Management* (New York: McGraw-Hill Book Co., 1962), pp. 73–130; or Franklin G. Moore, *Manufacturing Management* (4th ed.; Homewood, Ill.: Richard D. Irwin, Inc., 1965), pp. 538–74.

out of the place where the work is to be done; heat, if a factor; lighting; and all other components affecting the completion of the job. After this, the ratesetter reduces the work content of the job into individual items called work content elements, or cyclic elements. Noncyclic elements are taken into consideration, although they do not enter into every single cycle. Some noncyclic elements, for example, may involve occasional travel away from the work area to obtain a quantity of stock to work on, or visits to the washroom, etc. All the cyclic and the noncyclic elements combined make a cycle. A cycle results in the production of one unit or a single piece.

The ratesetter then observes an operator performing the particular cycle involved, using a stopwatch to time movements of the operator. The number of cycles he will observe is a matter of judgment. In doing so, the ratesetter forms an opinion as to whether the operator is performing at a normal pace, below normal, or above normal. The ratesetter then "normalizes" the performance he observes by applying a rating (leveling) factor if he believes that the operator was performing above or below normal. By applying this normalizing factor to the operator's average time in a cycle, the ratesetter will arrive at what is known as normal time for a cycle. After ascertaining normal time, the ratesetter makes allowances for personal fatigue and delay of the operator. Delay may involve keeping time records, or rests, or cleaning up in the work area. Thereupon the total elapsed time per piece is computed. "Standard" is the number of pieces which should be produced in an hour at a normal pace and is calculated by dividing 60 (the number of minutes in an hour) by the total elapsed time per piece. If, for example, the total elapsed time per piece is 36 seconds (or 0.6 of a minute) then standard is 60 divided by 0.6, or 100 pieces an hour.

The Refusal to Permit Time Studies by the Union

Since even the best of time study procedures were recognized by the company and union as containing several areas of subjective judgment, the contract provided for a four-step grievance procedure, the last step of which was arbitration. Whenever there was a dispute involving determination of standard rates which could not be solved without arbitration, the dispute would be submitted to a permanent arbitrator who himself was an industrial engineer. The permanent arbitrator then conducted his own time study of the job in question, and he would rule in the light of his findings.

On various dates prior to February 7, 1963, the union submitted four grievances to the company on certain piecework rates involving jobs within the bargaining unit. The union contended that these rates had not been properly established by the company under the governing provisions of the contract. These grievances were processed through the first two steps of the grievance procedure, but the company did not agree to the union's position. On February 7, 1963, the company's top officials met with top representatives of Local 133, including UAW International Union representatives, as required at Step 3 of the grievance procedure.

At this Step 3 meeting, the union representatives requested and received all the time study data used by the company in establishing the piecework rates of the jobs involved in the grievances. Kermit Mead, a representative and director of the time study and industrial engineering department of the International Union was present. He analyzed the data and asked company officials several questions about the data. These questions were answered fully. Mead then requested permission to make, on behalf of Local 133, his own time study of the operations involved in the four grievances. Mead told the company officials that unless he could make his own time studies, he would be unable to advise the union whether, in his opinion, the rates set for the disputed operations were in conformity with the provisions of the collective bargaining agreement. This was a requirement for him in order to advise the local union whether or not to proceed to arbitration of the grievances. Mead stated that merely studying the time data supplied by the company was not a sufficient basis for forming an opinion respecting the correctness of the rates, because there was no way for him to assess the validity of the time allotted by company's industrial engineers to the many subjective variables in each operation. Mead cited a number of subjective factors included among the grievances which he wished to evaluate himself. Among these were the methods by which the company's ratesetters had arrived at their leveling factors and allowance times for personal fatigue and delays, and whether sufficient allowances had been allotted for job conditions such as heat and stock loading conditions.

Company officials denied Mead's request to make his own time study. The company told the union: (*a*) that such a union study was unnecessary, since the company had furnished the union with sufficient information for it to determine whether the grievances should be taken to arbitration; (*b*) that the contract failed to grant the union the right to conduct an independent time study; and (*c*) that the permanent arbitrator, as he had for a number of years in all piecework rate grievance cases submitted to him, would conduct his own independent time study to determine whether the particular piecework price had been set according to the pertinent criteria established by the contract.

The company stated that the union should submit the four grievances to arbitration, if it was still dissatisfied with the results of the company time studies.

POSITION OF THE UNION

On February 11, 1963, the union filed an unfair labor practice charge against the company with the NLRB. The union charged that the company had violated Section 8 (a) (1) and (5) of the Labor-Management Relations Act in refusing to allow the union to conduct its own time studies on the disputed jobs. Section 8 (a) (5) makes it an unfair labor practice for an employer "to refuse to bargain collectively with the representatives of his employees, subject to the provisions of Section 9 (a)." The union contended that in refusing to allow the time studies (which the union regarded as necessary in order to properly negotiate its position) the company was, in effect, refusing to bargain in good faith. This contention was based on the argument that the data provided by the company was inadequate for the union's purposes.

The union argued that Section 8 (a) (5) of the act imposes an obligation upon an employer to furnish upon request all information relevant to the bargaining representative's intelligent performance of its function. This obligation extends to information which the union may require in order to police and administer existing agreements. The time studies requested by the union were in the nature of requests for information which were both relevant and necessary to enable the union to fulfill its function as the bargaining representative. Compliance with the good faith bargaining provisions of the act should require the company to cooperate with the union by making plant facilities available to the union to conduct its own time studies, where this is necessary for the union to properly make judgments as the bargaining representative of the employees.

POSITION OF THE COMPANY

The company contended that it did not violate Section 8 (a) (5) of the act, and that its actions in this case were proper. The company claimed that it was justified in denying the union's request for its own time studies, for three basic reasons: (*a*) such a study was unnecessary because the company supplied the union with sufficient information to enable it to decide whether to proceed to arbitration; (*b*) the contract did not grant the union the right to make an independent time study; and (*c*) the permanent arbitrator would conduct his own time study.

The company noted that for some years, grievances of this type had been processed without an independent time study being made at any stage prior to the submission of the grievance to the permanent arbitrator. In determining whether a grievance had merit, the arbitrator invariably made his own time study. The lack of a prearbitration time study was not a handicap to the union in the past, causing the union either to fail to process meritorious grievances or to process an excessive number of nonmeritorious grievances.

The testimony of Mead, the union's industrial engineer, did not establish that the information available from other sources (such as the company's time study data, and discussion with employees, stewards, and committeemen) was insufficient to permit a determination as to whether the grievance should be taken to arbitration. This was the only purpose for which the union time study was desired. Since the union did not prove either the necessity of access nor the unavailability of adequate alternative sources of information, there was no support for the union's charge that the company did not bargain in good faith with the union by denying the union access to company premises to conduct its own time study.

The union complaint should be dismissed.

QUESTIONS

1. Does Section 8 (a) (5) of LMRA require an employer to permit a union to conduct an independent time study on company premises? Is this question relevant to other conditions involved in a case situation? Does it appear that the Fafnir Company was attempting to impose arbitrary standards upon employees represented by the union?
2. Evaluate the union's argument that it needed its own time study in order to properly act as bargaining representative for the employees. Evaluate the company's argument that the grievance-arbitration procedure fulfilled its obligation to bargain over the issue of time standards.
3. Is the fact that the union had not requested its own time studies in the past germane to the case? What is at stake in terms of the relationships between parties?
4. Evaluate the precedent implications of this case to both management and union interests.

11. THE CONTRACT AND THE MEDIATION SERVICES

COMPANY: Cream Top Creamery, Incorporated

UNION: Milk, Ice Cream Drivers, and Dairy Employees, Local 783, International Brotherhood of Teamsters, Chauffeurs, Warehousemen, and Helpers of America (IBTCW)

THE UNFAIR LABOR PRACTICE CHARGE

On July 17, 1963, the company filed an unfair labor practice charge against the union alleging that the union had violated Sections 8 (d) (3) and 8 (d) (4) of the Labor-Management Relations Act.

Section 8 (d) of the act, among other things, states the following:

... That where there is in effect a collective-bargaining contract covering employees in an industry affecting commerce, the duty to bargain collectively shall also mean that no party to such contract shall terminate or modify such contract, unless the party desiring such termination or modification—

(1) serves a written notice upon the other party to the contract of the proposed termination or modification sixty days prior to the expiration date thereof, or in the event such contract contains no expiration date, sixty days prior to the time it is proposed to make such termination or modification;

(2) offers to meet and confer with the other party for the purpose of negotiating a new contract or a contract containing the proposed modifications;

(3) notifies the Federal Mediation and Conciliation Service within thirty days after such notice of the existence of a dispute, and simultaneously therewith notifies any State or Territorial agency established to mediate and conciliate disputes within the State or Territory where the dispute occurred, provided no agreement has been reached by that time; and

(4) continues in full force and effect, without resorting to strike or lockout, all the terms and conditions of the existing contract for a period of sixty days after such notice is given or until the expiration date of such contract, whichever occurs later.

104

BACKGROUND

The Cream Top Creamery, Inc., is a corporation with its office and principal place of business in Louisville, Kentucky. The company is engaged in the processing of milk and related milk products such as chocolate milk, orange drink, ice cream, etc., and their sale and distribution at wholesale and retail levels. Total company sales were about $900,000 for the fiscal year ending September 30, 1963.

IBTCW Local 783 is the collective bargaining agent for a unit of about 24 employees working for the company. The employees covered in the bargaining unit consist of retail and wholesale milk drivers, ice cream drivers, and plant employees; office clerical employees, guards, and supervisors are not in the bargaining unit. The contract between the company and the union at the time of this case was entered into on April 1, 1960. The last article, Article 36, of the contract made reference to the general termination dates of the contract and read as follows:

This contract shall be effective from and after the date hereof and shall continue through March 31, 1963, and continue from year to year thereafter, ending on March 31, of each year thereafter, but subject to the right of any party hereto to terminate same as of April 1, of any year following the year 1962, by giving not less than 60 days' written notice of its intention to do so.

Another article germane to this case—Article 34—concerned the area of welfare and pension funds. Section 3 of Article 34 of the contract covered payments to be made by the company to the pension fund for each employee for each month of a calendar year beginning with 1958. The monthly payment for 1958 was $5. Section 3 of Article 34 provided for an increase of $1 per month for each calendar year beginning with 1959. This would make the monthly payments for the years, 1963, 1964, 1965 equal to $10, $11, and $12 respectively.

Section 34 also embodied a special provision, Section 6, which dealt with the termination date associated with the pension and welfare commitments. The Section 6 provision read as follows:

Notwithstanding that this contract and the contracts which may follow it may be terminated prior to April 1965, it is agreed that until April 1965, neither the union nor any of its representatives nor any employee covered by this agreement shall make any requests that the amount which each Employer is required by Section 3 of this Article to pay to said Pension Fund be changed and during said period the Employers shall not have any obligations to negotiate or bargain with the union with respect to such change.

This pension fund agreement was drawn up in joint negotiations with eight other dairy companies in the area. However, each company signed a separate contract with IBTCW Local 783.

On January 30, 1963, Local 783 notified Cream Top Creamery of its desire to terminate the contract. The union made similar notifications to the other eight dairy companies which previously had joint negotiations with the union.

In the first week of April, 1963, the union and the company began negotiations for a new contract. However, the union had not notified the Federal Mediation Service or the Kentucky Department of Labor of its contract termination proposal or the existence of a contractual dispute. Prior to meeting, the union presented proposals to the company and the company presented counterproposals to the union. On April 20, the counterproposals of the company were rejected by the union. From that time on, negotiations dealt primarily with the union's proposals, and except for Item 3 of the union's proposals, the union and the company reached tentative agreement on all other issues during May, 1963.

Item 3 of the union's proposals provided for increasing the company's payment to the pension and welfare fund from $10, $11, and $12 monthly for 1963, 1964, and 1965, respectively, to $5 weekly for the first 2 years of a contract and $6 per week thereafter. The company did not include any changes in the pension fund payments in its counterproposals; the company's position was that changes in the pension fund payments were not a subject for negotiations until April, 1965. However, in response to a number of threats by the union of a strike starting June 1, 1963, if the company did not agree to the union's proposals for the increase in pension fund payments, the company did offer to make some increase in the payments. Since the other eight dairy companies which previously had jointly negotiated with the union had agreed to the changes in the pension fund payments as demanded by the union, the union rejected the company's offer concerning the pension fund payments. The company then requested an opportunity to make its offer directly to its employees who were members of the union. The union indicated that it had no objections to the company's calling a meeting of its employees and informing them of the increase the company was willing to make. Shortly thereafter, company representatives met with the employees, and discussed the proposed increase with them. The employees later informed the company through the union's senior business representative that they, too, had rejected the company's offer.

On June 1, 1963, employees of the union struck Cream Top Creamery in support of their union's demands for increases in the monthly pension payments to be made by the company.

On August 8, 1963, the union, by telegram, notified the Federal Mediation and Conciliation Service and the Department of Labor of the State of Kentucky, that the collective bargaining contract between it and the company would expire "in the near future." Mr. Martin Willinger, the company's secretary-treasurer, met with a representative of the Federal Mediation and Conciliation Service on two occasions following the notice given to the Service by the union, and he also had several telephone conversations with FMCS representatives.

On September 3, 1963, Commissioner Carl Cabe of the Kentucky Department of Labor addressed a letter to the Cream Top Creamery in which he informed the company of the notice which his department had received from the union. He also included in his letter a paragraph which stated that, "This is a routine notice as required by law which enables this department to contact the company and the union, advising them that this Department is at your disposal to assist you in any way possible."[1] Upon receipt of this letter on September 5, Mr. Willinger telephoned Mr. Cabe, and they briefly discussed the dispute. Mr. Willinger informed Commissioner Cabe that a strike had been in progress since June 1, 1963, and stated to him that nothing could be gained at that point by an attempt by Cabe to mediate the dispute; Commissioner Cabe agreed.

Subsequently, neither the Federal Mediation and Conciliation Service nor the Kentucky Department of Labor arranged to have representatives of the union and the company meet with their representatives to explore the possibilities of settling the dispute. The strike was still in progress when the case was heard by an NLRB trial examiner on September 30, 1963.

POSITION OF THE COMPANY

The Cream Top Creamery, in its unfair labor practice charge of July 17, 1963, and in amendments to this charge filed July 31 and August 31, 1963, claimed as follows:

Changes in the pension fund payments were not a subject for

---

[1] Included as an appendix to this case is information concerning Kentucky Revised Statutes Section 336.140, which empowers the commissioner of the state's Department of Labor to inquire into and mediate labor disputes.

negotiations until April, 1965, or 60 days prior to that date upon a written notification by the union for modification or termination. As of June 1, 1963, there was complete agreement on every other negotiable section of the contract, and any strike by the union thus would be in violation of Section 8 (d) (4) of the act.

Section 6 of Article 34 of the contract specified that April, 1965, was the earliest expiration date of the contract insofar as it provided (in Section 3 of Article 34) for monthly pension fund payments to be made by the company. Under the contract, the company had no obligation in 1963 to negotiate or bargain with the union with respect to a change in pension fund payments.

The union's strike against the company since June 1, 1963, was to enforce its demand for increases in the monthly pension fund payments made by the company; the union did not strike to enforce any demands relating to the other matters covered in the contract. Thus, the union's strike violated Section 8 (d) (4) of LMRA.

Further, the company maintained that the union did not give notification to the Federal Mediation and Conciliation Service or to the Department of Labor of the State of Kentucky within the 30 days after the union's January 31, 1963, notice to the company that it wished to terminate the existing contract. Since no agreement had been reached by the end of the 30-day period, the union had violated Section 8 (d) (3) of the act.

Therefore, by its strike actions and by its failure to notify federal and state mediation boards, the union had refused to bargain collectively, as required by the provisions of Sections 8 (d) (3) and 8 (d) (4) of the act, and therefore the union was guilty of unfair labor practices.

POSITION OF THE UNION

The union had several affirmative defenses for its actions. They were as follows:

First of all, the alleged violation of Section 8 (d) (3) by the union was a mere technicality of little importance. A technical mistake for the union's failure to give the required statutory notice was without a remedy, since the union and the company had bargained for two months following March 31, 1963, before the union initiated a strike on June 1, 1963.

Further, a business representative of the union testified that he had negotiated contracts for the union for 12 years, but in that time he had never called the Kentucky Department of Labor or its commissioner to conciliate or mediate a dispute.

Secondly, the union claimed that actually the strike was caused by the counterproposal of the company. The nominal concession by the company to increase its pension fund payments constituted a voluntary agreement by the company to waive the April, 1965, contract expiration date concerning these payments. On June 1, 1963, when the strike began, the contract date as it related to the pension fund payments actually was not in effect. Therefore, the union was not in violation of Section 8 (d) (4) of the act by striking, since the union had fulfilled its requirements to bargain collectively in relationship to the March 31, 1963, termination date of the contract.

Thirdly, since the strike was actually over the counterproposal of the company, the Section 8 (d) (3) notices to the FMCS and the Kentucky Department of Labor should have been given by the company, not the union.

Finally, neither the Kentucky Department of Labor nor the Federal Mediation and Conciliation Service had held any meetings between the parties following the notice which the union gave on August 8, 1963. Therefore, this notice as required by Section 8 (d) (3)—which the union claimed should have been given by the company—was really of little practical consequence to this dispute.

The union claimed that the unfair labor practice charge should be dismissed.

APPENDIX

The Kentucky Statute

Kentucky Revised Statutes Section 336.140 of Chapter 336, with the heading *Commissioner to Investigate and Mediate Labor Disputes*, empowers the commissioner of the state's Department of Labor to inquire into the causes of strikes, lockouts, and other disputes between employers and employees, to endeavor to effect an amicable settlement, and to create within the department boards to which disputes between employers and employees may be submitted on the request of the employer and the employees for mediation. Another section of the same chapter (336.150) provides that the commissioner may act as mediator and conciliator and appoint similar persons in labor disputes whenever his intervention is requested by either party, and he may offer his services as conciliator and mediator if any emergency by reason of a labor dispute is found to exist at any time. Whenever his services as conciliator and mediator are accepted by both parties to a labor dispute, he is requested promptly to investigate and undertake to conciliate and mediate the dispute without delay. There is a proviso that the authority of this section shall not apply where the authority of a federal agency has been invoked or a federal agency assumes jurisdiction. Moreover, if the commissioner has assumed the jurisdiction, and a federal agency thereafter assumes authority, the authority of the commissioner shall cease pending federal jurisdiction.

QUESTIONS

1. Was the union guilty of an unfair labor practice in striking in order to have the pension fund payments increased? Did the concession by the company to increase pension funds payments in June, 1963, constitute an agreement to waive the April, 1965, expiration date in the contract? Is this a key decision point in this case?
2. Evaluate the union's argument that the technical notification to the state and federal mediation boards was of little consequence to this case situation.
3. Evaluate the union's claim that the strike was caused by the counterproposal of the company.
4. What remedial action can be prescribed in order to assure that a union or company follows the notification procedures outlined under the Labor-Management Relations Act?

12. A COMPANY'S REFUSAL TO SUPPLY JOB AND WAGE DATA TO THE UNION

COMPANY: Curtiss Wright Corporation

UNION: International Union of United Automobile, Aerospace, and Agricultural Implement Workers of America (UAW), Local Union No. 300

PRINCIPAL ISSUE OF THE CASE

The principal issue in this case concerned itself with Section 8 (a) (1) and (5) of the Labor-Management Relations Act of 1947 which states, "It shall be an unfair labor practice for an employer to interfere with, restrain, or coerce employees in the exercise of the rights guaranteed in Section 7; . . . and to refuse to bargain collectively with the representatives of his employees, subject to the provisions of Section 9 (a)." Specifically, the issue in this case was whether or not the refusal of the company to supply wage rates, grades, ranges, job evaluation factors, and data concerning other economic benefits on personnel classified as "confidential" and "administrative" employees constituted bad faith bargaining by the company.

BACKGROUND

The Aeronautical Division of Curtiss Wright Corporation is located in Wood-Ridge, New Jersey. This division is engaged in the design, manufacture, sale, and distribution of aircraft engines, space and hydrospace propulsion systems, rotating combustion engines, missile components, and related products.

For many years, Local 300 of the International Union of United Automobile, Aerospace, and Agricultural Implement Workers of America has represented all production, salaried office clerical, and engineering employees at the company's Wood-Ridge plant, with certain specific exceptions. Among those excluded from the bargaining

111

unit in 1962 were approximately 900 confidential and administrative employees.

Confidential employees are defined as those employees whose work is "regularly concerned with, and who have access to, information or records which relate directly to the problem of labor relations or knowledge of which would be advantageous to the union in its negotiations with the company." The category of confidential employees includes: secretaries and stenographers who work principally and directly for executives, staff members, or managers; employees in the employee relations division; job analysts; and all employees who fix rates of pay for employees included in the bargaining unit.

Administrative employees are defined as those employees who "customarily and regularly exercise discretion and independent judgment in the performance of their duties." Included in this category are: any employee who acts in an administrative or executive capacity; an employee who under only general supervision performs work along specialized or technical lines requiring special training, experience, or knowledge; an employee who under only general supervision executes special assignments and tasks.

On April 2, 1962, the president of the union wrote the company's director of industrial relations requesting the following information with respect to confidential and administrative employees:

a) A summary of job classifications and/or titles.

b) A job description or summary of duties and functions.

c) A summary of the total number of such employees in each job classification and/or title.

d) The regular rate of pay, including the grade or range for each confidential and/or administrative employee classification or title.

The union gave the following explanation of its request in its letter to the company:

As you know, the union and the company have been confronted with numerous problems involving the relationship of "included" and "excluded" employees at the company's New Jersey plants and the work and function performed by each. Many of these problems have failed in informal resolution and have culminated in formal grievances which have been processed through various steps of the grievance procedure. Lack of relevant and material information concerning job functions, duties, hours, and rates of pay for excluded employees directly concerned with these disputes has severely handicapped the union in the administration of the collective bargaining agreement and processing of contractual grievances. Since the work of excluded confidential and administrative employees in many situations bears a close and substantial relationship to that performed by employees covered by the collective bargaining agreement, complete information concerning such excluded employees is essential for the union to discharge its obligations under the collective bargaining agreement and to intelligently administer that agreement.

Moreover, the foregoing information is requested by the union for any collective bargaining that may ensue between the parties on the subject of work functions and duties for included and excluded employees at the company's New Jersey plants.

We request that this information be furnished to us as soon as possible in a form that is convenient to the company. In the event you have any questions concerning our request, we will be glad to provide further details.

On May 9, the company's director of industrial relations replied to this request in a letter to the union president as follows:

For many years during which the relationship between this Division and your Union has been governed by collective bargaining agreements, in which certain provisions have properly excluded from your representation all confidential and administrative positions, the Division has been alert to its responsibility of making certain that such provisions have been followed. To that end, we have regularly reviewed this matter.

Because of our close attention over the years to this matter, we are certain that administrative and confidential positions excluded by our agreement are correctly excluded. However, on receipt of your letter of April 2, 1962, we again initiated a review and preliminary results verify the correctness of the exclusions. I have delayed reply to your letter until the preliminary results were available. Our review will continue over the next several months. If, in the course of the review, any specific incorrect exclusions are found, you will be advised, discussion arranged, and correction made.

Your request for complete information on rates of pay, job description, head count by job classification, etc., is denied. Your request for information concerning more than 900 confidential and administrative personnel is beyond the scope of matters to be bargained with Local 300; a compilation would be in such volume as to be unduly burdensome to the Division; nor is it pertinent to pending grievances or administration by you of the collective bargaining agreement, or for the purpose of future negotiations.

I suggest that we resolve any specific items in this matter in keeping with the provisions of the bargaining agreement, which is through the orderly process of the grievance procedure.

On your return from your national convention, I would be happy to meet with you on any further questions you may have.

On June 18, the union filed a charge with the National Labor Relations Board, alleging violation of Sections 8 (a) (1) and (5) of the Labor-Management Relations Act.

On September 10, the union again wrote the company, requesting information identical to that sought in its letter of April 2.

On October 9, the union and the company executed a new three-year collective agreement. The preceding contract had run for one year and had expired September 30. Both the old and new contracts contained a detailed grievance procedure, terminating in arbitration.

Early in December, 1962, the company notified the regional office of the National Labor Relations Board that the company would furnish the union a list of job titles of the administrative jobs and the names of the individuals occupying those jobs. However, the company stated:

> We believe that we are not obliged under the law to furnish the Union with this information.
>
> . . . .
>
> The submission of the listing to the Union is not to be considered as a precedent, nor as a waiver or abandonment of any rights or defenses. . . .

On December 14, 1962, the company furnished the union with the names, numbers, job classifications, and titles of all its administrative employees, and on December 28, the company furnished similar data covering its confidential employees. In making the latter information available, the company indicated that its views as to its lack of obligation to furnish this data were the same as with respect to the data covering administrative employees.

On January 15, 1963, the union wrote the company, asking for job descriptions and other summaries of duties for approximately 80 specifically named administrative and confidential job classifications. Included among these were: *Administrative Controlled Materials and Cancellations; Liaison Commercial or Military Customers; Analyst Service Engineering, Senior; Specialist Service Methods Programs; Administrative Service Product Performance.* Again on February 21, the union repeated its request of January 15. In addition to the information previously requested with respect to the 80 job classifications or titles, the union requested the number of employees, the wage rates, "the grades and ranges, if any," and the economic benefits other than wages received by employees for each job classification or title.

On February 8, and several times thereafter, the company and the union met to discuss the union's questions concerning the job classifications listed in the union's letter of January 15. At each of these meetings, the company provided the union with job descriptions or a summary of the duties and functions of the particular job being discussed. As a result of these meetings, the company and union concluded that:

a) The work being performed by employees in the administrative job classification of *Administrative Controlled Materials and Cancellations* was work which should have been performed by employees represented by the union.

b) Employees in the administrative job classifications of *Liaison Commercial or Military Customers, Analyst Service Engineering, Sr.*, and *Specialist Service Methods Programs* were performing some work which should have been performed by employees represented by the union.

As a result, the company agreed to the following changes:

a) The company recognized the job of *Administrative Controlled Materials and Cancellations* as a job covered by the collective bargaining agreement between the company and the union.

b) Six administrative employees were transferred to the bargaining unit job classifications of *Correspondent Technical, Analyst Service Engineering Liaison*, and *Analyst Service Methods*, and assigned to perform bargaining unit work which was previously being performed by the employees in administrative job classifications.

c) One employee classified as *Liaison Commercial or Military Customers*, one employee classified as *Analyst Service Engineering, Sr.*, and one employee classified as *Administrator Service Products Performance* were laid off.

Finally, on March 12, 1963, the union orally requested that in addition to being furnished job descriptions of company employees in the job classifications as set forth in the union's letter of January 15, 1963, the union should also be furnished with a list of "job evaluation factors" for these job classifications. The job evaluation factors are a part of the total "job description" sheet which the company prepares for each job in the bargaining unit and also for a number of the administrative jobs outside the unit. Each of these sheets contains on one side a narrative description of the duties and functions of the particular job. The reverse side is a printed form listing 11 job factors, and blank spaces opposite each for filling in the appropriate "degree" and the "basis of rating." The sum of the 11 degrees gives the total point rating of the job, which in turn determines the wage. The basis of rating on each factor is a sentence or two explaining the degree assigned. The 11 factors are: *Scholastic Requirements, Previous Related Experience, Qualifying Period,*

Scope of Duties, Initiative Exercised, Frequency of Verification, Contacts Required, Degree of Concentration, Working Conditions, Number Directed, and *Supervisory Responsibility.*

These job evaluation forms are used for employees in the bargaining unit, and also for a number of administrative employees. When the company on February 8 gave certain job descriptions of administrative employees to the union, the information provided consisted only of the narrative side of the job description sheet; the data as to the 11 factors had been withheld, which led to the union's oral request on March 12.

Stipulation

The case was heard by an NLRB trial examiner on July 8, 1963. The facts of the case were not in dispute, and in a large part these facts were agreed upon in the following stipulation:

On or about April 2, 1962, and at all times material herein since that date, including on or about May 9, and September 10, 1962, and February 28, 1963, the company has failed and refused and continues to fail and refuse to furnish the union with the wage rates, grades, and ranges, and other economic benefits of respondent's employees at its Wood-Ridge plant classified as confidential and administrative employees.

On or about March 12, 1963, and at all times material herein since that date, the company has failed and refused and continues to fail and refuse to furnish the union the "job evaluation factors" for the job classifications set forth in the union's letter of January 15, 1963.

POSITION OF THE UNION

In pressing its unfair labor practice charge before an NLRB trial examiner, the union claimed that the data it had requested, and to some extent had failed to receive, was relevant to the proper discharge of its function as a collective bargaining representative. The union pointed to what it considered an erosion of the bargaining unit and the creation of what it termed as an "imbalance" of administrative jobs. According to union estimates, in 1957 the union had from 4,500 to 4,700 employees in the bargaining unit, and the excluded group numbered about 2,100. But over the intervening years, the percentages had shifted until the excluded group exceeded the number within the bargaining unit. The union claimed that at least part of this situation was caused by having so-called administrative employees doing work properly allocated to persons in the bargaining unit.

In the union's view, the grievance procedure in the contract had proved inadequate and unsatisfactory as an exclusive method of correcting these "encroachments." According to union representatives, when they attempted to use the grievance procedure to correct a job situation, they found that adequate investigation and preparation of a grievance resulted in a sharp increase in the amount of time which union representatives lost from work; this in turn brought immediate complaints from the company. In the union's view the early steps of the grievance procedure as applied to this problem were largely wasted, since the company, without making a careful investigation, would simply answer that an employee in question was doing administrative work proper to his classification. Since the company had 768 administrative and 100 confidential jobs, the costs of arbitration to remedy the problem would be prohibitive. Further, the union argued that if it had the information it was requesting, it would be better able to ascertain whether a particular complaint from one of its members had merit and should be pressed as a grievance, or whether the union should simply write it off.

At the time of the NLRB hearing, the union had pending some 259 active classification grievances in the prearbitration stages of the grievance procedure; the union estimated that perhaps an equal number had been processed to final solution (or withdrawn) since 1955. Only three cases had gone to arbitration, and of those the union had won one and lost two.

In regard to job evaluation factors, the union argued that this information was necessary to determine whether the narrative job description was accurate or was misleading. For example, if the factor of *Initiative Exercised* was given a low degree, or if *Frequency of Verification* was given a high degree, such matters would tend to disprove a claim that the job carried true administrative responsibility.

As to wage rates, the union claimed that information concerning wages and other benefits received by alleged administrative employees would be helpful in determining whether such employees were properly classified as administrative. Such information also would be helpful to the union in determining whether at the next contract negotiations the union could reasonably seek better provisions in those respects for employees in the bargaining unit.

POSITION OF THE COMPANY

The company's basic position was that the union had no legal right to demand data which concerned employees outside the unit it represented, since this was information which was at management's discretion alone. The company claimed that the grievance and arbitration procedure furnished an adequate remedy for any errors in job classifications which might occur. The company further pointed out that job evaluation factors for confidential employees, in large measure, were already in the union's possession, since many of these employees were secretaries or stenographers whose jobs were identical—except for their confidential character—with those of similar employees within the bargaining unit.

The company stated that the various materials which the company gave the union on December 14 and 28, 1962, and also the job descriptions given at the meetings in February, 1963, and thereafter, were materials which the company gave as an "accommodation." But in the company's view, it would be within its legal rights in declining to give any such data, and this would not constitute bad faith collective bargaining.

QUESTIONS

1. Was the union justified in seeking the wage and job classification data from the company? Why was the union anxious to receive this type of information?
2. From a management standpoint, what is the danger in providing job classification and wage data to a labor union?
3. Evaluate the job evaluation factors and the evaluation system used by the company.
4. Does the NLRB have statutory authority to order the company to supply job and wage data to the union? Why, or why not?

13. WERE THE FIVE "SUPERVISORS" A COLLECTIVE BARGAINING UNIT?

COMPANY: Crimptex, Incorporated

"BARGAINING UNIT": Rafael Vega, Ramon M. Cuevas, Luis A. Nazario, Angel Cruz, and Angel Gonzalez

BACKGROUND

Although the offices of the president of Crimptex, Inc. are head-quartered in the state of Rhode Island, Crimptex is a Puerto Rican corporation with its principal office and plant at San German, Puerto Rico. Since 1958, the company has been engaged in the manufacture of yarn at the San German location.

In 1962, when operating during normal production periods, 25 machine operators were employed at San German to run 11 machine units used to produce Canlon, Crimptex's major product. Normally, three 8-hour shifts were scheduled, with starting times of 8 a.m., 4 p.m., and midnight; 8 to 10 machine operators were employed on a rotating basis on each shift. During the day shift, two maintenance mechanics were employed in the machine shop. A single maintenance mechanic was on duty during the other two shifts.

Rafael Vega, Ramon M. Cuevas, Luis A. Nazario, Angel Cruz, and Angel Gonzalez were assigned on a rotating basis to duties as maintenance mechanics on the three operating shifts. The company gave these men the job classification title of "supervisor," which was accepted by them as appropriate.

In 1958, Vega, Gonzalez, and Cruz attended a course in the United States where they were trained in the maintenance and operation of the machinery used in the San German plant. Upon their return, they were made responsible for assisting in the training of production employees. In addition, they repaired, adjusted, maintained, and serviced production machinery. Also, daily during the operators' relief and half-hour lunch periods, they performed production tasks, substituting for the operators.

On weekdays, during the hours from approximately 8 a.m. to 5 or 6 p.m., the plant manager, Henry Pelletier and/or his assistant Henry Enriquez were on duty in the plant. The "supervisors" on duty took their directions and instructions directly from either Pelletier or Enriquez when they were at the plant.

However, after 5 or 6 p.m. and on the weekends or holidays, neither the plant manager nor his assistant was normally at the plant except for unscheduled appearances. Occasionally, Pelletier would come to the plant at these times because of a telephone request from the maintenance mechanic "supervisor" on duty. It was during night-time hours, weekends, and holidays, that the maintenance mechanics as "supervisors" were technically responsible for the plant's performance.

The Certified Bargaining Unit

In June 1959, Crimptex, Inc. and the International Ladies Garment Workers Union, AFL–CIO, executed an agreement for a consent election to be conducted in a unit described as:

All production and maintenance employees employed by the Company at its plant at San German, Puerto Rico, excluding all professional and clerical employees, guards, and supervisors as defined in the Act.

The question of whether to include Rafael Vega *et al.* in this unit was brought up and discussed by the company, the union, and an NLRB agent. It was agreed, by the union and management, that the names of Rafael Vega, Ramon Cuevas, Luis Nazario, Angel Cruz, and Angel Gonzalez would not appear on the representation eligibility list. Vega and Cruz asked Pelletier if they could vote in the election; they were told that they could not because they were "supervisors."

The election was held on July 2, 1959, and the employees voted to be represented by the International Ladies Garment Workers Union. The names of Vega *et al.* did not appear on the eligibility list used in conjunction with this election. The five "supervisors" continued to perform their duties as before and were not made part of the ILGW Union.

Circumstances Leading to Layoffs

During the month of July, 1962, Crimptex's operations entered a seasonal lull, and production was scheduled on the basis of a two- or three-day work week. In August, all operations were halted completely, and all personnel were laid off, including the five "supervisors."

On August 19, 1962, the five "supervisors" sent a jointly signed letter to Henry Pelletier, the plant manager, demanding a management clarification of their authority and responsibilities as "supervisors." They also demanded on their behalf the following: increased salaries, improved vacations and sick leave benefits, and assurances against periodic layoffs. Pelletier responded to this letter on August 21, 1962, by informing the "supervisors" that their letter had been referred to the president of the company; he assured them that he (Pelletier) would contact them as soon as he received instructions.

After Pelletier received instructions by telephone, he arranged for a meeting and met with Vega and the others at his office on September 7, 8, and 10.

At their first meeting on September 7, Pelletier discussed with the five "supervisors" their demands. Pelletier offered them 2 weeks' vacation as compared to their present 1½ weeks, 15 days' sick pay, and 3 or 4 days' guaranteed pay during slack periods. Also, he requested that they return to work, since production orders had increased and their services were needed.

The five men responded by saying that they accepted the wage, vacation, and sick benefits offer; but they demanded, as a condition of their return to work, a guarantee of a five-day work week during slack periods, and that the benefits orally promised should be put in writing. Pelletier refused to accept these demands, and after an hour's discussion the meeting ended with the parties in disagreement only on the latter point—that the agreement be put in writing.

The second and third meetings ended much like the first, with both sides unable to agree that the terms be reduced to writing. However, before the third meeting on September 10, the "supervisors" sent a letter to the president of the company stating that they intended to "stay out of work" until they received a formal and satisfactory answer to their letter of August 19, 1962.

Upon being shown a copy of the letter, Pelletier said, "That is the best thing you can do; let's wait, then, for an answer to that letter." He suggested that they resume work on the basis of the benefits orally granted. The employees refused to work unless their demands had been agreed to in writing by the president of the company.

On the following day, September 11, Pelletier sent a telegram to Rafael Vega which read as follows:

> This is to confirm personal notice given you yesterday to report to your job in Crimptex on the 8 a.m. shift tomorrow Wednesday.

Each of the other "supervisors" received identical telegrams except for the reporting time. During the day, Pelletier and Enriquez talked individually with Gonzalez and Cruz, and with Nazario and Cruz together, telling them "to forget about the rest and go back to work."

That evening, the five men went to the plant and spoke with Pelletier. They again stated their demand that the terms agreed to orally should be put in writing. Pelletier refused to agree to their demand.

On September 13, Pelletier sent the following letter (which is produced in part) to each of the five "supervisors."

> Since the day of September 13 has gone by without your having reported to work, notwithstanding the notices given to you, nor your having informed of any impossibility to do so, I understand your not having reported to work demonstrates that you are not interested in continuing working for this company.

On September 18, the group of five men went to the San Juan office of the International Ladies Garment Workers Union and there spoke with two union officials. Each of the men signed a union authorization card. The following day the five met with Pelletier and unconditionally offered their services, withdrawing their previous demand of a written agreement. Pelletier told them that he had already hired replacements.[1]

Again on September 27, the five men went as a group and offered to return to work unconditionally. Pelletier answered that he had no work for them, since they had been replaced. (At this time, however, the men did not inform Pelletier that they had signed ILGWU authorization cards, nor did they request him to recognize and bargain with them as a collective bargaining unit.)

Subsequently, in separate charges filed on October 2, 1962, by Rafael Vega, Ramon Cuevas, and Luis Nazario, and separate charges filed on November 8, 1962, by Angel Cruz and Angel Gonzalez, the five former "supervisors" brought unfair labor practice charges against Crimptex, Inc. Specifically they claimed that:

1. Rafael Vega *et al.* constituted a labor organization within the meaning of Section 2 (5) of the LMRA, since as a group the five men had negotiated with management concerning wages, hours, and conditions of work.

---

[1] Testimony revealed that four men were hired to replace the five "supervisors." One was hired on September 18, another on September 19, and two on September 23. At the time of the case hearing, a permanent replacement for Gonzalez had not yet been hired.

2. Management had discriminated in regard to the tenure of their employment, thereby discouraging membership in a labor organization of its employees. Therefore, the company had engaged in unfair labor practices within the meaning of Sections 8 (a) (1) and 8 (a) (3) of the act.

POSITION OF THE FIVE "SUPERVISORS"

In their individual charges, the five "supervisors" contended that they were a group of unrepresented employees who were not included in the original agreement between Crimptex, Inc., and the International Ladies Garment Workers Union. They claimed that they were really only maintenance mechanic "leadmen," and not "supervisors" as defined by the act. However, by their unified efforts to present their collective and individual interests to Crimptex for the purpose of discussing economic demands, working conditions, and grievances, they constituted a bona fide labor organization within the meaning of the act.

Since Crimptex, Inc., and specifically Mr. Pelletier, did recognize and deal with these five employees collectively with regard to their wages, hours, and working conditions, the subsequent discharging of the five employees because of their refusal to return to work, i.e., their declaration of a strike against Crimptex, Inc., was in violation of the act. The company refused to reinstate the employees, although they made an unconditional request that they be given back their old jobs. Because of these actions, the group's position was that the company had violated Section 8 (a) (1) and also Section 8 (a) (3) of the Labor-Management Relations Act.

POSITION OF THE COMPANY

Crimptex, Inc., did not deny any of the basic facts of the case. However, its position was that: (*a*) Rafael Vega, Ramon Cuevas, Luis Nazario, Angel Cruz, and Angel Gonzalez were indeed supervisors within the meaning of the act and therefore not entitled to the protection of various provisions of the act; (*b*) they did not constitute a group of "employees" within the precedents set by the NLRB; (*c*) the mere fact that they acted in a united way when they presented common demands did not constitute a recognized labor organization; and (*d*) the discharge of the "supervisors" was for their failure to respond to the employment available and offered to them at the end of the seasonal layoff.

Other Duties of the "Supervisors" at Crimptex, Inc.

Testimony at the trial examiner's hearings focused primarily upon the nature and duties of the five "supervisors" at Crimptex. This was relevant to the company's contention that the five men were supervisors within the meaning of Section 2 (11) of the Labor-Management Relations Act and thus employees not entitled to the protection of the act.

It was determined that the five men as "supervisors" signed time charts which showed the hour when a machine was started, when it was shut down, and how much yarn was produced. Both the "supervisor" and the operator were required to initial the entries.

If an operator did not report for work in the evening or if one became ill while at work, the "supervisor" would report this by telephone to Pelletier, who either obtained a replacement or ordered adjustments to be made, with instructions to the "supervisor" as how to accomplish the adjustments. If the "supervisor" was not particularly busy that evening, he would occasionally substitute for the missing operator and not call Pelletier at all.

The "supervisors" had the responsibility of seeing to it that the operators were at their work stations and finding out why they were not. But they lacked authority to independently discipline such employees; they were expected to report any violations, absences, indolence, etc., to Pelletier through the use of written reports.

Crimptex displayed rules on the employee bulletin board for a number of years that required all employees to secure permission from their "supervisor" when absent or late, to abide by his instructions, and to receive permission from their "supervisor" when in doubt about job standards.

The "supervisors" also made recommendations concerning the discharge of employees. In one instance, Gonzalez sent an employee home before his shift was over because the employee had "incurred an act of discipline" and "was very undisciplined" to Gonzalez. On another occasion another employee was discharged because he assaulted Vega after the midnight shift was over. Vega had called this employee's attention to the fact that he was spending an excessive amount of time in the washroom. Pelletier testified at the trial hearings that both employee discharges resulted from the recommendations of the "supervisors" involved.

The company claimed that unless the men classified by the company as "supervisors" actually possessed supervisory powers, some 8 to 10 employees would have been working two night shifts and weekends without responsible supervisory direction.

QUESTIONS

1. What is the key issue upon which this entire case situation rests? What are the precedent-setting implications of this case?
2. What is the meaning of the term "supervisor" as defined under the Labor-Management Relations Act? Why were supervisors excluded from the protection of the act?
3. How might a company avoid situations such as this in establishing which employees are supervisors and which are not supervisors?
4. What constitutes a collective bargaining unit? Discuss.

14. UNION REPRESENTATION AND THE AUTHORIZATION CARD[1]

COMPANY: Gissel Packing Company, Huntington, West Virginia

UNION: Food Store Employees Union, Local No. 347, Amalgamated Meat Cutters & Butcher Workmen of North America, AFL-CIO

BACKGROUND

In 1960, Gissel Packing Company, Inc., reacted to a union organizing campaign by engaging in threats to refuse to recognize the union, to close or greatly curtail its plant operations at Huntington, West Virginia if the union gained bargaining rights, and to discharge various employees who joined or who were thinking about joining a union. The National Labor Relations Board ordered a representational election, and both the union and the company waged vigorous campaigns. The union lost the election, and correspondingly filed unfair labor practices against the company. An NLRB trial examiner found the various actions of the company to be unfair labor practices in violation of Section 8 (a) (1) of the Labor-Management Relations Act. But the union did not gain representational rights at this time.

During the period 1960 to 1963, the union continued a "low key" campaign trying to sign up employees in the union. In 1963, the union stepped up its organizational activity, and various company actions which vigorously opposed this organizing effort were taken.

---

[1] Because of circumstances surrounding this case, which was a "landmark" case that went to the Supreme Court for a final decision, the format presented here will be somewhat different than for other cases included in this collection. The case has been excerpted from a total presentation of this case included in *Law Reprints*, Labor Series Volume 2, No. 10, 1968-1969 term of the Supreme Court of the United States. (New York: Law Reprints Publications).

For example, Vice-President James Kaiser[2] told a new employee that the plant was nonunion, and that "any employee caught talking to a union representative would be discharged."

In September, 1964, Vice-President Kaiser, aware of the union's activities at two other Huntington plants, individually interrogated several employees concerning whether they had engaged in conversations concerning the union and threatened them with discharge if either was caught talking to a suspected union agent.

The union continued its organizing efforts in January, 1965, and between January 13 and 22, 31 of the 47 employees signed cards authorizing the union to represent them in collective bargaining. The card stated: "The undersigned hereby authorizes this union to represent his or her interests in collective bargaining concerning wages, hours, and working conditions."

On January 22, union representative Art Miles advised Vice-President Kaiser that the union represented a majority of employees and requested recognition and bargaining. Kaiser refused to talk about the union, and he referred Miles to the company attorneys. On the same day, Miles confirmed his telephone request for recognition in a letter to Kaiser in which he offered to submit signed authorization cards to the company, "so that there will be no possible doubt as to our majority status."

Also on this same day [January 22], Vice-President Kaiser told one of the employees "If the union got in, I'd just take may money and let the union run the place the way it wanted to."

On January 26, the company formally rejected the union's request in a letter which: (1) stated that the union had lost an earlier NLRB election and that the company did "not believe that there has been any change in circumstance or opinion of our employees since that time"; (2) stated that the company was "advised" that the union's organizing technique involved the obtaining of "signatures on so-called authorization cards by a variety of means and representations which are not compatible with a free exercise of an employee's choice." The company claimed that illegal union practices included "instances of direct misrepresentation in obtaining employees' signatures"; (3) denied that truck drivers were "a part of any appropriate bargaining unit"; and (4) invited the union to file for an NLRB election.

However, the company did not at this time utilize Section 9 (c) (1) (B) of the Act to petition the NLRB for an election to determine

---

[2] All names disguised.

the union's representational status.[3] In the early part of February, Vice-President Kaiser: (1) interrogated one employee as to whether he had heard anything about the union and if any union man had been around to sign him up; (2) asked another employee whether employee Irv Westphal was the leader of the union and stated that Westphal would be immediately discharged if Kaiser discovered him to be such a leader; (3) requested this same employee to report to him all he could learn about the union, including the names of the employees who had signed cards; (4) asked another employee if he knew anything about the union, what the union had offered him, and stated that he could offer him more than the union could; (5) asked still another employee if he would join in a "walk-out"; (6) told a group of employees, "the hell with the Union . . . I'm going to leave the plant and turn it over to them"; (7) said to a group of employees that he did not want "to hear any more about this Union stuff"—to "get out if they could not do their work"; and (8) to still another employee, Kaiser threatened that the union would have to "fight him first" and stated that it would "not get in."

In this context, on February 10 union Representative Miles by letter renewed the union's request for recognition, pointing out that "the coercion and intimidation and illegal interrogation and threats which occur between the time an election is petitioned and the actual election by the employers is most difficult for us to combat." Miles again offered to deliver the signed cards to the company for check against payroll records to prove the union's majority. Vice-president Kaiser answered on February 12, asserting that the union's "approach . . . bolsters our opinion that you do not honestly represent a majority of the employees." No other reason for

---

[3] Section 9 (c) (1) of the Labor-Management Relations Act reads as follows: Wherever a petition shall have been filed, in accordance with such regulations as may be prescribed by the Board—(A) by an employee or group of employees or any individual or labor organization acting in their behalf alleging that a substantial number of employees (i) wish to be represented for collective bargaining and that their employer declines to recognize their representative as the representative defined in Section 9 (a), or (ii) assert that the individual or labor organization, which has been certified or is being currently recognized by their employer as the bargaining representative, is no longer a representative as defined in Section 9 (a); or (B) by an employer, alleging that one or more individuals or labor organizations have presented to him a claim to be recognized as the representative defined in Section 9 (a); the Board shall investigate such petition and if it has reasonable cause to believe that a question of representation affecting commerce exists shall provide for an appropriate hearing upon due notice. Such hearing may be conducted by an officer or employee of the regional office, who shall not make any recommendations with respect thereto. If the Board finds upon the record of such hearing that such a question of representation exists, it shall direct an election by secret ballot and shall certify the results thereof.

doubting the union's majority was given. Replying on February 16, the union made a final unsuccessful attempt to achieve recognition from the company, again offering the authorization cards for inspection.

In March and April, various company managers continued an anti-union campaign: (1) by interrogating employee Lyman Hayes as to whether employee Gene Carr had said anything about a union, and directing Hayes to stay away from Carr who would be "bad for him"; (2) by further inquiries of Hayes as to whether employee Gil Trump had induced Hayes to attend a union meeting or sign a card; (3) by engaging in surveillance of a union meeting; (4) by asking employee Dwight Hopkins in the presence of employee John Kellogg whether he attended the meeting, and telling him that Mr. Kaiser had knowledge of such union meeting attendance; and (5) by changing the hours of work of Hopkins and Kellogg and subsequently discharging them with a profane reference in respect to what they could do with the union.

Subsequently, the union filed unfair labor practice charges against the company alleging violations of Sections 8 (a) (1), 8 (a) (3), and 8 (a) (5) of the Labor-Management Relations Act.

Findings of the National Labor Relations Board

The Trial Examiner, whose decision was upheld by the NLRB, concluded that the company interfered with, restrained, and coerced employees in violation of Section 8 (a) (1) of the act by interrogating employees about their union activities and the conduct of the union, by asking them to learn of the union activities of others, by threatening them with discharge, by promising economic benefits, and by creating the impression of and engaging in surveillance of union-related activities. The Board also concluded that employees Hopkins and Kellogg were discriminatorily discharged in violation of Sections 8 (a) (3) and (1) and further concluded that the company violated Sections 8 (a) (5) and (1) of the Act in refusing to recognize the union which a substantial majority of employees had designated as their bargaining agent by signing appropriately worded authorization cards in a clearly appropriate unit.

The Board rejected the company claim that it had a good faith doubt concerning the union's majority status for the following reasons:

1. The company ignored the union's offer to submit for exam-

ination and comparison with payroll signatures the signed authorizations upon which the union relied.

2. The company failed to file an employer's representation petition with the NLRB.
3. The company's asserted reasons for refusing to recognize the union were unsubstantiated.
4. The company's course of unfair labor practice conduct both before and after the union's request for recognition constituted (a) an "absolute refutation" of the company's good faith claim, (b) a program to destroy the union's majority, and (c) "a positive rejection by the company of the principle of collective bargaining." The Board also rejected the contention of the company that a union can never establish its majority on the basis of cards but can do so only in a Board-conducted election.

The Board ordered the company to cease and desist from the unfair labor practices, to offer reinstatement with back pay to the employees discriminatorily discharged, to bargain with the union upon request, and to post appropriate notices.

The Decision of the Court of Appeals

The case was appealed to the U.S. Court of Appeals for the Fourth Circuit. This court held that substantial evidence supported the Board's findings and remedial orders in connection with the company's coercion of its employees in the exercise of their rights in violation of Section 8 (a) (1) of the act and discriminatorily discharging two employees because of their union membership and activity in violation of Sections 8 (a) (3) and (1). However, *the court rejected the Board's conclusion that the company had refused to bargain in violation of Sections 8 (a) (5) and (1).* The court said:

> In recent cases we have had occasion to point out that authorization cards are such unreliable indicators of the desires of the employees that an employer confronted with a demand for recognition based solely upon them is justified in withholding recognition pending the result of a certification election. The reasoning elaborated in those decisions applied with equal force here.

Appeal to the Supreme Court

At this point, the union through its counsel, and the NLRB through its solicitor general, petitioned the Supreme Court to review the lower court's ruling. Therefore, each party was required to submit to the Supreme Court arguments to support its position. The major elements of each side's arguments were as follows.

THE POSITION OF THE COMPANY

The company presented three major arguments:

1. That an employer is not obligated by the act to bargain with a union solely on the basis of authorization cards allegedly signed by a majority of employees.

In support of this first argument, the company pointed to a growing trend on the part of the NLRB in using the authorization card method as a means of union certification. The company claimed that this trend was clearly not in the spirit of the act's original passages.

Developing the argument historically, the company noted that in 1935 an employer was first required to bargain collectively with the representative of his employees. There was a requirement that the representative be designated or selected for the purpose of collective bargaining by a majority of the employees, but there was no specific manner in which determination was to be made as to whether or not a majority of employees wanted such representation. The Wagner Act allowed the NLRB to "take a secret ballot of employees, or utilize any other suitable method" to ascertain such representatives [NLRA, Section 9 (c)].

In 1947, the Labor-Management Relations Act (Taft-Hartley) revisions to the Wagner Act were passed. The LMRA did not amend Section 8 (a) (5), and Section 9 (a) was largely unchanged. Section 9 (c), however, was completely revised to allow, for the first time, a petition by an employer when only one union was requesting representation, and to provide if a question of representation existed that the Board should direct an election by secret ballot and certify the results. Thus, argued the company, the Wagner Act language, allowing other forms of determination. was stricken.

To illustrate that the Board should have been cognizant of the limitation placed upon it by Section 9 (c), company counsel quoted from an NLRB report written in 1948 which stated:

Section 9 (c) of the Act, as amended, prescribes the election by secret ballot as the sole method of resolving a question concerning representation, and leaves the Board without the discretion it formerly possessed—but rarely exercised—to utilize other suitable means of ascertaining representatives.

The Gissel Company's point of contention here was that the Board's "good faith doubt" criterion for certification of the union in this case was the utilization of a "suitable means" which was a prerogative that was banned in 1947. The Board erred in holding hearings and investigations to determine if the union was the rightful representative of the employees. The mere fact that hearings were held indicated that a "question of representation" existed and, therefore, as the 1947 amendment (Section 9 (c) advises, when there is a question concerning representation the Board has no choice but to hold an election. Since there was a question of representation (at least in Gissel's mind), the Board erred in not immediately holding an election.

2. Authorization cards are an unreliable indicator of an employee's actual preference as to representation by a labor organization.

This contention was supported by several arguments. The company pointed to statistics which showed that in the fiscal year 1967, 7,882 elections were conducted by the Board, and four out of ten were lost by the unions. The company noted a speech made by the then NLRB Chairman that in 57 elections where unions presented authorization cards from over 70% of the employees, they won 43, or 75% of them. Thus, unions lost one in four elections where employees were given a free choice, even though their card-based apparent approval would indicate that a loss would be a statistical rarity. These statistics indicate that unions do not automatically win elections. The Gissel Company might have been among the one out of four whose union would lose an election despite an alleged majority.

In supporting this second argument, the company pointed to statements from other circuit courts to support this contention. The Sixth Circuit with the concurrence of the Second Circuit had written:

> As both the courts and the Board recognize, the use of authorization cards is a 'notoriously unreliable method of determining the majority status of a union' . . . To base a recognition and bargaining order on such questionable procedures is a 'strong medicine to be used only with restraint.' (*NLRB* vs. *Fashion Fair, Inc.,* 6th Circuit, 1968).

Supporting this second argument from another angle, the company questioned the method by which signatures were obtained by citing remarks made by the Fourth Circuit in another case—*NLRB* vs. *S. S. Logan Packing Co.*:

... It is well known that many people, solicited alone and in private, will sign a petition and, later, solicited alone and in private will sign an opposing petition, in each instance, out of concern for the feelings of the solicitors and the difficulty of saying "No". This inclination to be agreeable is greatly aggravated in the context of a union organizational campaign when the opinion of fellow-employees and of potentially powerful union organizers may weigh heavily in the balance ... Without adequate supervision, solicitors of authorization cards may resort to a wide variety of other threats.

The company also supported its position by quoting from the AFL-CIO *Guidebook for Union Organizers* (1961): "NLRB pledge cards are at best a signifying of intention at a given moment. Sometimes they are signed to 'get the union off my back.' "

3. The Board failed to sustain its burden of proof that the company had no good faith doubt as to the union's majority status. The company relied most heavily on three points to support this third argument.

  a) Due to the company's previous history of unfair labor practices, the trial examiner and the NLRB approached this particular case with preconceived conclusions.

  b) Being guilty of 8 (a) (1) and (3) does not automatically make an employer guilty of 8 (a) (5).

  c) Therefore, notwithstanding alleged 8 (a) (1) and (3) violations, the Board still has the burden of proving that a good faith doubt was lacking.

The company here claimed that the Board had not proved any 8 (a) (5) violation, but had simply assumed as much because of the finding of 8 (a) (1) and 8 (a) (3) violations. In fact, the company contended, the Board never did discharge its responsibility of providing proof because the company did have its doubts about the union's claimed majority status. This argument was fortified by pointing to the fact that, in 1960, the union claimed a majority only to be defeated in the NLRB-held election. The company concluded by arguing that since the facts were the same in 1965 as in 1960, why shouldn't they have doubts? The Board should be ordered to rescind its order for the company to bargain with the union, and an election should be held to determine the status of union representation.

POSITION OF THE NATIONAL LABOR RELATIONS BOARD

The NLRB countered with two major arguments of its own:

1. An employer is obligated to bargain with a union which

presents valid authorization cards signed by a majority of the employees, unless there is a "good faith doubt" as to majority. The employer's other unfair labor practices were a relevant factor in determining whether the company relied upon such a doubt in refusing to bargain.

The Board claimed that the union involved had attained majority status through solicitation of authorization cards from the employees. After the union had attained this status and had requested the employer to recognize and bargain with them, the employer had engaged in extensive unfair labor practices which foreclosed the possibility of an immediate fair election. This justified an inference that the company's refusal to bargain with the union was not prompted in good faith by a doubt of the union's majority status.

The Board asserted that repeated serious unfair practices are relevant both to demonstrate the employer's improper motivation and to identify cases in which more than a simple cease-and-desist order would be required to restore the previous situation.

2. Where the Board has found a refusal to bargain in violation of Section 8 (a) (5), it may appropriately enter a bargaining order even though subsequently the union may have lost its majority.

The Board claimed it is not limited to a cease-and-desist remedy; it may properly order the employer to bargain with the union without first requiring the union to show that it still represents a majority of the employees. The Board many times has expressed the view that the unlawful refusal of an employer to bargain collectively with its employees' chosen representatives disrupts the employees' morale, deters their organizational activities, and discourages their membership in unions. Further, where there has been a refusal to bargain accompanied by serious unfair labor practices against a union which has obtained authorization cards from a majority of employees, it is likely that its majority status will be dissipated as a result of the unfair labor practices and the time required for the Board to issue its decision and remedial order. Merely to issue a cease-and-desist order and to direct an election in this situation would both prejudice the employees' right freely to determine whether they desire a representative and profit the wrong-doing employers.

Since the Board had concluded that the company here violated Section 8 (a) (5) of the act by refusing to bargain with the representatives of a majority of the employees, the bargaining orders issued by the Board as a remedy for these violations were necessary and proper to effectuate the policies of the act.

POSITION OF THE UNION

In summary form the major arguments presented by union counsel before the Supreme Court were as follows:

1. The 1947 Taft-Hartley Amendments to the National Labor Relations Act did not divest the Board of its authority to order an employer to recognize a union whose majority status is based on authorization cards.

2. In 1956 the Supreme Court acknowledged an employer's obligation to recognize a labor organization designated by a majority of employees upon signed authorization cards.

3. Congress made no changes in Section 8 (a) (5) or Section 9 in 1959, but by adding Section 8 (b) (7) to the act increased the value of a certification while maintaining an employer's obligation to recognize a union designation by the majority of its employees.

4. Designation by a majority of employees on unambiguous authorization cards obtained without misrepresentation or coercion is as reliable an indicator of employee wishes as an election.

5. The good faith of an employer is not relevant to his duty to recognize the bargaining representative designated by a majority of his employees. The union here cited several cases where the Board and the courts made it unmistakably clear that "good faith" is totally irrelevant. Thus it has been held that an employer acts at his peril when he mistakenly, albeit in good faith, refuses to recognize the union because he believes the unit description to be improper. This rule has been extended by the Board to cases where the union's unit description in its request to bargain was unclear, and indeed, where it varied in some degree from the unit ultimately found to be appropriate. Counsel for the union argued:

Thus the mental attitude of the employer is not relevant to either of the basic elements of his duty to recognize, i.e. the appropriate unit or majority status. It is thereby difficult to perceive by what legerdemain the good faith state of mind of the employer becomes a valid defense to a violation of the duty to recognize where the union's majority status is proved by means other than an election.

In practical terms it is the issue of "good faith" that in large part has created difficulty in respect to refusal to recognize Section 8 (a) (5) violations. The Board, the courts and the legal writers, without benefit of psychoanalysis or psychiatric tools, the science of cybernetics or subliminal testing, vainly have sought to delve into the cerebrations of an employer to determine whether a refusal to recognize was predicated upon a "good faith" doubt as to the majority status of the union. Some have suggested that the test should be based upon whether the employer rejects the principle of collective bargaining or whether he seeks undue delay to gain time in which to undermine the union.

The union asked that the decision of the Fourth Circuit Court should be reversed, and that the full order of the NLRB requiring the company to bargain with the union should be upheld.

QUESTIONS

1. Evaluate each of the successive decisions made by the National Labor Relations Board and the Court of Appeals prior to the case being heard by the Supreme Court.
2. Evaluate the major arguments of the company, the union, and the National Labor Relations Board in supporting their respective positions before the Supreme Court.
3. Does the fact that the company was found guilty of violations of Sections 8 (a) (1) and 8 (a) (3) of the act have a bearing upon the question of a Section 8 (a) (5) violation? Why, or why not?
4. Are union authorization cards valid enough indicators of sentiments of employees that the Board should have the latitude to use these cards in determining union majority status under certain circumstances? Discuss.
5. Would it be desirable that the act be amended to require that all cases of union representation be decided by an NLRB supervised election? Discuss. [Note: Under Executive Order 11491, union representation among federal government employees is decided *only* by a federally supervised election.]

15. DISCRIMINATION CHARGES DURING A UNION ORGANIZING CAMPAIGN

COMPANY: Northwest Propane Co., Inc., Farmington, Michigan

UNION: Local 614, International Brotherhood of Teamsters, Chauffeurs, Warehousemen and Helpers of America

BACKGROUND

During a union organizing campaign at the Northwest Propane Co. of Farmington, Michigan, a series of events occurred which brought multiple unfair labor practice charges filed by the Teamsters Union against the company. Each of these incidents will be described separately, although they did not necessarily occur sequentially as presented in this case.

The Discharge of Employee Don Meyers[1]

Northwest Propane Company sells propane gas and related products at Farmington, Michigan. Its business is seasonal, and its peak season occurs between November and March. During the slack season, the company usually reduces its work force.

Company offices and the main plant are situated along a main highway known as Northwestern Highway. The office building is approached by a large driveway which leads from the highway and passes along the front of the office. Offices of the company president and other executives are in the front of the office building, directly overlooking the driveway and also the highway.

Around May 12, 1971, Rollie Johnson, one of the company's employees, phoned an organizer of the union. The organizer advised Johnson that he would go to the company's premises the following day to handbill and to solicit authorization card signatures.

---

[1] All names disguised.

137

At around 4 p.m. the next day, the organizer went to the company's premises and stayed there for about an hour and forty minutes. During the time that he was handbilling, he wore a bright blue jacket on the back of which was written the word "Teamsters" in gold letters. He stationed himself at the driveway entrance leading into the company's property. While he was there the company President, Ken Schader, drove into the property, parked his car on the driveway, looked in the organizer's direction, and then went into the main office building. Sometime later, Schader and office manager Anton Gibson repeatedly looked out the window of the office building to observe the union organizer.

While the organizer was handbilling the employees, employee Rollie Johnson, employee Jack Tobin and a third employee, Don Meyers, left the company premises in Meyers' Mustang car. After driving south on Northwestern Highway, they reversed direction and crossed the highway stopping on a crossover area approximately 150 feet from the company office. Johnson, who initially had contacted the organizer, waved his hand and called to the organizer; Johnson was seated on the passenger side of the front seat of the car. Tobin, who was seated on the right hand passenger seat in the back of the car, also called and waved to the organizer. At this moment, both Tobin and Meyers observed President Schader standing in his office window.

After the union organizer had left the company premises, he met with a group of employees at a local restaurant. All the employees present signed authorization cards. These employees included Tobin, Johnson, and Meyers.

The following afternoon, company President Ken Schader terminated Meyers. Schader told Meyers he had been terminated because business had slowed down, and the employer could not use Meyers' services. Meyers was employed as a truck driver, and he had a weak, defective left hand which made it difficult for him to load and unload gas cylinders. Schader reminded Meyers that he had been told previously in April that his employment would not be continued during the upcoming slack season.

The Discharge of Employee Jack Tobin

Employee Jack Tobin heated his home with propane gas and also owned a rental property heated by propane gas. Tobin purchased the gas for his two properties from Northwest Propane Company.

In early May, Tobin received a call from the owner of the property adjacent to his rental property. The owner asked Tobin to remove three propane gas cylinders which were lying near the rear of Tobin's rental property. These cylinders had been ordered by Tobin for use at his rental property. However, the rental property was vacant, and the cylinders had not been hooked up but were lying unattended on the ground for several months. That same day Tobin loaded the cylinders in his car and brought them to his residence.

On the Monday after Tobin took the three propane gas cylinders home, he told office manager Gibson that he had the cylinders at his home. Subsequently, pursuant to instructions by Gibson, Tobin brought two of the cylinders back to the company storage area, but the third cylinder remained at his home.

A few days later, because Tobin had not received his own bulk delivery of propane gas from the company, Tobin told the office manager that if he did not receive his bulk delivery, he would probably have to hook up the remaining cylinder to maintain heat and hot water in his home. Gibson replied that he could do so. Subsequently, Tobin hooked up the remaining cylinder to the heating system in his home.

On May 25, President Schader discharged Tobin for "stealing" this gas cylinder.

The Discharge of Employee Joyce Dees

In late May, the office manager, Anton Gibson, told the bookkeeper and another employee that, "If the Union gets in, the employer will close the business!" The bookkeeper, Joyce Dees, was one of the union's supporters. On June 7, she went to President Schader and complained that during the preceding several weeks, office manager Gibson had followed her whenever she went to the restroom or got a drink of water. In response to Schader's inquiry, Ms. Dees stated that the office manager had been following her because she was talking to her fellow employees about the union.

Later the same day, Ms. Dees was informed by Schader and Gibson that she was being discharged effective immediately. They told her that she was discharged because she had various work deficiencies, including failure to finish her bookkeeping work on time, rudeness to customers, and general disruption of the office by talking to other employees about the union on company time.

The union filed unfair labor practice charges on behalf of each of these employees and also a general complaint against the company alleging an overall pattern of antiunion activity.

POSITION OF THE UNION

In the case of the employee Don Meyers, the union claimed that Meyers had been illegally discharged in violation of Section 8 (a) (3) of the Labor-Management Relations Act because of his union activities. The union claimed that Meyers was discharged because he was observed as the owner and driver of a car whose passengers waved to the union organizer, and because Meyers had signed a union authorization card. The union claimed that this discharge action was part of the company's total pattern of activities designed to interfere with and discriminate against the union organizing campaign. The union requested that Meyers be reinstated and be given full back pay for employment that he had missed.

In the case of employee Jack Tobin, the union argued that Tobin similarly was discharged because of his union activities, thus violating Section 8 (a) (3). The union claimed that Tobin did not steal any propane gas cylinders. Tobin had been a good employee for four years, and his discharge did not occur until after the company had learned that Tobin was involved in the union campaign and a request for a representational election had been filed. Concerning the alleged stealing of the gas cylinder, the union claimed that this was strictly a fabricated charge and pointed out that Tobin actually had received permission from the office manager to hook up the one cylinder to his heating system in his home. The union requested that Tobin be reinstated with full back pay for any period of employment missed.

In the case of employee Joyce Dees, the union again claimed that the company had violated Section 8 (a) (3) by discharging Ms. Dees for her union sympathies and activities, not the alleged work deficiencies which company management had stated. Ms. Dees had been a satisfactory employee for over five years. The union argued that she could have been discharged at any time previously in the five years for work deficiencies. The union also pointed out that office manager Gibson had told Ms. Dees that her talking about the union with fellow employees on company time was part of the company's reasons for taking disciplinary action against her. The union requested that Ms. Dees be reinstated to the position of bookkeeper, and that she be granted full pay for wages missed during the time of her termination.

The union also filed a general complaint which claimed that the company had violated Section 8 (a) (1) of the act by continued surveillance of its employees' union activities and by threatening employees with closing of the business if a union was successful in the organizing drive. The discharge actions against the three employees cited previously were part of a concerted total management effort to defeat the union. The union requested that the company be ordered to cease and desist from discouraging union membership and, in any other ways, from interfering with the process of having a fair representation election held at the company premises.

POSITION OF THE COMPANY

The company denied that it had embarked on a systematic effort to spy on employees involved in union activity. The company claimed that its actions taken against the three employees in this case were reasonable and fair under the circumstances and only coincidental with the union organizing campaign.

In the case of employee Don Meyers, the company pointed out that he had been told that his employment would not be continued during the slack season. Meyers was not physically capable of performing as much work or of performing his work as satisfactorily as other employees because of his defective left hand. The fact that Meyers was observed riding in a car with two other employees who waved to a union organizer was not related to the termination of Meyers. The company claimed that Meyers' termination was strictly due to economic reasons, plus the fact that Meyers was not physically capable of carrying out the required job duties.

In the case of employee Jack Tobin, the company claimed that this discharge action was strictly for the attempted theft of the gas cylinder involved in the case. The company claimed that it was clearly against company policy for any employee to have unauthorized private possession of company-owned gas cylinders for private use. There was a communications' misunderstanding between Tobin and the office manager concerning the hooking up of the cylinder to his private premises. All of the three cylinders in question should have been returned to the company premises, since they were not being utilized at Tobin's rental property where they had been delivered. Tobin knew that he had no right to hook up the cylinder at his home, but he did so anyway. Consequently, claimed the company, Tobin was discharged for his actions which the company considered to be as "stealing the cylinder," and the discharge was not due to his union activities.

Concerning employee Joyce Dees, the company again claimed that she was discharged for work deficiencies, and not for union activities.

Ms. Dees had been wasting considerable time talking to employees about the union on company time; she knew she was not permitted to do this. Her discharge was the culmination of various types of poor job performance which had existed over a long period of time. The fact that her discharge came partly as a result of her talking to other employees about the union was because this was "the straw which broke the camel's back." The company further claimed that its statement to Ms. Dees regarding closing the business was meant not as a threat, but rather it was a reflection of the fact that increased operating costs associated with a union in its situation might cause the company to go out of business.

The company claimed that it had not violated the Labor-Management Relations Act by its various actions and that all of the unfair labor practice charges against it should be dismissed.

QUESTIONS

1. Evaluate the union charges of unfair labor practices concerning each of the three employees. What remedies, if any, should be effected?
2. What is meant by the union's charge of the company's "total pattern of activities" designed to interfere with and discriminate against the union organizing campaign?
3. How can the NLRB determine whether the incidents were isolated or part of a systematic management effort in violation of the law? Discuss.
4. Why must the burden of proof in this case rest upon company management to demonstrate that its actions in this case were for reasons that clearly did not have an antiunion origin?

16. WAS THE EMPLOYEES' REFUSAL TO WORK OVERTIME PROTECTED BY LABOR LAW?

COMPANY: Polytech, Incorporated, Overland, Missouri

EMPLOYEE GROUP: Philip Bergt, Jack Shepley, Thomas Hall, Ernest Dowling, George Lesseg [1]

BACKGROUND

The company manufacturers transparent plastic sheets and related products at its plant in Overland, Missouri. At the time of this case, the company employed some 12 to 15 employees divided into fabrication and casting departments.

The casting work required the lifting of heavy molds and was performed under hot and uncomfortable conditions. The casting of 73 transparent plastic sheets were scheduled for each working day. At this time there were seven casting employees, including one woman. Casting usually was completed within the regular working day, but sometimes it required overtime of an hour or so for completion of the scheduled 73 sheets. Production occasionally was scheduled for a Saturday to gain a workday, and clean-up work was also regularly scheduled as overtime work.

The seven casting employees had worked seven hours on Saturday, March 13, 1971, and eight hours on Saturday, March 20. They also worked overtime two or three days in each of the following two weeks. Company President Dan Gehrmann, had told the employees toward the end of March that he expected them to cast the scheduled 73 plastic sheets each day.

On April 5, 1971, one employee, Del Reinke, was absent. Another employee, Jack Shepley, was inexperienced. Production fell behind schedule, and it was apparent that there would be overtime required

---

[1] All names in this case are disguised.

that night to complete the scheduled 73 sheets. After the morning break, Thomas Hall told leadman Philip Bergt that he was not going to work that night. Bergt said that that "sounded fine" to him. At lunch, Bergt and Hall spoke to Jack Shepley, Ernest Dowling, and George Lesseg about not working that night. The five men agreed at the afternoon break around 2 p.m. that they would not work that night. The one female employee in the casting department, Minnie Gersting, was not told about the plan to refuse to work any overtime.

The normal quitting hour was 4 p.m. At 3:40 p.m., George Lesseg started to close down the glass washer, and the other men worked to complete the work in process. The Company Vice-President, Mrs. Dan Gehrmann, entered the casting room about this time and asked Lesseg why he was shutting down the glass washer, saying, "We are not done yet; we have more to come." Lesseg answered that the men were "tired of staying late almost every night," that they were tired that day, and they had decided not to work that night. Mrs. Gehrmann told Meyer to run the washer until 4 o'clock. Meyer turned the washer back on and Mrs. Gehrmann walked out. She returned a few minutes later with Mr. Gehrmann. She asked the five men if they were going to work that night. As each man answered "no," she said, "Well, we don't have any work for you, then, for the next two days." She asked the men what they were trying to prove. They replied that they were not trying to prove anything, but that they were tired that day and did not want to work. The five men left the plant at 4 o'clock and returned to work on April 8 after completing a two-day suspension without pay.

Although the five employees were not represented by a labor union, shortly thereafter employee Philip Bergt on behalf of the entire group filed unfair labor practice charges which claimed that the company's suspension of the employees was in violation of rights guaranteed to groups to act on a concerted basis even though they are not represented by a labor union.

POSITION OF THE EMPLOYEE GROUP

Counsel for the employee group argued that the employees' refusal to work overtime on April 5 was a single strike of limited duration to protest against working conditions and the assignment of what the men considered to be excessive overtime. Counsel argued that several cases decided by the National Labor Relations Board and the courts indicated that when a group of unrepresented employees chose to take united action because of unsatisfactory working conditions or to protest employer practices, this type of concerted action could be entitled to the protection of the Labor-Management Relations Act as guaranteed in Section 7. In particular, a case involving the First National Bank of Omaha was cited, where a group of unrepresented employees refused to work overtime because of dissatisfaction with the employer's overtime policy. In this case the NLRB held that such employee action was protected under Section 7, since the refusal to work overtime was limited in duration and was not part of a total pattern of employee activities designed to dictate policies to the employer in the future.

Employee Thomas Hall testified that, at the meeting of April 5, the employee group discussed only to refuse working overtime on that evening; they did not discuss future problems or actions that they might take. Counsel for the employee group argued that this was a single concerted action by a group of unrepresented employees—similar to the Omaha case—designed to protest what they considered to be undesirable working conditions and excessive overtime. Counsel argued that this was the only practical alternative open to this group of employees under the circumstances, since they were not represented by a union with an enforceable grievance procedure. By suspending the employees for two days, argued counsel for the employee group, the company had illegally interfered with the rights of employees guaranteed under Section 7 of the act and thus was guilty of an unfair labor practice under Section 8 (a) (1) of the Labor-Management Relations Act. The employee group requested that they be compensated for the earnings that they lost during the two days of their suspension, and that the company be ordered to cease and desist from this and other such unfair labor practice actions.

POSITION OF THE COMPANY

Company representatives argued that the refusal of the employee group to work overtime in this case was tantamount to a rebellion against carrying out a legitimate work order. According to the company, the work on April 5 was not unusual. The employees had completed the casting of heavy sheets during regular hours, and they had comparatively light work to perform during the overtime period. The statement of the employees that they would not work overtime because they had been working "almost every night and were tired" was calculated to put the company on notice that the men might walk out again whenever they felt they had been working too much overtime. The company argued that management was within its rights to issue a two-day suspension, since the company could not tolerate such rebellious conduct. Management was not trying to discourage the men from registering a legitimate protest against working overtime. In fact, Mrs. Gehrmann had asked the men to tell her what the walkout was all about. The employee group refused to do so and simply stated that they were tired and did not want to work any more overtime. Without some management response to this situation, there could be a complete breakdown in employee discipline throughout the plant. In summary, the company argued that the employees' refusal to work overtime constituted an attempt by the employee group to work overtime on their own terms and to dictate policy to the company. This required imposition of a management disciplinary response which, in this case, was reasonable and not excessively punitive. The company argued that the unfair labor practice charge was without merit and should be dismissed.

QUESTIONS

1. Was the employees' refusal to work overtime "concerted action" which was entitled to the protection under the Labor-Management Relations Act, Section 7? Why, or why not?
2. Evaluate the employee group argument that, "this was the only practical alternative open to this group of employees under the circumstances, since they were not represented by a union with an enforceable grievance procedure." Why do you agree or disagree with this argument?
3. Why did company management consider the refusal of the group to work overtime as being tantamount to a rebellion against carrying out a legitimate work order?
4. Was management's disciplinary action in this situation justified? Reasonable? Was it legal under the law?
5. On what fundamental issue does a decision in this case ultimately rest?

17. CAN THE EMPLOYEES REFUSE TO CROSS ANOTHER UNION'S PICKET LINES?

COMPANY: Diamond National Corporation, Superior, Montana

UNION: Union No. 3-249, International Woodworkers of America, AFL-CIO

BACKGROUND

Diamond National Corporation has plants at Superior, Montana, Albeni Falls, Idaho, and Coeur D'Alene, Idaho. Employees at all three plants are represented by local affiliates of International Woodworkers of America (IWA), AFL-CIO.

At the time of this case, the collective bargaining agreement which covered employees of these three plants contained the following relevant provisions:

Article 14—Strikes and Lockouts

Section 1. At no time shall employees be required to act as strikebreakers or go through picket lines or armed guards. . . .

Section 2. If the Plant is affected by any labor dispute, both parties agree to do all that is feasible to bring about a prompt and fair settlement. . . .

Section 3. Irrespective of all other provisions of this Agreement, it is understood and agreed that the Union will notify the Company in writing not less than ten (10) consecutive calendar days in advance of the date and time that any strike action is to be commenced. Under no circumstances shall such notice be given until after: first—a meeting has been held between top Western States Regional Council of IWA . . . and the Union being dissatisfied with the results of that meeting; second—the Union requests the intervention of the Federal Mediation and Conciliation Service, and either that Service has advised both parties in writing that it refuses to assert jurisdiction, or that Service has had the opportunity of holding at least one meeting of the parties in an effort to resolve the dispute involved.

Article 18—Grievance Procedure

Section 1.   In the event there by any dispute as to the Interpretation of any provision of this Agreement, or any grievance arising out of the operation of this Agreement, the matter shall be referred to the Shop Committee immediately. . . .

Section 3.   It is agreed that during the period of this Agreement there shall be no strikes, cessation of work, picketing, or lockouts, until the procedures specified in this Article have been exhausted.

In August, 1969, Diamond National Corporation let a contract for remodeling work at the Superior plant to a nonunion contractor. The company set up a reserved gate for the contractor's employees. A local of the Carpenters union began to picket both the main and the reserved gates protesting the use of nonunion employees for this remodeling work. Diamond National employees who were represented by the Woodworkers union refused to cross the picket line.

At a meeting with union representatives, the company took the position that the employees were on strike in violation of Section 3 of Article 18 of the collective-bargaining agreement. The union representatives, on the other hand, asserted that the employees were exercising their right not to cross a picket line as guaranteed in Section 1, Article 14 of the contract. Following the meeting, the company sent the union a letter, with copies to all employees. The letter outlined possible legal remedies for an alleged breach of the no-strike clause, but urged the employees to return to work promptly and promised no reprisals if the employees did so. The picket line was removed the following day, and the employees returned to work. There were no reprisals.

Somewhat similar incidents took place at the Albeni Falls plant on September 11 and at the Coeur d'Alene plant on September 15. The same sequence of events occurred: unidentified pickets appeared at these plants and the company employees refused to cross the picket lines. The company wrote letters to the union and the employees; these letters outlined possible legal steps to remedy the alleged breach of the no-strike clause; pickets did not appear on the following day; and the employees then returned to work. However, at the Coeur d'Alene plant the company took a firmer stance. In the letter to employees of that plant, it threatened to discharge all employees who did not report for work. It also imposed two-day disciplinary layoffs on three union stewards who were active in encouraging employees not to cross picket lines.

On September 14, Diamond National management received reports that the unidentified pickets who had earlier appeared at the

Albeni Falls and Coeur d'Alene plants were going to picket the Superior plant. On September 15, Diamond National dispatched a letter to the union and the employees of the Superior plant reading as follows:

Gentlemen:

We have heard rumors that roving pickets, on strike from a Diamond National Plant at Marysville, California where a lumber and sawmill workers' union is involved, may establish a picket line at our Plant tomorrow. If such a picket line is established and our Superior employees choose to "honor" it, such action will constitute a most serious violation of our Working Agreement with your Union.

The Agreement makes it completely clear that you are not to strike our operation except under certain spelled out procedures. We believe that a strike under circumstances mentioned above would completely violate our Working Agreement, in which event our attorney has indicated that we might take any or all of the following courses: (1) sue your Union and its leadership for damages occasioned by the illegal strike; (2) seek an injunction to bar such strike action; (3) file unfair labor practice charges against your Union and its leadership, for taking such action without prior negotiations and following the steps required by our Working Agreement; (4) terminate all employees or just the leaders for engaging in conduct in violation of our Working Agreement; (5) terminate the Working Agreement because of its violation.

In the event our employees go on strike under the circumstances first above mentioned, they will have subjected the Union and themselves to possible legal action.

However, no pickets showed up to picket at the Superior plant. Employees reported to work as usual, and the company took no action against any employees. However, shortly thereafter, the union filed unfair labor practice charges with the National Labor Relations Board, contending that the company's letter had violated Section 8 (a) (1) of the Labor-Management Relations Act.

POSITION OF THE UNION

The union argued that the company had violated Section 8 (a) (1) by sending its letter of September 15 to the Superior plant employees and the Woodworkers union. The union argued that Section 1 of Article 14 of the collective bargaining agreement guaranteed employees the right to refuse to cross another union's picket line, and that Section 3 of Article 14 and Section 3 of Article 18 of the agreement were applicable to disputes only between the Woodworkers union and the company regarding various provisions and benefits for Superior plant employees. The union said that the company was wrong in stating in its September 15 letter that employees who refused to cross unidentified picket lines at the Superior plant would thereby breach the existing collective bargaining contract and expose themselves to legal liability and disciplinary action. The union contended that, by its erroneous letter and other pressure tactics, the company had coerced, restrained, and interfered with the rights of employees as guaranteed by Section 7 and Section 8 (a) (1) of the Act.[1] The union argued that the company should be found guilty of an unfair labor practice, that it should be required to cease and desist from such activity, and that the company should be required to send a letter to the employees and the union rescinding the letter which it had sent to them on September 15, 1969.

POSITION OF THE COMPANY

The company contended that the articles in dispute in the contract were independent of one another. The company noted that introductory words of Section 3 of Article 14, "irrespective of all other provisions of this Agreement," emphasized that this provision was to have paramount status in the labor agreement, and that refusal to cross a "stranger" picket line would be a strike that first required following the detailed procedures set forth in Section 3 of Article 14. The company claimed that its letter of September 15 correctly stated that the strike or proposed strike would be a direct violation of Section 3 of Article 18 of the bargaining agreement and that the company was justified in describing the steps that it could take to remedy the situation. For these reasons, the company argued that the unfair labor practice charges should be dismissed.

QUESTIONS

1. Could this case conceivably have been heard by a arbitrator under a grievance procedure? Why, or why not?
2. Why are the provisions of Article 14 and Article 18 of the labor agreement somewhat contradictory and confusing? Why does intent and meaning of the agreement become a crucial point of contention?
3. Were the company's actions and letters in this case motivated from a desire to weaken or break the union strike action, or were they merely an attempt by

---

[1] The union had also submitted unfair labor practice charges regarding the earlier letters that were written concerning the incidents at the other plant and had filed unfair labor practice charges regarding the disciplinary layoffs of the union stewards at the Coeur d'Alene plant. The regional director of the NLRB had declined to issue complaints based upon these earlier charges.

management to force the union to observe the agreement as management interpreted it? Discuss.

4. In effect, the NLRB is being asked to issue a decision interpreting the meaning of clauses in the collective bargaining agreement. Does the Board have the legal authority to do this? Are issues such as this better left to the parties themselves, or should they be handled through a grievance-arbitration procedure?

18. WAS A PREARRANGED AGREEMENT TO RECOGNIZE THREE UNIONS LEGAL?

COMPANY: Wickes Corporation, Wickes Manufactured Housing Division, Lansing, Mich.

UNION: International Union, United Automobile, Aerospace and Agricultural Implement Workers of America (UAW)

BACKGROUND

Wickes Manufactured Housing, a division of Wickes Corporation, manufactures single-family residential units. Around March 1, 1971, the company opened a plant in Mason, Michigan. Shortly thereafter, management contacted Carpenters Local 1191, Plumbers Local 388, and Electrical Workers (IBEW) Local 655 (collectively referred to as Tri-Trades), and asked for a meeting "to discuss Tri-Trades' labor agreements as they related to modular homes." In early April, the company and Tri-Trades discussed the possibility of recognizing Tri-Trades as the bargaining representative of the employees. The company and Tri-Trades entered into a series of bargaining sessions. On June 15, they reached agreement on the terms of a collective bargaining contract subject to Tri-Trades securing signed authorizations cards from a majority of the employees.

After the contract was agreed upon, Tri-Trades arranged for a union meeting to be held in Holt, Michigan, some 15 miles away from the company's facility. On June 16, the day of the scheduled meeting, a secretary in the company office gave a janitor about 200 Tri-Trades authorization cards and instructed him to attach the cards to the employees' timecards. A foreman also posted a notice informing the employees of a Tri-Trades union meeting scheduled for that evening. At the request of a Tri-Trades representative, the plant manager announced the meeting over the plant address system of the plant.

At the union meeting that evening, Tri-Trades representatives informed employees of the previous negotiations and contract agreement. When a number of employees expressed opposition to certain features of the contract, one of the Tri-Trades representatives stated that, "We had two weeks to ratify a contract . . . or else there would be no union at all at the . . . plant."

Ultimately, a secret ballot "yes" or "no" vote was taken. The voting resulted in a predominantly "yes" vote, 74 to 9. Thereafter, most of the employees present signed and turned in the authorizations cards that had been appended to their timecards.

On the following day, Tri-Trades submitted the signed cards to the company and requested formal recognition. By a letter dated June 22, the company granted recognition, and on June 23, it executed the previously agreed-upon contract.

In the meantime, on the day after the Tri-Trades meeting, (i.e., June 17) one of the employees, Bill Brock,[1] contacted the United Automobile Workers Union (UAW). He was given several UAW authorization cards, and before the start of his shift the following day, he began soliciting card signatures at the plant gate. After Brock had obtained a few signatures, Plant Superintendent Gil Smith approached him. In response to the superintendent's inquiry, Brock stated that he was employed by Wickes Corp. Superintendent Smith then went through the gate.

Shortly before the start of his shift, Brock stopped soliciting card signatures and went through the gate. However, he was stopped by Smith who told Brock that he had been discharged.

On June 22, Brock returned to the plant to pick up his paycheck. He was met by his foreman, Bob Tora, and Superintendent Smith who told Brock of his "shortcomings as a worker." The next day, however, Brock was offered his job back. Brock accepted the offer, and after he was reinstated Brock was paid for the time he had missed because of his discharge.

Brock was not reinstated to his former job which included layout work. Instead, he was assigned to a sanding operation which was described by Brock as being "the worst job in the plant." Within a few days, however, Brock was reassigned to his previous layout work. But on his first day back on layout work, Brock was given a written reprimand which asserted that an error he had made resulted in "delaying the job three man-hours."

Around July 1, a foreman told another employee to take off a UAW button he was wearing or "he'd be fired."

On July 8, while Brock was talking to another employee

---

[1] All names disguised.

concerning some materials that he needed in connection with his work, foreman Tora approached him and told Brock to stop talking about union business on company time. Although Brock denied the foreman's charge, later that day he was given a disciplinary note signed by the foreman and the superintendent. This note stated that Brock had been repeatedly observed by Tora "promoting UAW on company time."

Later, while Brock was punching out, he individually notified other employees who also were punching out that a UAW meeting was going to be held. Two days after the UAW meeting, Wickes Corp. posted a rule which stated that "no solicitation for any reason will be permitted on company property during working time." At the time the rule was posted, one copy of the rule was personally handed to Brock by Tora with the statement, "This is especially for you."

Shortly thereafter the UAW filed unfair labor practice charges against the company, claiming that Wickes Corporation had violated various sections of the Labor-Management Relations Act and requesting remedial actions accordingly.

POSITION OF THE UNION (UAW)

The union maintained that the Wickes Corporation had violated Section 8 (a) (2) of the Labor-Management Relations Act by recognizing three unions as representative of the employees and agreeing to a collective bargaining contract with these unions before a majority of the employees had designated these unions as their bargaining representatives. The union argued that many of the employees did not understand the vote taken on the evening of June 16, 1971, as a vote for ratification or rejection of the contract that had been prearranged between the company and the Tri-Trades unions. The UAW union claimed that the company had no legal right to assume that Tri-Trades had obtained a majority status for employee representation purposes. This prearranged system of recognition and the contract were in clear violation of the obligation of an employer not to interfere with the rights of workers to freely choose which union or unions they wanted to represent them.

The union further argued that the company had violated Section 8 (a) (3) of the act when it discharged a known union adherent (Brock) and reprimanded him twice after reinstating him, since the company's actions were due to Brock's activities on behalf of the UAW. The pattern of activities which company representatives displayed clearly were discriminatory toward Brock and his sympathies with the UAW.

The union also claimed that the company violated Section 8 (a) (1) of the act by posting a "no solicitation" rule, since the purpose of this posting was to curtail union organizing activity on behalf of the UAW. The union noted that, at the time the "no solicitation" rule was posted, Brock was told that the rule was especially for him. Further, the union claimed that, despite the rule, the company continued to permit the holding of football and other "pools," and also permitted Tri-Trades' representatives to solicit dues checkoff authorizations during working time.

The union further claimed that the company violated the act by threatening another employee with discharge if he did not remove the UAW union button that he was wearing.

The union requested that the company be required to withdraw its recognition of Tri-Trades as the bargaining agent for the employees and that its contract with Tri-Trades be declared illegal. The union requested that the company be ordered to cease its discriminatory activities on behalf of Tri-Trades and against employees sympathetic to the UAW. The union further argued that a representation election should be held in the future to establish the true representation rights for employees in the plant.

POSITION OF THE COMPANY

The company claimed that the Tri-Trades unions were the free choice of the employees in their plant. Despite the fact that a general meeting had been held between company management and Tri-Trades, there was a free and open election in which the employees overwhelmingly voted for the Tri-Trades unions to represent them and to ratify the agreement that had been developed between company and Tri-Trades' representatives.

The company claimed that employee Brock had been reprimanded for his failure to perform his job duties and for soliciting employees on behalf of a union on company time. The company claimed that disciplinary actions against Brock had been rescinded, except for those actions which clearly were related to Brock's inability to perform his job properly. The company had the right to prohibit Brock from soliciting employees on company time. The company claimed that it did not object to Brock advocating the UAW union, but that his union solicitation activities had to be conducted off of company premises.

The company requested that the agreement with Tri-Trades be recognized as a valid agreement, and that the unfair labor practices against the company be dismissed.

QUESTIONS

1. Why did the United Automobile Workers Union file unfair practices charges against the company when such charges might just as logically also have been filed against the Tri-Trades unions?
2. Why would the company enter into an agreement of this nature with the Tri-Trades unions prior to an official authorization election from the employees involved?
3. Was the election in which the employees voted for the Tri-Trades unions to represent them and to ratify the prearranged agreement sufficient evidence of their choice to have Tri-Trades as the legal bargaining agent for the employees? Discuss.
4. What decision should the NLRB reach in this case? What remedial actions, if any, should be taken?

19. THE PREELECTION POLL CONTEST

COMPANY: *Glamorise Foundations, Inc., Williamsport, Pa.*

UNION: *Local 306, International Ladies' Garment Workers Union, AFL-CIO*

BACKGROUND

A representational election was to be held among employees at the Williamsport plant of Glamorise Foundations, Inc. The election was scheduled to be held during the last week of July, 1971. On June 30, 1971, about a month before the scheduled election, company management sent a notice to the employees announcing a contest. This contest was one in which employees were invited to guess the number of "no" votes which would be cast in the forthcoming union representational election. Supervisory personnel helped distribute flyers to employees captioned in large letters as follows: "IT IS IMPORTANT TO VOTE. HERE'S A CONTEST TO INTEREST YOU TO VOTE ON ELECTION." Among other things, the flyer also stated, "We all know that the employees will reject the International Ladies' Garment Workers Union. But who can give us the score?" The winning entry was to be identified by a numbered receipt which the employee was to retain, and employees were told that it was not necessary for them to sign their names. The employees were given until the close of the following day to deposit their entries in a box placed near the plant's timeclocks. After the end of the next day, the box was sealed and it was not to be opened until after the election results were known. A $50 U.S. savings bond and a $25 bond were to be given to the two employees who came closest to guessing the total of "no" votes cast in the election.

Upon announcement of this contest, the union immediately protested the contest as being illegally interfering with and trying to influence the outcome of the election.

Subsequently, the company decided not to open the sealed box in which the contest entries were placed because a union representative stated at the conclusion of the union representation voting in late July that he was filing objections to the election outcome because of the company-sponsored contest. Management decided to keep the contest entries sealed pending a ruling by the National Labor Relations Board. The union did lose the election and immediately filed unfair labor practice charges against the company relating to the preelection contest.

POSITION OF THE UNION

The union filed exceptions to the outcome of the election under Section 9 (c) of the Labor-Management Relations Act, claiming that the company contest was illegal interference in violation of Section 8 (a) (1) of the act. The union claimed that the company contest essentially was a poll of employee sentiment concerning the outcome of the election. This type of poll, in the union's opinion, was a type of "straw ballot" which was aimed at influencing employees in their decision concerning union representation. Further, the union claimed that the poll was designed to help the company obtain information concerning union sentiments, since employees would talk about the various votes that would be taken, and a general discussion of estimates was sure to come to the attention of the company. The union argued that the poll was a very significant factor in the result of the election, and it requested that the results of the election be set aside and that a new election be held free of any illegal employer interference.

POSITION OF THE COMPANY

The company contended that the contest which it sponsored was not a private poll of employee sentiment. The company claimed that it was merely a type of "raffle" intended to stimulate interest in the election, and therefore the election should be permitted to stand on its merits. No employee was coerced to participate in the poll, and safeguards were included to guard the identity of any employee until after the actual representational election was held. There was no intent on the part of the company to interfere illegally with the free choice of the employees concerning the matter of union representation. The company claimed that the union was simply using this issue as a means to obtain another election. The company requested that the unfair labor practice charges be dismissed, and that the election results be certified.

QUESTIONS

1. Was the company poll a type of "straw ballot" aimed at influencing employees in their decision concerning union representation? Why, or why not?

2. Evaluate the union charge that such a poll might help the company obtain information concerning union sentiments, even though the poll itself was secret and results would not be available until after the election.

3. Evaluate the company's argument that the poll was merely a type of "raffle," and that the union was simply using the issue as a device to obtain another election.

4. Is there a difference in the legal right of a union to try to measure employee sentiments concerning union representation prior to an election as compared to management's rights in this regard? Discuss.

5. If the Board should rule that the company preelection poll was illegal interference, was the poll of sufficient magnitude to justify a new election? Why, or why not?

20. RESTRICTIVE USE OF THE PLANT'S PUBLIC ADDRESS SYSTEM

COMPANY: The Heath Co., a wholly owned subsidiary of Schlumberger Technology Corp., St. Joseph, Michigan

UNION: United Steelworkers of America, AFL-CIO

BACKGROUND

A union representation election was scheduled for October 27, 1970, to be held in the Heath Company plant. The proposed bargaining unit consisted of about 700 production and maintenance employees. A few weeks before the election, the company personnel director prepared a list of about 25 to 35 supervisors and non-bargaining unit employees. An administrator in the personnel department subsequently contacted these individuals for the purpose of tape recording antiunion speeches for broadcast by the company over its public address system. About a dozen of those individuals contacted agreed to make such speeches for the company. No management representative was present during the twelve separate taping sessions. Although the antiunion talks were monitored before being broadcast by company management, there was no attempt by management to write or otherwise influence the content of the speeches.

Six of the 12 taped speeches were played over the company's plant public address system on October 22 and 23. They consisted of noncoercive but otherwise favorable testimonials on the company's behalf and against unionization.

All but one of the speechmakers were supervisors within the meaning of Section 2 (11) of the Labor-Management Relations Act. The exception was Maria Hoover,[1] a nonbargaining unit employee.

After listening during work time to the broadcast of the antiunion speeches over the public address system in the plant, several

---

[1] Name disguised.

employees asked an official of the personnel department whether they could use the system to reply to those testimonials. They were denied access to the system on the ground that only management was entitled to use it. In any event, they were told, other means were available for contacting prounion employees. The employees who asked to use the public address system were given permission to use the cafeteria during lunch to present the union's case to their fellow employees.

On October 27, the representation election was held. Of the 692 eligible voters in a unit of all production and maintenance workers in the plant, 293 cast valid ballots for, and 355 cast valid ballots against, the union. There were five challenged ballots and two were void.

Subsequently the union filed an unfair labor practice charge, contending that the company had illegally interfered in the election process.

POSITION OF THE UNION

The union contended that the actions of the company constituted election interference in violation of Section 8 (a) (1) of LMRA. Specifically, the union held that it should not have been denied access to the public address system to reply to the six antiunion testimonials given over the system by procompany employees. These testimonials, given only several days prior to the election, were, in the union's opinion, very influential in the outcome of the election, which was very close.

The union claimed that the use of the public address system by the company to present "antiunion propaganda" during work hours to all employees was an unfair advantage. The public address system should have been made equally available to the union, but the company prohibited such access in violation of the union's rights.

The union also objected to the company's actions in soliciting supervisors and nonbargaining unit employees to deliver the speeches. The union particularly claimed that the company had coerced a nonsupervisory employee, Maria Hoover, to deliver an antiunion speech. This, too, claimed the union, violated Section 8 (a) (1) of the act. For these reasons, the union argued that the results of the representation election should be set aside, that a new representation election should be held, and that the company should be ordered to stop its illegal interference during the period prior to the next election.

POSITION OF THE COMPANY

The company held that it did not engage in illegal preelection conduct in soliciting its supervisors to tape record and broadcast statements over the public address system. These statements, by the union's admission, were not coercive and did not include any threats or promises of benefit to workers dependent upon the outcome of the union representation election.

The company claimed that it did not exert pressure on Maria Hoover to make the statement, which she agreed to do. Further, her statement was only about a minute in duration, and it could hardly have had any major impact on the outcome of the representation election.

But, primarily, the company claimed that the union had no inherent right to utilize the company's public address system on an equal basis to reply to the six statements which the union considered to be antiunion. Although it was not required to do so, the company did permit union supporters to use the cafeteria during lunch time to present their views. This afforded reasonable opportunity to union supporters to explain their positions to employees.

The company requested that the unfair labor practice charges be dismissed, and that the results of the representation election be upheld.

QUESTIONS

1. Should the union have been given equal access to the company public address system to reply to the antiunion statements made by the company supervisory personnel? Why, or why not?
2. Evaluate the union's arguments that the alleged antiunion statements by supervisors were "very influential in the outcome of the election" and constituted an "unfair advantage" to the company side.
3. Was the company guilty of an unfair labor practice in soliciting supervisors and nonbargaining unit employees to deliver the so-called antiunion speeches? Why, or why not?
4. Was the company obligated to permit union supporters to use the cafeteria during the lunchtime to present their prounion views? Did this provide a reasonable balance for the speeches made over the company public address system by the supervisory and nonbargaining unit personnel?
5. If the NLRB rules that unfair labor practice charge or charges should be upheld, were the violations of sufficient magnitude to justify a new election? Discuss.

21. WITHDRAWING OF A TRADITIONAL CHRISTMAS BONUS

COMPANY: Century Electric Motor Co., Gettysburg, Ohio

UNION: International Union of Electrical, Radio, and Machine Workers, AFL-CIO, and Its Local 768

BACKGROUND

The plant in which this case occurred was located at Gettysburg, Ohio. Small electric motors were manufactured for use in water systems. Century Electric Motor Company had purchased the plant from Tait Manufacturing Company in June, 1967. During Tait's ownership, from 1957 until the sale to Century, Tait had paid plant employees a bonus each year at Christmas time. Since 1959 bonuses had regularly consisted of $10 for an employee's first year of service, plus $5 for each additional year. The payments had been made, however, without any provision in the collective bargaining agreement.

When Century purchased the plant, Tait advised Century management that the bonuses at Christmas were discretionary, and that the practice was subject to modification or revocation at any time. Nevertheless, Century agreed with the union to continue the obligations and relationships existing under Tait's collective bargaining agreement. Although the agreement contained no provision for any Christmas bonus and although Century had owned the plant for only the last half of 1967, Century made payment of a bonus for that year similar to the bonuses Tait had made in the past.

This payment was made by decision of the plant officers and not by action of the company's board of directors. When the directors held their first meeting in 1968, they reviewed the affairs of the corporation and the actions of the plant officers. The chairman of the board thereupon told the officers that the company was operating at a loss, and that there would be no more payments of

Christmas bonuses until the business was making a discernible profit.

On November 27, as the end of 1968 approached, the plant officers reviewed all accounting reports available through October 31, 1968. Based upon these reports, they decided that they would not be entitled under the instructions given them by the board to make payment of a Christmas bonus for that year. The plant officers called a meeting of the employees that same day and announced to them that, "this has been a poor year from a sales standpoint, and the income has been such that it was necessary for us to forego paying a Christmas bonus this year."

Contract Negotiations

The union and the company had for some weeks been engaged in negotiation sessions on a new collective bargaining agreement. The previous agreement, made by Tait and assumed by Century, had an expiration date of November 8, 1968. The parties had by November 22 reached an understanding, or accord, on almost every major issue involved between them. A final session was held on December 10 at which all remaining issues pertaining to such things as contract language, super-seniority for stewards, and shop classifications were agreed upon. On that date, the contract was written into final form and executed.

The new agreement, like the prior one, was without any provision relating to Christmas bonuses. Further, there was included in its closing article a "wrap-up" or "zipper" provision which stated as follows:

The parties acknowledge that during the negotiations which resulted in this agreement each side had the unlimited right and opportunity to make demands and proposals with respect to any subject or matter not removed by law from the area of collective bargaining, and that the understandings and agreements arrived at by the parties after the exercise of the right and opportunity are set forth in this Agreement. Therefore, the Company and the Union, for the life of this Agreement, each voluntarily and unqualifiedly waives the right, and each agrees that the other shall not be obligated, to bargain collectively with respect to any subject or matter not specifically referred to or covered in this Agreement, even though such subjects or matters may not have been within the knowledge or contemplation of either or both of the parties at the time they negotiated or signed this Agreement.

The Union Serves a Demand

The union waited until a week had gone by after the signing of the agreement and then served the company with a demand that it meet and negotiate on the question of a 1968 Christmas bonus. The company did meet with the union, but the company took the position that there was nothing to negotiate concerning a 1968 bonus. Company management asked the union why it had not indicated its disagreement by bringing the question up at the December 10 session before the new collective bargaining agreement was executed, if it felt that the company did not have a right to take the position it had taken in the November 27 announcement.

The union officials responded that the bonus was not mentioned in the December 10 meeting simply as "a deferential courtesy." Since the plant had paid a Christmas bonus for some ten years, the union claimed it had assumed that the subject of the Christmas bonus nevertheless would be discussed prior to a final decision. The company responded that the matter of the Christmas bonus was purely within its descretion, and that it would not bargain with the union concerning this matter. Shortly thereafter, the union filed an unfair labor practice charge which alleged that the company had violated Section 8 (a) (5) of the Labor-Management Relations Act by unilaterally eliminating the Christmas bonus and thereafter refusing to bargain about this matter with the union.

POSITION OF THE UNION

The union basically argued that the Christmas bonus had become such a traditional part of the company's total compensation package that, in effect, it had become a condition of employment. The company could not unilaterally withdraw this Christmas bonus from the employees without discussing the matter with the union as required under Section 8 (a) (5). There was nothing in the contract to indicate specifically that the union had given up and waived its right to bargain over the Christmas bonus. The contract was silent on this issue, and the so-called "zipper" clause in the contract did not negate the union's right to raise the Christmas bonus issue as a subject for bargaining. Under the provisions of well-established labor laws and rulings, argued the union, the company must bargain over a mandatory subject of bargaining unless the union has specifically agreed not to bargain over such an issue. The union never agreed specifically to the company's unilateral abolition of the Christmas bonus.

The union argued that the company should be found guilty of an unfair labor practice in violation of Section 8 (a) (5), that a Christmas bonus should be granted to the employees for 1968, and that the company should be ordered to bargain over the issue of a Christmas bonus for future years.

POSITION OF THE COMPANY

The company argued that the union had waived its right to bargain over the Christmas bonus by its acquiescence and by not mentioning the issue of the Christmas bonus during 1968 contract negotiations. Failure on the part of the union to discuss the question of the Christmas bonus until after the contract had been signed on December 10 indicated that the union had waived its right to bargain about the matter. Further, the contract "zipper" clause specifically negated the company's obligation to bargain during the contract period concerning any subject not mentioned in the contract. Therefore, argued the company, it was not obligated to bargain over the Christmas bonus issue. The company requested that the unfair labor practice charge be dismissed.

QUESTIONS

1. Evaluate the intent and meaning of the "wrap-up" or "zipper" provision in the agreement upon which much of the dispute in this case hinges.
2. Was the Christmas bonus a matter completely within company management discretion, or had the bonus become a subject of collective bargaining as argued by the union? Evaluate the union's statement that the Christmas bonus "had become such a traditional part of the Company's total compensation package that, in effect, it had become a condition of employment."
3. Did the union waive its right to bargain over the Christmas bonus by (a) not mentioning the issue of the Christmas bonus during the 1968 contract negotiations, and (b) by agreeing to the "zipper" clause in the contract? Why or why not?
4. Does the fact that company management changed over the period of time of the Christmas bonus have direct or indirect bearing on the issues involved? How?
5. If the company should be found guilty of an unfair labor practice, must the company: (a) pay a Christmas bonus for 1968, and/or (b) bargain over the issue of a Christmas bonus for all forthcoming years?

22. THE EMPLOYEE WHO WORKED ON DR. MARTIN LUTHER KING'S BIRTHDAY

COMPANY: Bechtel Corp. on behalf of employee Dan Hasler[1]

UNION: Laborers' International Union of America, Local 832, AFL-CIO, Morgantown, Maryland

BACKGROUND

Bechtel Corporation is a major company which engages in the business of constructing power plants throughout the country. At Morgantown, Maryland, the company was involved in a project to construct a major power plant. Bechtel employed as laborers members of Local 832 of the Laborers' International Union which was located in this area.

During the three years that the Morgantown project was in progress prior to this case, there had been a tacit agreement between the company and Local 832 which permitted members of the local to observe Dr. Martin Luther King's birthday as a holiday if they wished to do so. This was a voluntary policy; however, most of Local 832's members refrained from working on this particular day.

In 1971, the union's members were informed by the union on January 14th that there would be no work on Dr. King's birthday, January 15th. On January 15th, Dan Hasler, a member of the union who had been employed on the project from its beginning, showed up at the Morgantown job site to obtain a set of knee pads which he intended to use for a personal project at home. Upon arriving at the job site, Hasler was asked by the project's general superintendent if he would like to work that day with the carpenters who already were at work. Carpenters were members of another union who were not observing Dr. King's birthday as a holiday. Hasler agreed to remain at

---

[1] Names disguised.

the job site and worked with the carpenters for a full eight hours. On the following day, January 16, all of the workers, including Hasler, returned to work.

Early that morning, the Local 832 shop steward learned that Hasler had worked on Dr. King's birthday while the remainder of the Laborers' union local had been at home. On January 18th the general labor foreman, who was a member of Local 832, delivered a safety lecture to a gathering of the union's members who were present for the lecture. This foreman made a statement concluding that violators of safety regulations would be subject to layoff by the company and the union. Following the safety lecture, the union's business agent held a meeting for all of the labor foremen who were working on the Morgantown project and who were members of the union.

After some discussion of the safety problems, the conversation turned to the matter of Hasler's having worked on Dr. King's birthday. Some of the labor foremen were very resentful of the fact that Hasler had worked. Others were rather indifferent to the whole matter.

Eventually, Hasler's foreman sent him to talk to the union business agent. After talking with Hasler, the agent told him that, at 2 p.m. that day, by vote of the union Executive Committee, he was to be laid off for an indefinite period for having worked on Dr. King's birthday in violation of the agreement that the union had with the company.

Due to a combination of circumstances, however, Hasler was not laid off until a month later. When he was laid off by the union, Hasler immediately filed unfair labor practice charges against the union, claiming that his rights as a union member and employee had been violated. The company contacted the union, and Hasler shortly thereafter was reinstated to his former position on the job. Nevertheless, the unfair labor practice charges were pressed by the company on behalf of employee Hasler, and eventually they were heard by an NLRB trial examiner.

POSITION OF THE COMPANY

On behalf of employee Dan Hasler, the company held that the Laborers' union had violated Section 8 (b) (2) and Section 8 (a) (3) of the Labor-Management Relations Act by discriminating against Hasler because of his violation of the union's policy of not working on the birthday of Dr. Martin Luther King. The company argued that

Hasler had every right to work on Dr. King's birthday, since there was nothing other than a general agreement that this would be a voluntary holiday. The company argued that Hasler was being discriminated against because of a matter which was outside the Labor-Management Relations Act. According to the Labor-Management Relations Act, a union may only discriminate against a union member for his failure to pay or tender periodic dues uniformly levied by a union. However, Hasler had consistently paid his dues. The company requested that the union be found guilty of an unfair labor practice, that Hasler be made whole for any loss of earnings caused by the discriminatory layoff instigated by the union, and that the union should be directed to desist in this kind of activity against its own members.

POSITION OF THE UNION

The union did not deny that it had threatened employee Hasler with the loss of his job on January 18 due to his having worked on Dr. King's birthday. However, the union pointed out that the actual layoff of employee Hasler did not occur until about a month later. The union held that Hasler's layoff was because he repeatedly had violated certain safety regulations. Further, the union claimed that a general reduction of the work force had resulted in Hasler's being laid off from the Morgantown project about 30 days after the incident involved in this case. The union pointed out that other members as well as Hasler had been laid off by the union for various reasons, but primarily due to a reduction in the labor force. The union claimed that the company was using this incident as a way of embarrassing the union, and that the company was insensitive to the feelings of the membership regarding Dr. King's birthday. The union asked that the unfair labor practice charges be dismissed.

QUESTIONS

1. Did the union violate the Labor-Management Relations Act by not permitting employee Dan Hasler to work under the circumstances of this case? Why, or why not?
2. Evaluate the union's argument that the company was using this incident as a way of embarrassing the union, and that the company was insensitive to the feelings of the membership.

3. Section 8 (b) (2), as related to Section 8 (a) (3) of the Labor-Management Relations Act, primarily focuses upon the question of discrimination which would encourage or discourage membership in a labor union. Were the union's actions in this case in violation of this aspect of the act? Why, or why not?
4. Why would the company pursue such a case as this on the behalf of one of its employees in what could essentially be considered as an intraunion issue?

23. THE TURNCOAT UNION MEMBERS

COMPANY: The Boeing Company, Michoud, Louisiana Plant

UNION: Booster Lodge No. 405, International Association of Machinists and Aerospace Workers, AFL-CIO

BACKGROUND

Booster Lodge No. 405, International Association of Machinists and Aerospace Workers, AFL-CIO, and the Boeing Company, were parties to a collective bargaining agreement which was effective from May 16, 1963 through September 15, 1965. Upon the expiration of the contract, the union commenced a lawful strike against Boeing at its Michoud, Louisiana plant, as well as at various other locations. This work stoppage lasted 18 days. On October 2, 1965, a new bargaining agreement was signed, and the economic strikers returned to work the following day. Both the expired agreement and the newly executed contract contained maintenance-of-membership clauses, which required all new employees to notify both the union and the company within 40 days of their acceptance of employment if they elected not to become union members. It also required those who were union members to retain their membership during the contract term.

During the strike period, some 143 employees of the 1,900 production and maintenance employees represented by the union at the Michoud plant crossed the picket line and reported to work. All of these employees had been union members during the 1963–65 contract period. Twenty-four of the employees who worked during the strike made no attempt to resign from the union during the strike. The remaining 119 submitted voluntary resignations from the union, in writing, to both the union and the company. Sixty-one of these employees who resigned did so before they crossed the picket line and returned to work; the other 58 resigned during the course of the strike, but after they had crossed the picket line in order to work. All of these resignations were submitted after the expiration of the 1963-1965 contract, and before the execution of the new agreement. Union members had not been warned prior to the strike that disciplinary measures could, or would, be taken against those who crossed the picket line to work, nor had any such discipline been imposed on members of Booster Lodge 405 prior to this time.

The Union Takes Action

In late October of 1965, the union notified all the members and former members who had crossed the picket line to work during the strike that charges had been preferred against them under the International Union constitution, for "Improper Conduct of a Member" due to their having "accepted employment . . . in an establishment where a strike existed." They were advised of the dates of their union trials, which were to be held even in their absence if they did not appear. Also, they were notified of their right to be represented by any counsel who was a member of the International Association of Machinists and Aerospace Workers. The International Union constitution provision permitted the imposition of disciplinary measures, including "reprimand, fine, suspension, or expulsion from membership, or any lesser penalty or combination," where a member had been found guilty of misconduct after notice and a hearing.

Disciplinary actions accordingly were imposed on all individuals who had worked during the strike. No distinction was drawn between those persons who had resigned from the union during the course of the strike and those who had remained union members. Employees who did not appear for trial before the union trial committee and those who appeared and who were found "guilty" were fined $450 each, and they were barred from holding a union office for a period of five years. The fines of about 35 employees who appeared for trial, apologized, and pledged loyalty to the union, were reduced to 50 percent of the earnings they received during the strike.[1] In some of these cases the time period during which these persons were prohibited from holding union office was decreased to a period based upon the number of days of strike-breaking activity each respective person had engaged in. None of the disciplined individuals processed intraunion appeals.

---

[1] Employees who worked during the strike earned between $2.38 and $3.63 per hour, or between $95 and $145 per 40-hour week. In some instances, earnings during the strike period were supplemented by the inclusion of bonus or premium rates for weekend and overtime work.

Although none of the $450 fines had been paid at the time of this case, reduced fines were paid in some instances. The union sent out written notices to all individuals who had not paid the fines that the matter was being referred to an attorney for collection, that suit would be filed if the fines remain unpaid, and that reduced fines would be reinstated to $450 in the event of nonpayment. The union actually filed suit against nine individual employees to collect the fines (plus attorney's fees and interest). None of these suits had yet been resolved at the time of this case.

POSITION OF THE COMPANY

On February 18, 1966, the company filed charges with the National Labor Relations Board, alleging that the union had violated Section 8 (b) (1) (A) of the Labor-Management Relations Act, which states that it is an unfair labor practice for a labor organization to "restrain or coerce employees in the exercise of rights guaranteed in Section 7." Included among those rights is the right to refrain from engaging in any of the protected concerted activities enumerated at the beginning of Section 7.

The company argued that the union was in violation of 8 (b) (1) (A) in four areas: (1) by fining those employees who had resigned from the union before they returned to work during the strike; (2) by disciplining those employees who had resigned after returning to work to the extent that the fines were imposed for their working during the strike after their resignation; (3) by fining members for crossing the picket line to work; and (4) by fining members of the union on whom discipline was imposed to an extent which was an unreasonable amount.

The company argued that the levy of any fine in this type of situation was calculated to force individuals to pay money to the union and engage in conduct which would be against their will, and this would be true regardless of the ultimate collectibility of the fine. The company argued that the threat of a fine and the imposition of a fine, even if it is not collected by the union, coerces employees to forego their statutory rights not to honor the union's picket line, rather than to exercise their own free judgment in a labor-management dispute.

The company requested: that the union be deemed guilty of an unfair labor practice; that it be ordered to cease and desist from such activity in the future; that the fines levied on the various union members involved be deemed uncollectible; and that the various disciplinary actions imposed by the union on its members be declared unenforceable.

POSITION OF THE UNION

The union argued that its actions in disciplining members and former members who had crossed the picket line during the strike were legal and appropriate under the law and under the union constitution. The union claimed that this was an internal matter which must be left to the handling of the union itself if it was to be effective. The union argued that the significance of its membership relationship was the union's established authority over its members. In joining a union the individual member becomes a party to a negotiated union contract and the union constitution. Without waiving protected Section 7 rights under the Labor-Management Relations Act to refrain from concerted activities, a union member recognizes that, by joining a union, he consents to the possible imposition of union discipline upon his exercise of that right. Without some form of internal control of its members, a union could hardly engage in concerted activities for the overall good of the total membership.

The union argued that even when a member resigns from a union in the middle of a strike he is not relieved from the burden of union discipline with respect to post-resignation activity. The union claimed that it had the same right to discipline those who had resigned in the middle of the strike, and who had crossed the picket line as it did those members who did not resign from the union, since in both cases this was an internal matter, not subject to the Labor-Management Relations Act. Further, the union argued that the amount of the fines it imposed was an internal matter over which the NLRB had no jurisdiction. The union requested that the unfair labor practice charges be dismissed.

QUESTIONS

1. Evaluate the company's argument that a "threat of a fine and the imposition of a fine by the union, even if not collected, coerces employees to forego their statutory rights not to honor the union's picket line."
2. Does a labor union have the right to control its members through various

forms of discipline, even where such discipline appears to force union members to give up certain of their freedoms in the work place? Discuss.

3. Does it make any difference in this case whether an employee resigned from the union before crossing the picket line? Why, or why not?

4. Why does the union argue that once a strike begins, regardless of the subsequent behavior of various members, it retains disciplinary control over the members involved?

5. Does the NLRB have any jurisdiction to rule on the reasonableness of the union fines if such fines are considered legal under the law? Discuss.

24. THE EMPLOYER'S PREDICTIONS AND THE REPRESENTATION ELECTION

COMPANY: Lenkurt Electric Co.

UNION: San Francisco & Vicinity Printing Pressmen, Offset Workers and Assistants' Union No. 24, International Printing Pressmen's & Assistants' Union of North America, AFL-CIO

BACKGROUND

The Lenkurt Electric Company is engaged in the design and manufacture of communications equipment for sale in interstate commerce. It maintains a manufacturing plant at San Carlos, California. At the time of this case, the company employed approximately 3,500 employees of whom some 2,800 were represented by various unions. The remaining personnel were primarily supervisory and administrative personnel, engineers and other professional employees, and the employees in department 83, the publications service department. The employees in department 83 prepare and publish the printed material which the company ships with the products it sells.

On August 29, 1966, the union filed a representation petition with the NLRB seeking an election for certification as the bargaining representative of 14 unrepresented employees in the Publications Production division of department 83. These employees operated certain printing equipment used in the production and duplication of printed matter. After a representation hearing, the regional director for the Board ordered that an election be held on October 14, 1966.

About two weeks before the election, the manager of the department, Mr. Theo Herald,[1] held a series of informal meetings with various employees to discuss the unionization issue.

In his conversations with the printing department employees, Mr. Herald suggested that if the employees were to unionize, it was possible that a more strict regimentation of working hours would be

---

[1] Name disguised.

implemented. He explained that under the present working conditions, company policy with respect to coffee breaks, lunch hours and conversations while working had been fairly casual in the printing department, while employees were strictly controlled as to coffee breaks, lunch hours and general attention to their labors in the unionized departments of the plant. Mr. Herald further explained that if the printing department employees were unionized, the basis of their compensation would likely be changed from monthly salary to that of an hourly rate, which was the basis for compensation of other union employees in the plant. Also, employees should anticipate that there would be a more strict observance of time worked, rest periods, late arrivals and similar matters. These comments were based largely on his own personal observations of other employees in the plant who were unionized and had gone to an hourly basis of compensation.

Mr. Herald further suggested that working conditions might be made more difficult as a result of unionization, because the company might seek to reduce operating costs by using less expensive paper stock in the printing department. He explained that, while the employees usually worked with "premium stock" paper, if it were necessary to reduce costs he would probably introduce lower quality stock, which might cause more problems for the operators of the various machines.

In the course of these meetings, Mr. Herald also stated that sick leave and other fringe benefits, particularly the company's policy of providing working smocks and laundry service to the employees, might be changed by unionization. With respect to sick leave, Mr. Herald explained that it was his understanding that employees with the International Brotherhood of Electrical Workers Union, which represented most of the employees in the plant, did not get paid if they did not come to work. The possibility of discontinuing the laundry service and working smocks was described as potentially necessary to reduce costs and to "remain competitive."

Subsequently, the representational election was held as scheduled. The election resulted in a rejection of the union by a vote of seven to five, with two ballots being challenged. The union thereafter filed an unfair labor practice charge and objections to certain conduct of the company which allegedly affected the outcome of the election.

POSITION OF THE UNION

The union contended that manager Theo Herald's remarks to

employees in the two weeks prior to the representation election violated Section 7 of the National Labor Relations Act, thereby violating Section 8 (a) (1) of the act. The union held that Mr. Herald's remarks "restrained and coerced these employees in the free exercise of their rights under Section 7. . . . "

The union argued that the preelection statements made by Mr. Herald, considered in the context in which they were made, constituted an implied threat that the company would deprive its employees of certain benefits and employment, and would impose more rigid working conditions if the union were elected as the employees' bargaining representative.

The union argued that the company should be found guilty of an unfair labor practice, and that the results of the representational election should be set aside. As a remedy, the union argued that the company should be required to recognize the union as the bargaining agent for the printing department employees, or at the very least, a new representational election should be held free of employer interference.

POSITION OF THE COMPANY

The company contended that Manager Theo Herald's statements simply were "fair comment and permissible predictions of the consequences of unionization." The company held that such statements were protected under Section 8 (c) of the Labor-Management Relations Act which states:

The expressing of any views, argument or opinion, or the dissemination thereof, whether in written, printed, graphic, or visual form, shall not constitute or be evidence of an unfair labor practice under any of the provisions of this Act, if such expression contains no threat of reprisal or force or promise of benefit.

The company argued that Mr. Herald's statements did not constitute either an expressed or implied threat of retaliation should the union gain bargaining rights at Lenkurt Electric Co. His statements mostly were predictions of possible disadvantages which might arise from economic necessity or because of union demands or policies, and all of these predictions had factual basis. The company requested that the unfair labor practice charge should be dismissed.

QUESTIONS

1. Did Mr. Theo Herald have the legal right to discuss the question of unionization with his employees? Why, or why not?

2. Were the statements made by Mr. Herald in the course of his meetings with employees within the permissible limits under Section 8 (c) of the Labor-Management Relations Act, or were they implied threats that were illegal under the act? Discuss.
3. Why is it difficult for the NLRB to draw a clear dividing line between the provisions of Section 8 (c) as compared to the requirements of Section 8 (a) (1)?
4. Evaluate the company argument that Mr. Herald's statements were "predictions of possible disadvantages which might arise from economic necessity or because of union demands or policies, and all of these predictions had factual basis."

25. THE COMPANIES' LOCKOUT DURING NEGOTIATIONS

COMPANIES: Inland Trucking Co., co-partner with Wesley Meilahn, doing business as Oshkosh Ready-Mix Co., Cook & Brown Lime Co., and Waupun Ready-Mix, Oshkosh, Wis.

UNION: General Teamsters, Warehouse and Dairy Employers, Local Union No. 126

BACKGROUND

Oshkosh Ready-Mix (Oshkosh RM) and Waupun Ready-Mix are engaged in selling and delivering ready mixed concrete to the building and construction industry. Cook & Brown Lime Company is engaged in fabricating steel products and in selling and delivering ready mixed concrete, fuel oil, steel products, and other related products.

Cook & Brown had bargained with the union for over thirty years. Oshkosh RM had a labor agreement with the union since 1964. Waupun's ownership changed hands in 1965, after a previous agreement with the union had expired. In 1965, all three employers negotiated union contracts, which were to expire on May 1, 1968.

Cook & Brown and Oshkosh RM negotiated jointly with the union in the 1968 bargaining sessions. Prior to the start of these negotiations, one of Waupun's owners told the union that Waupun wanted to delay discussion of its contract until after the Oshkosh RM contract had been negotiated, since he wished to continue the prior arrangement under which Waupun and Oshkosh RM had similar agreements except for a 25-cent wage differential.

The Waupun contract was discussed at some of the negotiations between the union and the other two employers. Whenever such discussions occurred, however, they were kept separate from the Oshkosh RM and Cook & Brown negotiations, and took place after the end of regular negotiations for the day. Moreover, Waupun consistently took the position that negotiations for Waupun were to be delayed until the Oshkosh RM negotiations were concluded.

There was no agreement between the union and Waupun that the Oshkosh RM contract terms would control the Waupun agreement.

Six bargaining sessions were held between March 29 and April 30. On April 30, the union was told that there would be no further offer from the employers; if the current offer was not accepted, an employer attorney said, the companies would lock out their employees when the contracts expired.

On May 1, the union telegraphed each employer to advise that it had no intention of striking when the current contracts expired and that it would give the employers at least a week's notice before a work stoppage.

Upon receipt of this message on May 1, each of the three employers handed their employees notices stating that the "union's refusal to compromise its wage demands has created an unfortunate situation which forces us to engage in a lockout." The employees were instructed "not to report for work until further notice."

As of May 2, Cook & Brown had 29 employees on its payroll, including 8 on seasonal layoff; Oshkosh RM had 8 employees at work and two on layoff; and Waupun had 4 employees on its payroll, all at work. None of these employees were permitted to work during about a two and a half month period while negotiations continued intermittently between the companies and the union. Nevertheless, the companies continued to operate, using supervisors, management personnel, and new employees to do work normally done by the locked–out employees. The new employees were given to understand that their tenure might be only temporary.

It was not until July 19, 1969, that agreement on a new contract was reached, and the locked-out employees then were permitted to return to work.[1]

As a result of the employee lockout, the union filed an unfair labor practice charge alleging that the companies had engaged in an action which discriminated against employees and which was in violation of employee rights guaranteed under the Labor-Management Relations Act.

POSITION OF THE UNION

The union did not contend that the lockout was unlawful at its

---

[1] Not all of the locked-out employees returned to work. Some found permanent employment elsewhere.

inception, but it did contend that the companies violated the LMRA by maintaining the lockout while employing replacements for the locked-out employees and thus continuing operations during the negotiating period.

Specifically, the union held that the companies violated Sections 8 (a) (1) and 8 (a) (3) of the LMRA by engaging in conduct discriminatory to union membership and destructive of employee rights protected by the act.

The union argued that the real purpose of the lockout was to try to force a capitulation of the union to the companies' terms by depriving the employees of their livelihood for an indefinite period, thus penalizing them for their resistance to those terms and tending to weaken and divide their bargaining power.

Such conduct was in clear violation of the rights of employees guaranteed under Section 7 of the act to bargain collectively through their selected representatives and to engage in concerted activities for the purpose of collective bargaining or other mutual aid or protection.

The union asked that the companies be found in violation of the act, and that all employees affected by the lockout should be reimbursed for all wages and benefits of which they were deprived during the illegal lockout.

POSITION OF THE COMPANIES

The companies defended their lockout actions as a reasonable and legal approach within the collective bargaining process. They argued, first of all, that they were justified in their actions by the fact that their contracts had expired and the union was free to strike. Since the contracts had expired, the companies were under no legal obligation to retain the employees on the payroll, even though negotiations were continuing with the union.

But the companies' main argument was based upon a previous NLRB case which had been carried to the Supreme Court of the United States.

In a case involving the American Ship Bldg. Corp., the Supreme Court held "that an employer violates neither Section 8 (a) (1) nor Section 8 (a) (3) of the LMRA when, after a bargaining impasse has been reached, he temporarily shuts down his plant and lays off his employees for the sole purpose of bringing economic pressure to bear in support of his legitimate bargaining position."

Footnote 8 to the opinion of the Court said: "we intimate no view whatever as to the consequences which would follow had the employer replaced its employees with permanent replacements or even temporary help."[2]

The companies contended, in effect, that the question left open in the American Ship case required an answer favorable to employers. Counsel for the companies argued as follows:

"Stated another way, the Supreme Court has interpreted the Act as sanctioning the use of the lockout by employers as an economic tool to be utilized either offensively or defensively within the process and procedure of collective bargaining as well as sanctioning an employer's hiring and use of temporary employees during the defensive lockout. In view of this settled law, the companies are simply asking for the logical extension of this law to include the hiring and use of temporary employees during the period of an offensive lockout as a legitimate right of employers. The circumstances of this case present a rational and logical basis upon which to close the heretofore incomplete perimeter of employer's rights when they resort to the lockout device as an economic tool in the process and procedure of collective bargaining."

The companies requested that the unfair labor practice charges should be dismissed.

QUESTIONS

1. Evaluate the union argument that "the real purpose of the lockout was to try to force a capitulation of the union to the companies' terms by depriving the employees of their livelihood for an indefinite period, thus penalizing them for their resistance to those terms and tending to weaken and divide their bargaining power."
2. Was company management legally free to resort to a lockout because the contract with the union had expired? Why, or why not?
3. Evaluate the company's argument concerning its rationale for use of an offensive lockout and hiring temporary employees based upon the American Ship case.
4. Assuming that bargaining is carried on in good faith, must a company wait until a union actually strikes before it resorts to actions, such as hiring replacement workers, designed to bring economic pressure on the union? Discuss.

---

[2] *American Ship Bldg.,* v. *Labor Board* (1965), 380 U.S. 300, 318, 58, LRRM 2672.

Part II

Problems in Union–Management Relations

CASES FROM LABOR ARBITRATION

GRIEVANCE PROCEDURES, ARBITRATION, AND THE RESOLUTION OF CONFLICT*

The potential for conflict exists within every organization. This is true whether we think of the family unit, business organizations, social groups, or government agencies. These conflicts may range from minor differences of opinion to open warfare resulting in physical violence. Yet, humane democratic institutions attempt to resolve intraorganizational and interpersonal conflicts in an orderly manner. While conflict can be destructive, and it often is, it need not be so. Differences of opinion, when openly confronted and fully aired, can and often do lead to new understandings and subsequent improved relationships on the part of those involved.

The avoidance of conflict is important; its resolution is critical to personal, group, and organizational viability. Conflict creates within individuals and organizations alike tensions and diversions which hinder or prevent the attainment of goals. Furthermore, striving to attain goals in itself creates tension and conflict. It is imperative that these conflicts be resolved in such a manner that striving to attain the goals of the organization will not be thwarted. Hopefully, conflict will produce new understanding and harmony, which will propel the organization toward its goals at an increased pace.

While an organization is concerned with the attainment of its goals and objectives, individuals within the organization are also concerned about the attainment of their own goals and objectives. Hence, the potential for conflict between an organization and the individuals within it arises. For example, an organization's need for productivity may come into conflict with an individual's need for security in his advancing years. As a consequence, differences may develop over the relative importance of productivity and length of service in determining layoffs.

Not all individuals within an organization share the same objectives. For example, young employees may attach less importance to length of service in determining promotions than older employees.

---

*This section provides a brief introductory overview of some of the major considerations and issues inherent in the grievance arbitration process. For more detailed information and analytical presentations, a selected bibliography is included at the end of this section.

Interpersonal and intergroup conflict within organizations arises from such differences.

Ours is a democratic society which places a high value upon justice and especially upon the protection of individual rights. The democratic ideal has stimulated the concept of participation in organizations. The high value attached to protection of human rights has stimulated the development of various mechanisms which aim to promote the administration of laws, policies, rules, and procedures in a humane and equitable manner, giving full consideration to human dignity and welfare.[1]

APPEAL PROCEDURES

Concern for human rights in our society has resulted in the development of various means whereby injured parties may appeal decisions made by those exercising power over them. In fact, almost every type of organization has developed one or more appeal procedures.

All government agencies have developed appeal procedures which enable employees to seek redress from acts of agency administrators. Labor unions have developed internal procedures for the protection of members from bureaucratic harassment. The International Union of United Automobile, Aerospace, and Agricultural Implement Workers of America has expended unusual effort to provide its members a fair opportunity for defense against union decisions concerning them, and has provided well-defined and speedy avenues of recourse in the event of unjust acts by officers and administrators. Religious institutions have developed appeal procedures which provide members with avenues of recourse against the clergy. For example, the Roman Catholic Church has developed elaborate procedures which members might employ to seek redress.

Business organizations also have developed appeal procedures. They exist in both union and nonunion companies. Many nonunion organizations have developed formalized complaint and grievance procedures which guarantee employees the right to appeal decisions made concerning them by their supervisors. In most instances, recourse may be sought all the way up through the organization to the president.

---

[1] For an excellent discussion of this issue in arbitration see: Walter E. Baer, *Discipline and Discharge Under the Labor Agreement* (New York: American Management Association, 1972), pp. 25–43.

Formalized appeal procedures seem to become more necessary as organizations become larger and more institutionalized. Further, the more demanding and more urgent the goals and objectives of the organization, and the more that they press upon the individuals in the organization, the less freedom the individual is able to exercise. The hierarchical and authoritarian nature of organizations tends to produce dependency of the subordinate on the superior. Dependency, in turn, tends to create frustration in the individual seeking freedom of self-expression on the job. Inability to exercise freedom of self-expression, in turn, tends to block the individual in his search for satisfaction through work.

Thus, formalized complaint and grievance procedures provide an opportunity for individuals to exercise greater control over their environment and to expand the opportunities for them to achieve their life goals through work.

COMPLAINT AND GRIEVANCE PROCEDURES

Appeal procedures are generally formalized in unionized organizations in complaint and grievance procedures which are included in the collective agreement. These formalized procedures vary considerably from organization to organization. Typically, however, they provide that, at the first step, the employee takes his complaint to either his immediate supervisor or his union steward. The supervisor, the steward, and the employee discuss the complaint and hopefully arrive at an amicable settlement. Most complaints are settled on an informal basis at this first step. If the parties are unable to agree, either because the supervisor disagrees with the request of the employee or because he lacks the authority to make a decision, the complaint is appealed to the second step of the grievance procedure. Typically, the grievance committee of the union and the plant superintendent attempt to negotiate a settlement. However, complaints which are not settled at the first step of the grievance procedure may not be settled at the second step either; they are then usually appealed to the third step of the grievance procedure. At this level, the handling of the grievance is quite formalized; the parties negotiating the settlement may include members of top management of the company and members of the international office of the union. Approximately 95 percent of all collective agreements provide that if the parties are unable to arrive at a decision at the third (or fourth) step of the grievance procedure, either party may petition for arbitration of the dispute by a third party. Mediation and conciliation by an outside party is always possible at any stage prior to the rendering of a decision by the arbitrator.

Grievance procedures serve many purposes in organizations. First, they serve to locate problems which exist in the relationship between the union and the company, and also to locate problems which exist within both organizations. Second, they tend to open the channels of communication between employees and management. They are especially helpful in stimulating communication upward from employees to management, sometimes to the discomfiture of the managers! Third, the grievance procedure is the instrument which enables the parties to initiate action, to interpret provisions of the collective agreement, and to apply the contract to new and changing aspects of daily relations between the employees and management. Finally, it serves as a valuable source of data at contract negotiation periods.

ARBITRATION

Arbitration constitutes the final step in a grievance procedure for settling disputes. It begins where the other procedures leave off, since the parties are presumed to have explored every avenue of negotiation and compromise before resorting to an arbitrator. When the parties turn to arbitration, they voluntarily agree to refer their dispute to an impartial third person. The arbitrator's determination will be made on the basis of the evidence and arguments presented by the disputants, who agree in advance to accept the decision of the arbitrator as final and binding.

Arbitration is usually viewed as a judicial process. However, the parties do influence this process by the internal policies which each has adopted with respect to it. For example, either the company or the union may follow a policy of carefully screening disputes which are referred to arbitration. Their objectives may be to present to arbitration only those cases which have merit and which the appealing party believes it has a good chance of winning. On the other hand, one or both parties may operate on a "percentage" basis. If they adopt this approach to arbitration, they may elect to appeal doubtful cases on the theory that arbitrators will tend to compromise. According to this reasoning, they expect to win certain points that they might otherwise have conceded. Of course, this approach to arbitration can be shortsighted; the theory that arbitrators will "split" decisions is generally not valid, since most arbitrators try to judge each case on the specific issues involved in the case. Thus, while the arbitration process is essentially a judicial one, in certain respects it is an extension of collective bargaining.

Arbitration has become an important means for the resolution of conflict. First, it has prevented open conflict, which tends to be very costly in terms of income lost to workers and profits lost to companies. Second, arbitration creates a better climate for the resolution of conflict. The parties resolve, as a matter of principle, to settle their disputes amicably. It promotes a spirit of cooperation which tends to pervade the entire grievance-handling process. Third, the parties know in advance that if they do not settle a dispute between themselves, it will ultimately be settle by a third party. While this may, in a few instances, prevent the parties from behaving in a mature and responsible manner, as a general rule arbitration has helped to develop mature dispute settlements. Finally, no-strike and no-lockout provisions in a collective agreement are possible only if an alternate means for ultimate settlement exists. If a union gives up the right to strike over a grievance during the life of the agreement, it must be assured that some other method for settlement of disputes is available.

Harry Shulman, former Dean of the Yale School of Law, and one of our most distinguished labor arbitrators, summed up his view of the role of arbitration and of the arbitrator as follows:

> The arbitration is an integral part of the system of self-government. And the system is designed to aid management in its quest for efficiency, to assist union leadership in its participation in the enterprise, and to secure justice for the employees. It is a means of making collective bargaining work and thus preserving private enterprise in a free government.
>
> . . . .
>
> The important question is not whether the parties agree with the award but rather whether they accept it, not resentfully, but cordially and willingly. Again, it is not to be expected that each decision will be accepted with the same degree of cordiality. But general acceptance and satisfaction is an attainable ideal. Its attainment depends upon the parties' seriousness of purpose to make their system of self-government work, and their confidence in the arbitrator. That confidence will ensue if the arbitrator's work inspires the feeling that he has integrity, independence, and courage so that he is not susceptible to pressure, blandishment, or threat of economic loss; that he is intelligent enough to comprehend the parties' contentions and empathetic enough to understand their significance to them; that he is not easily hoodwinked by bluff or histrionics;

that he makes earnest effort to inform himself fully and does not go off half-cocked; and that his final judgment is the product of deliberation and reason so applied on the basis of the standards and the authority which they entrusted to him.[2]

LIMITS AND OBJECTIONS TO ARBITRATION

Voluntary arbitration is a valuable device for settling disputes during the life of a contract, when the arbitrator's function is primarily that of interpreting the language or intent of the parties. Both management and unions generally reject arbitration as a method for determining the language of the contract. The contract is "law," since it represents critical areas of managerial and union decision making. Matters in dispute often are considered by the parties to involve issues of "principle," "rights," or "prerogatives." Neither management nor unions wish to permit an outside third party to resolve such important issues. Not only do they fear losing control over their destinies, but they also fear that a provision of an agreement determined by arbitration could never be changed. This is in contrast to their belief that if an arbitrator's ruling on a clause of an existing contract indicates to a party that the clause is unsatisfactory, that party can hope to change or eliminate that clause in the next contract negotiation.[3]

Arbitration is most useful when the parties resort to its use sparingly and only as a last resort. Constructive conflict can lead to new insights and understandings by the parties. Agreements reached after serious negotiation also tend to be more acceptable than those imposed from outside. Serious negotiation further helps to develop maturity and responsibility. If the parties turn to an arbitrator as a means to escape a serious confrontation or to "save face," they reduce their potential for developing their collective bargaining skills and the maturity essential for a satisfactory relationship. In fact, arbitrators often make comments about unsatisfactory grievance handling such as the following: "This case should never have gotten to arbitration," or, "The parties should have been able to resolve this case themselves."[4]

---

[2] Harry Shulman, "Reason, Contract, and Law in Labor Relations," *Harvard Law Review*, 1955, Vol. 68, p. 999.

[3] James J. Healy, *Creative Collective Bargaining* (New York: Prentice-Hall, Inc., 1965), pp. 78-79.

[4] For a view of arbitration which is less idealistic than that of Shulman see: Paul R. Hays, *Labor Arbitration: A Dissenting View* (New Haven: Yale University Press, 1966).

ARBITRATION PROCEDURES

Arbitration clauses in collective agreements must be individually tailored to meet the specific needs of each union-management relationship. The American Arbitration Association, however, has developed a standard arbitration clause which is quite commonly used and which provides a model which can be tailored to meet specific needs of a particular union-management situation:

> Any dispute, claim or grievance arising out of or relating to the interpretation or the application of this agreement shall be submitted to arbitration under the Voluntary Labor Arbitration Rules of the American Arbitration Association. The parties further agree to accept the arbitrator's award as final and binding upon them.[5]

However, many collective agreements are much more restrictive than the American Arbitration Association clause. For example, the following clause limits both the issues subject to arbitration and the authority of the arbitrator:

Step 4. In the event any employee's grievance is not settled to the satisfaction of the Union in the previous steps, the Union shall, within the time herein set out, request the appointment of an arbitrator. The selection of the arbitrator shall be carried out by the parties in accordance with the rules of the American Arbitration Association. The parties will jointly stipulate the question to the arbitrator, or if they are unable to agree to a stipulation, each party shall submit to the other its written statement of the question at least five days in advance of hearing thereof, and both statements shall be submitted to the arbitrator.

The arbitrator shall have authority to decide only matters involving grievances which were processed and handled in accordance with the Grievance Procedure and which involve a dispute as to the meaning of terms found in this Agreement, or as to the existence of facts which affect the manner in which the terms found in this Agreement are applied. He shall have no authority to rule on any of the matters excluded from the Grievance Procedure or from arbitration by this Agreement and shall have no authority to add to, subtract from, or modify any of the terms of this Agreement, nor to establish any conditions not contained in this Agreement.[6]

The American Arbitration Association also has developed a standard set of rules and procedures which govern any arbitration which it administers. If American Arbitration Association rules are not utilized by the parties, the arbitration section of the collective

---

[5] American Arbitration Association, *Labor Arbitration, Procedures and Techniques* (New York, 1960), p. 7.

[6] Agreement between Whirlpool Corporation (Fort Smith Division) and International Union Allied Industrial Workers, AFL-CIO, Local 370, July 28, 1966, p. 23.

agreement must contain a statement of policy indicating that disputes shall be arbitrated and also must enubicate other rules governing the conduct of arbitration proceedings. Issues which must be met in the arbitration clause include:

1. What is arbitrable? The clause quoted above provides that any dispute arising out of or relating to the interpretation or application of the agreement may be submitted to arbitration. On the other hand, the parties sometimes wish to exclude certain matters from arbitration, such as determination of production or quality standards. Presumably, the parties prefer to decide what course of action they will take, including the possibility of strike or lockout, if they fail to reach an agreement at the last step of the grievance procedure at the time when the deadlock occurs.

2. How is the arbitrator appointed, including what procedure shall be followed if the parties are unable to agree upon an arbitrator? Shall the parties appoint a "permanent" arbitrator to hear all disputes, or should an "ad hoc" arbitrator be appointed for each dispute?

3. What are the rules and procedures governing the conduct of an arbitrator? This includes methods for initiating an arbitration, time and place of hearings, swearing of witnesses, representation by legal counsel, recording of the proceedings, filing of briefs, rules of evidence, time within which an award will be made, and to whom it will be delivered.

4. Who bears the cost of an arbitration? Typically, but not always, the parties will agree to share equally in these costs.

Disputes are brought to arbitration by one of two routes, either by a "submission" from the parties or by a "demand for arbitration" filed by either party. A submission agreement is a statement signed by both parties indicating the specific nature of the issue under contention and the specific relief which the injured party is seeking. A demand for arbitration is a formal request made by either of the two parties to the other for arbitration of an issue in dispute.

Among the major types of evidence and testimony presented and considered by arbitrators are the following:[7]

1. The contract language.
2. Intent of the parties.
3. Past practice.

---

[7]William E. Simkin, *Acceptability as a Factor in Arbitration under an Existing Agreement* (Philadelphia: University of Pennsylvania Press, 1952), p. 40.

4. Practice at other plants in the same industry or in other industries.
5. Equity.
6. Arbitration precedents.
7. Good industrial relations practices.

The American Arbitration Association identifies ten common errors committed by the parties in arbitration:[8]

1. Using arbitration and arbitration costs as a harassing techinque.
2. Overemphasis of the grievance by the union or exaggeration of an employee's fault by management.
3. Reliance on a minimum of facts and a maximum of arguments.
4. Concealing essential facts; distorting the truth.
5. Holding back books, records, and other supporting documents.
6. Tying up proceedings with legal technicalities.
7. Introducing witnesses who have not been properly instructed on demeanor and on the place of their testimony in the entire case.
8. Withholding full cooperation from the arbitrator.
9. Disregarding the ordinary rules of courtesy and decorum.
10. Becoming involved in arguments with the other side. The time to try to convince the other party is before arbitration, during grievance processing. At the arbitration hearing, all efforts should be concentrated on convincing the arbitrator.

The parties to a dispute seek an award from the arbitrator. The purpose of the award is to arrive at a final and conclusive decision with respect to the controversy. The arbitrator must not exceed the authority given him under the terms of the collective agreement. Some agreements, for example, specifically state that the arbitrator may not add to, detract from, or otherwise modify any part of the collective agreement. Even where this is not specifically stated in a collective agreement, this restriction is generally implied in the submission of a dispute to the arbitrator. The award of the arbitrator is unassailable by either party, and it will be upheld in the courts unless: the arbitrator exceeds the authority granted him by the parties; fraud or some other breach of ethics is proved; or the result is contrary to law (e.g., an arbitrator enforces an illegal union security provision).

The cases found in this section all resulted from actual disputes which were processed through grievance procedures in their respective collective agreements, remained unsettled, and were subsequently submitted to arbitration. You will have at your disposal, in a

---

[8] American Arbitration Association, *op. cit.,* pp. 20-21.

condensed form, all the information available to the arbitrator. You have the opportunity of experiencing actual arbitration situations and of arriving at decisions with respect to the disputes.

SELECTED BIBLIOGRAPHY

Abersold, John R., and Wayne E. Howard. *Cases in Labor Arbitration: An Arbitration Experience.* Englewood Cliffs, N.J.: Prentice-Hall, Inc., 1967.

Baer, Walter E. *Discipline and Discharge Under the Labor Agreement.* New York: American Management Association, 1972.

Bangs, John R., and Frank A. Fraser. "The Impact of the Courts on Arbitration and the Right to Manage," *California Management Review,* 5:51–60 (Summer, 1963).

Brandt, Floyd S., and Carroll R. Daugherty. *Cases in Labor-Management Behavior.* Homewood, Illinois: Richard D. Irwin, Inc., 1967.

Coulson, Robert. "Experiments in Labor Arbitration," *Labor Law Journal,* 17:259–65 (May, 1966).

Davey, Harold W. *Contemporary Collective Bargaining.* 3d ed., Englewood Cliffs, N.J.: Prentice-Hall, Inc., 1972.

Elkouri, Edna and Frank Elkouri. *How Arbitration Works.* Rev. ed. Washington, D.C.: The Bureau of National Affairs, 1970.

Fleming, Robben W. "Reflections on the Nature of Labor Arbitration," *Michigan Law Review,* 61:1245–72 (May, 1963).

Fleming, Robben W. *Labor Arbitration Process.* University of Illinois Press, 1965.

Heneman, H. G., and Dale Yoder. *Labor Economics.* 2d ed., Cincinnati: Southwestern Publishing Co., 1965.

Handsaker, Morrison. "Grievance-Arbitration and Mediated Settlements," *Labor Law Journal,* 17:579–83 (October, 1966).

Jones, Dallas L. (ed.) *The Arbitrator, the NLRB, and the Courts.* Washington, D.C.: Bureau of National Affairs, 1967. Proceedings of the Twentieth Annual Meeting, National Academy of Arbitrators.

Peters, Edward, and Paul Prasow. *Arbitration and Collective Bargaining:Conflict Resolution in Labor Relations.* New York: McGraw-Hill Book Company, 1970.

Rose, George. "Do the Requirements of Due Process Protect the Rights of Employees Under Arbitration Procedures?" *Labor Law Journal,* 16:44–58 (January, 1965).

Stone, Morris. *Labor-Management Contracts at Work: Analysis of Awards Reported by the American Arbitration Association.* New York: Harper and Brothers, 1961.

Stone, Morris. *Labor Grievances and Decisions.* New York: American Arbitration Association, 1970.

Tracy, Estelle R. *Arbitration Cases in Public Employment.* New York: American Arbitration Association, 1969.

Updegraff, Clarence M. *Arbitration and Labor Relations.* Washington, D.C.: The Bureau of National Affairs, 1970.

Wallen, Saul. "Arbitrators and Judges Dispelling the Hay Haze," *California Management Review,* 9:17–24 (Spring, 1967).

Wortman, Max S., Jr., and Fred Luthans. "Arbitration in a Changing Era," *Labor Law Journal,* 15: no. 5 (May, 1964).

Wortman, Max S., Jr., and George C. Witteried. *Labor Relations and Collective Bargaining - Text and Cases.* Boston: Allyn and Bacon, 1969.

Yoder, Dale. *Personnel Management and Industrial Relations.* 6th ed., Englewood Cliffs, N.J.: Prentice-Hall, inc., 1970.

index to Cases for Part II

198

Case Number and Title	Cases by Topic Outline					
	Seniority and Employee Rights	*Discipline*	*Work Assign- ments and Job Bidding*	*Management Rights*	*Wages and Benefits*	*Technological Change*
48. Sick Leave Pay During a Strike					X	
49. Caught with Pot		X				
50. Gun or Bottle?		X		X		
51. A Drink "to Cut the Dust"	X	X				
52. Sex Discrimination in the Food Processing Plant	X		X			X
53. The Controversial Bus Driver	X	X				
54. The Bomb Threat			X	X	X	
55. The Reluctant Retiree	X			X	X	
56. Must the Company Select A Female Credit Trainee?	X		X	X		
57. Can the Company Eliminate the Quatropulper Helper's Job?			X	X		X

26. THE CASE OF THE MISTAKEN OVERTIME

COMPANY: Standard Packaging Corporation, Johnson Foil Division

UNION: International Association of Machinists, District No. 9

BACKGROUND

Jerry Smith[1] reported for work at 11 p.m. on a Saturday night shift, November 12, 1966, through an error on his part. He had not been scheduled to work and he had not been called in, although a small crew was scheduled to work this shift.

At about midnight, Smith's regular foreman, Donald Smelser, entered the plant on a trouble call and questioned him regarding his presence in the plant. After some discussion both realized that Smith had reported in error.

Smelser informed Smith that he could finish out the shift; Smith worked eight hours. This was Smith's seventh consecutive day of work, and by contract he was paid at the rate of double time.

Howard Bell filed a grievance because Smith worked on a seventh day although he was junior to Bell in seniority. Bell claimed equal pay for the time Smith worked (eight hours at double time). He maintained that in accordance with the well-established practice at Johnson Foil, overtime is offered to employees in accordance with their seniority and their ability to perform the work involved. The issue was taken to arbitration.

POSITION OF THE UNION

The union argued that if Smelser had sent Smith home after he found him working, no grievance would have been filed. However, since the company and the union both agreed that the past practice had been and still was to let the most senior employees work all overtime, the union should be upheld in this case and Bell should

[1] All names disguised.

200

be paid for all time at the appropriate rate that the junior employee was paid.

POSITION OF THE COMPANY

The company contended that it should not be required to pay another employee for 16 hours. In consideration for the employee who reported by mistake, the company allowed Smith to work out the full shift instead of sending him home with one hour's pay. The claim of the union was unjust and inequitable. No union employee, neither Bell nor anyone else, suffered any loss of work or income because the company acted in a considerate manner. No one was scheduled to perform such work that evening. If Smith had not erroneously reported for work, no one would have worked in that job. The company's action in allowing him to continue to work after he was discovered should be commended and not condemned.

QUESTIONS

1. If Jerry Smith had worked the entire Saturday shift without having talked with his foreman, would Smith have been entitled to payment for the unscheduled work on his part? Why, or why not?
2. Is Howard Bell entitled to overtime pay under the agreement for offering overtime to employees in accordance with their seniority and ability? Why, or why not?
3. Evaluate the company's argument that the claim of the union was unjust and inequitable. Evaluate its argument that no union employee, including Bell, "suffered any loss of work or income because the company acted in a considerate manner."

27. IS CONTRIBUTING TO THE DELINQUENCY OF A MINOR JUST CAUSE FOR DISCHARGING AN EMPLOYEE?

COMPANY: Babcock and Wilcox Company, Tubular Products Division, Beaver Falls Works, Beaver Falls, Pennsylvania

UNION: United Steelworkers of America, Local No. 1082

BACKGROUND

The grievant was 19 years old when he was first employed by the company on February 5, 1963. During his period of employment, he was classed as a laborer and worked in the steel plant of the company. The company agreed that during his term of employment he was a satisfactory employee who had not received any disciplinary penalty until the incident of this case.

On November 26, 1963, the grievant was arrested on the charge of "contributing to the delinquency of a minor," which is a misdemeanor under Pennsylvania law.

According to testimony taken at the grievant's trial, the grievant and a teenage girl had engaged in a "single incident of improper sexual conduct" at 5 p.m., in broad daylight, in the grievant's automobile, on a day in July, 1963.

The grievant was then 19 years of age and married, and the girl was 13 years of age. There was no evidence or suggestion that this improper conduct was accomplished by the use of force. The incident was not reported by the minor to her mother or to any other person for at least two months after it occurred.

On March 18, 1964, in the County Criminal Court, the grievant, represented by counsel, pleaded guilty to the charge of "contributing to the delinquency of a minor." He was sentenced to be imprisoned for six months in the county jail. A petition for parole was filed and on May 19, 1964, he was released for the remainder of his term of sentence.

Management officials of the company, having knowledge of the legal proceedings, refused to grant the grievant's application for a leave of absence. On April 17, 1964, the company sent a notice to the grievant informing him that he was suspended, and on April 24, 1964, he was notified of his discharge.

On April 24, 1964, the grievant filed the following:

Grievance

I was suspended for five days and effective April 22 or 23 it was converted into a discharge.

I notified the Company that for reasons I could not be at work for a short period of time.

I feel that discharge is too severe, especially when my record of employment is good.

This is a violation of the Contract.

The company refused to rescind the discharge. The dispute was not settled during prior steps of the grievance procedure, and it was referred to arbitration.

POSITION OF THE UNION

The union argued that no proper cause existed for discharge, and requested that the grievant be reinstated to his former position.

The union argued that the grievant did not violate the common decency or the morality of the community in any manner which was directly related to the employment relationship. The union contended that only if the grievant had hurt the company name should he be dismissed. It is not the part of the company to punish employees for their off-the-job actions. While the grievant's improper conduct constituted a violation of the criminal statutes of the state, it received no publicity in the community and did not involve the company or fellow employees in any way.

The union argued that if an employee's offense occurs off plant premises and outside of working hours, and it is not shown to have any impact on the employment relationship, discharge of the employee involved is not justified under a contract provision which requires "just cause" for dismissal. Management has no authority to punish every act of immoral conduct in the community, merely because an employee is involved. The police power of the state is vested in designated public officials. Therefore, the grievant should not be discharged because of this incident.

The union also emphasized the point that the grievant's prior work history had been excellent. He had never been absent from work prior to the absence caused by his two months in jail. The union did not ask for back wages, but it did argue that there was not just cause for discharge of the grievant in these circumstances.

POSITION OF THE COMPANY

The company contended that the discharge was for just and proper cause and should be upheld, because the grievant was guilty of conduct which violated the morality of the community. The basis for this discharge is specifically reserved to management by plant rules that have been posted for many years. The following excerpt from the plant rules is pertinent:

2. The following offenses may be just cause for dismissal:
    (12)   Conduct which violates community decency or morality of the community.

The company also argued that the grievant's failure to be present for work during the two months of his jail sentence justified the discipline imposed. For these reasons, management argued that the grievance should be denied and the discharge of the grievant upheld.

QUESTIONS

1. Was the company justified in discharging the grievant in this case? Why, or why not?
2. Evaluate the company's contention that the discharge was in violation of its plant rules concerning "community decency or morality." Evaluate its argument that the grievant's failure to be present for work during the two months of his jail sentence justified the discharge action.
3. Evaluate the union's argument that the discharge action did not meet the "just cause" contract provision for dismissal. Should the discharge of an employee be limited to circumstances surrounding conduct only on the job? What other circumstances might be relevant?

28. DETERMINATION OF QUALIFICATIONS AND ABILITY IN THE JOB BIDDING PROCEDURE

COMPANY: International Minerals and Chemical Corporation, Accent International Division, San Jose, California

UNION: International Chemical Workers Union, Local No. 294

RELEVANT CONTRACT CLAUSES

Article IX

Section 3—Filling Permanent Vacancies. For the permanent filling of all newly created or vacant jobs, except Laborers, the Employer shall: ... (*b*) Select from the list of Employees who so bid, that Employee, provided the qualifications and abilities of two or more bidders are equal, who has accumulated the greater Seniority rights, excepting that:

. . . .

Section 5—Determination of Qualifications and Abilities. It is recognized that the determination of qualifications and abilities is primarily a function of the Employer.

It is also recognized that such determination will be made in a fair and equitable manner.

BACKGROUND

In compliance with Article IX, Section 3 of the contract on the filling of permanent vacancies, the company posted a job bid on May 27, 1963, for two first-class maintenance employees. Twelve employees bid on this job, including Barker, Robinson, and Lapp.[1]

On June 3, 1963, at a meeting between the parties, the company announced that Barker and Lapp had been chosen to fill the positions, and that Lapp was the first choice of all four maintenance

---

[1] All names disguised.

supervisors based on a comparison of the bidders' qualifications and abilities. The union agreed with the choice of Barker but not with the choice of Lapp, because Lapp had lower seniority than most of the other bidders.

On June 4, 1963, Turner, one of the unsuccessful bidders, filed a grievance alleging a violation of Article IX, Section 5, on the ground that the selection was not made in a fair and equitable manner. At a meeting between the parties on June 7, 1963, the company informed the union that the unsuccessful bidders had been bypassed because Lapp was more qualified and able, even though he had less seniority. However, the company agreed to ask its maintenance supervisors to restudy the job bids and to reevaluate the qualifications and abilities of the bidders. The company admitted that it had selected Barker because he had been in the maintenance department longer than any of the other bidders, and also because he had long requested a change in work shift.

A reevaluation was then made on the following basis: the four maintenance supervisors each made 5 choices among the 12 bidders, assigning five points for a first choice, four points for a second choice, three points for a third choice, and so on, within a list of specified factors.

The factors used by the supervisors in the determination of the qualifications and abilities of the candidates were as follows: (1) training and experience in the following areas of maintenance work: electrical, machining, pipe fitting, welding, carpentry, mechanical, instrumentation, rigging; (2) quality and quantity of work performed; (3) amount of supervision required; (4) overall knowledge of the plant layout, equipment, and process; (5) acceptance of responsibility for work assignments; and (6) ability to direct the efforts of, and assist in the "on the job" training of, second-class maintenance employees.

The supervisors' combined (composite) evaluation scores resulted in Lapp as first choice and Robinson second. Robinson thus replaced Barker as the company's original choice for one of the two jobs. The union was informed of the results of the reevaluation and selections on June 14, 1963.

The union objected to the method used by the company in reevaluating the bidders. The company then asked the union to suggest an alternative method for selecting candidates. The union offered no alternative method, stating that its suggestions had been rejected in the past, and demanding that workers with the highest seniority should be selected on job bids where the company is unable to fairly determine differential qualifications and abilities.

The grievance was eventually submitted to arbitration.

POSITION OF THE UNION

The union contended that the method by which Lapp and Robinson were selected over the other bidders was not fair. Some of the supervisors who evaluated the bidders had not been in a supervisory capacity very long and had not observed the performance of the bidders long enough to be able to grade them thoroughly. The union submitted that some of the job bidders had never worked for some of the evaluating supervisors; that Robinson had worked for one supervisor only three or four days and for another supervisor only on Saturdays; that two of the supervisors had been in the job of supervisor less than three months at the time they graded the bidders.

Further, the union challenged the supervisors' evaluation scoring method as containing biases and prejudices which were not true representations of the bidders' job qualifications.

The ratings were strictly opinions, not substantiated by any factual evidence and abilities. In support of this contention, the union submitted that Turner, though in third place in the composite score, had himself trained Lapp in welding, and that his right to the job was recognized by the company when he was later promoted to first-class maintenance work (at a time subsequent to the filing of this grievance and before the grievance was taken to arbitration). In addition, the union submitted that Jones, a bidder with 16 years' seniority, was also qualified to perform first-class maintenance work, but he was not included among the top choices by the supervisors' evaluation procedure.

The union argued that it was the contractual obligation of the company to determine the differential qualifications and abilities of a job bidder in a fair and equitable manner. The company, having failed to do so, should select the two men with the highest seniority for the first-class maintenance jobs.

POSITION OF THE COMPANY

The company claimed that past practice and contract language showed that it was management's responsibility to determine qualifications and abilities of bidders. Seniority was a factor only when bidders were equal in ability. The selection of Lapp and Robinson was made as fairly and equitably as possible by those supervisors who were in the best position to judge the qualifications and abilities of employees in the department. Not only did the union fail to come up with some alternate way of making a selection, but it had not shown that any unfair discrimination or collusion was present in the method by which the company made a selection between bidders for the two jobs.

The company testified to the effect that bidders had been selected many times in the past on the basis of qualifications and abilities over employees with greater seniority. Furthermore, in all prior contracts the determination of qualifications and abilities was agreed by the parties to be primarily a function of management. Up to and including the 1959 contract, if the union believed the selection made by the company was unfair, the transfer of the employee was delayed until the union and the company could carefully consider the matter. That provision was negotiated out of the current contract.

In answer to the union's charges that some supervisors were not qualified to evaluate the job bidders, the company replied that: those supervisors who had only recently become supervisors had previously worked in their departments in other capacities; that employees were transferred from one supervisor to another supervisor quite regularly; that all supervisors had the opportunity to observe all the employees in their departments; and that when a bidder worked outside the maintenance department, his outside supervisor was consulted.

Therefore, the company contended that the evaluation of the supervisors was made on a fair and equitable basis, and that the selection of Lapp and Robinson for the first-class maintenance positions should be upheld by the arbitrator.

QUESTIONS

1. What is the central issue in this case situation? What is meant by the contract provision that determination of qualifications "will be made in a fair and equitable manner?"
2. What is the strongest argument presented by the union in this case situation? What is the strongest argument presented by management in this situation?
3. Can supervisory opinion be a valid method for determining qualifications and ability in a job bidding procedure? Discuss. What significance can be given to the fact that the reevaluation procedure used by management led to a different decision than its original selection of job bidders?
4. Is the arbitrator in this case authorized to suggest a procedure by which qualifications and ability in the job bidding procedure may be established?

29. FUNERAL LEAVE DURING AN EMPLOYEE'S VACATION

COMPANY: Food Employer's Council, Incorporated, Los Angeles, California

UNION: International Brotherhood of Teamsters, Chauffeurs, Warehousemen, and Helpers of America, Local Union No. 683

BACKGROUND

This grievance arose under the agreement between the parties in effect for the period September 7, 1964 to September 7, 1967, inclusive. In this agreement, companies in the Food Employer's Council of Los Angeles agreed to grant three days' funeral leave, with pay, upon the death of certain defined members of an employee's family. Article XII, the Funeral Leave provision of the contract states:

Employees shall be allowed three days' funeral leave with full pay for a death in the immediate family. Immediate family shall be defined as the employee's parents, spouse, children, and siblings.

In March, 1965, a male employee and his family were enjoying a paid vacation in Oklahoma when notice was received of the death of the employee's father in San Diego. The employee left his family in Oklahoma and flew to San Diego to attend the funeral. Thereafter, he returned to his family and completed his vacation.

Upon returning to work from his vacation, the employee requested that the company grant him three days' funeral leave pay, or grant him a three-day extension of his vacation with pay. Management denied this request. The employee filed a grievance and, with the matter unresolved, the parties submitted the question to arbitration.

POSITION OF THE UNION

The union argued that the language of Article XII was direct and unambiguous. It clearly states the employer's obligation to grant three days of funeral leave with pay to employees who suffer the tragedy of a death in the immediate family.

Since the clause contained no exceptions to this obligation, the union claimed that funeral leave should be payable whether an employee was at work or on vacation.

POSITION OF THE COMPANY

The Council claimed that it was not the intent of any of the companies to grant funeral leaves to employees who suffered a death in their family at a time when they were absent from work and already receiving pay during the period of absence. Article XII speaks of employees being "allowed" funeral leave; therefore, it denotes some degree of management prerogative in ascertaining an employee's eligibility for such a benefit.

In support of its position, management cited the sick-leave and vacation clause provisions of the current agreement. The sick-leave clause did not entitle employees to sick-leave benefits if they were on vacation. Under the vacation clause, an extra day's vacation was granted if a recognized holiday occurred during an employee's vacation; but no such provision existed in regard to funeral leave. Management claimed that these clauses supported – by consistent reasoning – the Council's position that funeral leave should not be granted to an employee who is on vacation. The grievance should be dismissed.

QUESTIONS

1. What is the meaning of the clause "shall be allowed" in Article XII of the contract? Is this clause open to interpretation?
2. Evaluate the union's argument that the Council was obligated to pay the funeral leave to the employee who was on vacation.
3. Evaluate the Council's reasoning that the employee was not entitled to funeral leave pay. What are the precedent implications of this case to both union and management interests?

30. MAKING COFFEE ON COMPANY PREMISES

COMPANY: Sheridan Machine Company

UNION: International Union of Electrical, Radio and Machine Workers, Local No. 104

On February 10, 1961, the company posted the following notice on all bulletin boards located in the plant:

Over the years the matter of making coffee, etc., has expanded to the point where the lost time involved has become very costly.

We have had installed in the plant brewed coffee machines for the convenience of office and engineering employees. Those employees who do not wish to bring their own beverage in a thermos will find the quality of the coffee in these machines quite good. Also, the proceeds from these machines will go into the employees' fund the same as that from the other vending machines.

Therefore, in the interest of good management and the efficient operation of the plant, the making of coffee, etc. is to be discontinued. Effective Monday, February 13th, 1961, all coffee pots, urns, and hot plates are to be removed from the premises. No food preparations will be permitted after this date. All food and beverages not brought from home are to be obtained from the vending machines.

BACKGROUND

Management of the Sheridan Machine Company proceeded to enforce the provisions of the February 10 notice. The union filed a grievance to protest the company notice and its enforcement. Since the union and company were unable to settle the issue concerning the practice of employees brewing coffee and making other food preparations on the premises of the company, the grievance was submitted for settlement to an arbitrator.

Both parties to the grievance agreed to the following facts: coffee making by the employees had been permitted for a considerable length of time, estimated to be 14 years by representatives for the union. Representatives for the company estimated that this activity had continued throughout a period covered by the negotiations of the three previous contracts. However, the question of coffee making by employees was not raised during the negotiations of the last three contracts. Both parties agreed that the right of an employee to drink coffee was not at issue, this right being granted freely by the management.

POSITION OF THE UNION

The union contended that the issuing of the notice was illegal, since it was prohibited by the past-practice clause of the 1960 contract. Page 3 of the 1960 contract would indicate that the unilateral abolition of the right of employees to make their own coffee is a direct violation of the contract agreement, which says:

> Practices and policies now in effect and not covered by this agreement shall continue in effect for the duration of this agreement unless changed by mutual consent between the Company and the Union.

The union, to support its position, offered the following evidence. (1) Many employees were dissatisfied with the quality of coffee furnished by the machines installed by the company. (2) Expenditures for coffee by employees would be raised by as much as $3 per week. (3) The expense of bringing coffee from home increased because of periodic thermos bottle breakage. (4) The time involved in making coffee is minimal; the activity does not interfere with plant efficiency. (5) Plant efficiency is increased because of higher morale, with morale being boosted by the making of coffee to the individual taste. (6) Some supervisors in recent years had joined workers' coffee "pools." (7) The issue was raised previously in a meeting attended by management in which a tool room foreman's order to his employees to cease making coffee was overruled by management, when the union offered the past-practices argument to support its protest. Management thus had acknowledged the validity of the union's position. (8) In negotiations of the 1957 and 1960 agreements, management had an opportunity to raise this issue, but it failed to do so.

POSITION OF THE COMPANY

Management contended that only the right to have coffee available constituted a past practice. The method of making coffee was not a past practice but was within management discretion.

Management contended that the question had not been raised seriously until recently for three reasons: (1) the participation by workers in making coffee had substantially increased and had been extended recently to include the preparation of short-order dishes during working time in preparation for mealtime; (2) the introduction of a wide variety of utensils such as hot plates, sandwich grills, frying and cooking pans constituted a fire hazard; (3) a wide enough variety of coffee to suit an adequate number of tastes was now available in the new machines installed by management.

Management further contended that these abuses interfered with plant efficiency, thus violating a management right stated in paragraphs 3 (a) and 3 (b) under Article II, Section 1 of the contract as follows:

It is the responsibility of the Management of the Company to maintain discipline and efficiency in its plant.

In this regard, management contended that the practice of coffee making took a substantial amount of time away from work, which detracted from plant efficiency and therefore must be curtailed. Management's notice was both reasonable and within its rights to manage the plant in an efficient, profitable fashion.

QUESTIONS

1. Should this grievance be considered as a trivial dispute? Why is this the type of grievance which can be of serious consequence to both union and management interests?
2. Was management justified in posting its notice of February 10? Does management in this case have the right to prohibit the use of various utensils on its plant premises?
3. Which clause of the contract must be considered as being overriding in this case: the "practices" clause or the "management rights" clause? Are these clauses in basic conflict with each other?
4. What is the fundamental issue at stake for the management of the plant in this case?

31. THE SUPERVISOR WITHOUT SENIORITY

COMPANY: Ohio Valley Company

UNION: Retail, Wholesale, and Department Store Union, Local 21

On the day before he was to take over as acting foreman in the Sweet Goods department, Samuel Clements informed the plant superintendent that he could not accept the position.[1] The union had informed him that he would lose his seniority rights in the bargaining unit if he accepted the temporary promotion. The superintendent was unable to dissuade the union from its stand on the issue. The company filed the following grievance in a letter to the union, dated December 29, 1964:

You are hereby notified that the Company is grieving the action taken today by the officers of the bargaining unit to dissuade Samuel Clements from taking a temporary and acting foremanship by threatening to terminate his seniority if he accepts said job. If the Union will not give immediate, written assurance of its intent not to attempt to strip Samuel Clements of his seniority if he accepts said job, the Company asks that this matter be referred to an arbitrator as provided for in the bargaining agreement.

The Company contends that the Seniority section of the contract does not provide for termination of seniority due to promotion either to temporary or permanent foremanship, and therefore anyone so promoted would retain his seniority so long as nothing happened that is spelled out in the contract to cause seniority to terminate.

The Company further contends that it has the unilateral right to grant leave of absence from the bargaining unit to Samuel Clements while performing the job in question and that this right derives from Section 5, paragraph 5, of Article X and from Sections 1 and 2, Article IV, both of Division II of the bargaining agreement.

The Company therefore asks that an arbitrator rule on the merits of its arguments and asks that the Union compensate the Company for the time spent in preparing Samuel Clements for the job because such preparation was wasted due to the action of the Union.

---

[1] The names of all individuals have been disguised.

BACKGROUND

Illness required Henry Holtzman, foreman in the Sweet Goods department, to ask for a leave of absence during his anticipated hospitalization and convalescence.

The plant superintendent, Christopher Jense, interviewed Samuel Clements concerning his interest in serving as acting foreman during Holtzman's temporary absence. Clements saw this as a chance to gain experience which would be beneficial for later opportunities for promotion. Therefore, he agreed to accept the job on this temporary basis.

A week prior to the date on which Holtzman's leave was to begin, Clements was started on a week's training program in order that he would be prepared to handle the temporary position of acting foreman.

Three days prior to the date on which Clements was to assume the position of acting foreman, the superintendent posted a notice in the plant, informing employees that Clements would be temporarily an acting foreman in the Sweet Goods department for the period that Holtzman was off duty.

Employees who were members of the bargaining unit protested to the grievance committee of the union; the grievance committee, in turn, wrote the company that it was their opinion that:

An employee offered and accepting promotion to supervisor surrenders his rights to all provisions of the Contract and cannot retain or accumulate seniority within the bargaining unit, there being no provision in the Contract for retention or accumulating of seniority by employees promoted outside the unit.

As a result of this protest, Clements refused to accept the temporary promotion, since he did not wish to jeopardize his seniority position.

The company assigned responsibility for supervision of the Sweet Goods department to another foreman, who supervised this department as well as his own during the six-week period. The company, however, stated to the union that the work load had increased to where it was no longer reasonable to expect a supervisor to make up for the absence of another supervisor for sustained periods of time.

The company and the union subsequently attempted to resolve the problem. The union suggested that a possible approach might be to have the employee serve as a "working foreman" who would not be permitted to use any discretion with respect to discipline or hiring or firing. The union believed that this would remove the objection to having the employee remain in the bargaining unit. However, the company objected, since the job would remain in the bargaining unit, and thus it would be filled through the bidding procedure. According to the company, filling the job through the bidding procedure would be in conflict with its historic practice of exercising its right to choose a foreman without resort to the bidding procedure.

POSITION OF THE COMPANY

The company argued that the union erred in its action because:

1. The collective agreement did not state that an employee in the bargaining unit loses his seniority if he accepts the temporary position of foreman and is outside the bargaining unit during that period.

In fact Article X, Section 5, lists the reasons for terminating seniority, but none of these include the promotion of a member of the bargaining unit to a supervisory position, either permanently or temporarily.

2. The promotion of an employee to the temporary position of foreman should be considered as a "leave of absence."

Furthermore, nothing in the collective agreement spells out either all the reasons for granting leaves of absence, or the mechanism for doing so, or the duration of leaves.

3. The company had always exercised unilateral control in the matter of granting leaves of absence, although the company agreed that it was bound by the restriction that employees must be treated uniformly and fairly.

4. This case must be regarded as a leave of absence. It is not a frivolous one, since its purpose was to fill a definite and legitimate need. Where else should a company look for managerial talent other than from within its own personnel?

If "our people find that they will lose their seniority the minute they accept a temporary foremanship, then they will be blocked from advancement and the company will have to go outside to obtain supervisory personnel."

5. Article I only denied the union the right to bargain collectively for a supervisor; it did not "exclude an employee temporarily assigned to a supervisory position from continuing to hold membership in this bargaining unit."

Thus, an employee who is temporarily promoted to a supervisory position should be considered as having been given a leave of absence; he should retain his seniority while on inactive status with respect to the bargaining unit.

POSITION OF THE UNION

The union position was as follows:

1. Article I, Section 1, excluded from all provisions of the agreement supervisors as defined in the Labor-Management Relations Act.[2] Thus, an employee offered and accepting promotion to supervision surrendered his rights to all provisions of the contract and could not retain or accumulate seniority within the bargaining unit. There was no provision in the contract for retention or accumulation of seniority by employees promoted outside the unit.

Seniority is defined as "length of continuous service in the company's employment," but this has no application to supervisors since supervisors are excluded from all provisions of the agreement. Seniority rights exist only by virtue of the agreement and are nonexistent outside the bargaining unit.

2. "Continuous service" in the company's employment can only mean continuous service within the bargaining unit, so that acceptance of promotion outside the unit is equivalent to a voluntary quit which is provided for under Section 5 of Article X. A promoted employee in fact leaves the bargaining unit and enters an area of employment where the union does not and cannot represent him.

3. An employee promoted to supervision should return to the bargaining unit only as a new employee. The union asserted that it would be grossly unjust to allow an employee who accepts promotion to a supervisory position to retain or accumulate seniority within the bargaining unit. This would permit him, when he moved back to the bargaining unit, to displace an employee whose duties had remained in the bargaining unit.

---

[2] Labor-Management Relations Act of 1947, Section 2.

APPENDIX

Applicable Clauses of the Collective Agreement

Article I—Recognition

Section 1. The Company recognizes the Union as the exclusive representative for the purpose of collective bargaining with respect to rates of pay, wages, hours of employment and other conditions of employment for all production, maintenance, and wholesale route sales employees of the Company's Middleport, Ohio, plant, excluding office, clerical employees, managers, and all guards, professional employees, and supervisors as defined in the National Labor Relations Act, including the two supervisory maintenance employees.

Article IV—Management

Section 1. The Union agrees that the management of the business, including the direction of the working force; the right to hire, to plan and direct and control all business operations; the right to establish, change or introduce new or improved production methods, standards or facilities; is the sole and exclusive prerogative and responsibility of management. All other rights not specifically nullified by this Agreement are retained by the Company.

Section 2. The Company is vested with the right to relieve employees from duty because of lack of work or other legitimate reasons; to promote, suspend, demote, transfer, discipline and discharge for proper cause. The Company will not exercise these rights contrary to this Agreement.

Article X—Seniority

Section 1. Seniority is defined as the length of continuous service in this Company's employment, so that the oldest employee in point of service shall have the greatest seniority and the employee last hired shall have the least seniority. It is understood that the sales and shop employees are in separate departments and there shall be no bidding or bumping from one department to the other. For purposes of this Agreement, there are only two departments, sales and shop.

Section 3. When a vacancy occurs or a new job is created within the bargaining unit, the Company shall post a notice on the bulletin board giving the description of the job and the rate of pay. Employees in the department desiring that job may bid therefor within seventy-two (72) hours from the time of posting. The employee bidding for the job who has the greatest seniority will be given the job, provided he has the necessary physical fitness and ability to perform the duties of the job efficiently. If no one bids on the job for a period of seventy-two (72) hours from the time of posting, the Company may fill the job by transfer or by hiring someone from outside the plant. During the time of replacement the Company may temporarily fill the job in any manner it sees fit, provided that no hourly paid employee is required to take a reduction in hourly rate of pay. No more than two (2) changes will be made under this job posting provision by hourly paid employees.

Shop employees may bid successfully only once in any three (3) month period unless the job posted is a new job. Any bidder failing to perform satisfactorily on a job after reasonable training will be placed in whatever opening is available. Should the bidder that failed to learn the job not be able to handle the available opening or if there is no available opening he will be placed on the job of the most junior employee of the bargaining unit.

. . . .

Section 5. Seniority shall be broken and employment terminated for the following reasons:

(1) If an employee voluntarily quits;

(2) If an employee is discharged for cause and not reinstated under the grievance procedure;

(3) If an employee fails to report to work, or fails to notify the Company of his inability to report for work as promptly as reasonably possible, without, in either case, a reasonable excuse for such failure;

(4) If an employee is called back to work after a layoff and fails to report within four (4) days, after being called by registered letter posted to his last address filed with the Company. If the employee is not able to report for work within such four (4) day period he shall, within such time, apply in writing by registered mail for leave of absence for good cause, stating the reason with reasonable proof, and the time he will return to work;

(5) If an employee on leave of absence fails to return to work on the day following the expiration of the leave of absence, and,

(6) If any employee has been laid off for a period of one year and during said period of one year has not been recalled to perform any services for the Company. The first day after the last day said employee performed services for the Company shall be deemed to be the anniversary date for the purpose of computing said one-year period.

QUESTIONS

1. Why is it unusual for a company to file a grievance to a labor union? Is this an important right to a company management?

2. Evaluate the positions of the company and the union in this case situation. Does this case have precedent implications that go beyond the matter of temporary service as a foreman?

3. May a supervisor be a member of the collective bargaining unit in a plant under provisions of labor law? Explain.

4. Why is this case of significance to employees who are interested in possible advancement to foreman or other management positions? Should a union be willing to accept an individual back into the bargaining unit with no loss of seniority if such an individual fails to "make the grade" in a foreman or management position?

32. NO VACATION PAY

COMPANY: Purex Corporation, Limited

UNION: International Chemical Workers, Local No. 189

On April 27, 1962, Peter Francken[1] quit his job at the Omaha plant of Purex because of ill health. The company declined to grant his claim for compensation for vacation credit on the ground that he had quit before attaining his anniversary date of employment. The union filed the following grievance on April 26, 1962, on behalf of Francken:

Francken with seniority of 7/18/57 is entitled to 2 weeks' vacation pay. From July 18, 1961, to April 25, 1962, Francken has completed his 41 weeks requirement to earn 2 weeks' vacation pay. Francken has also given the Company proper notice that he was leaving the employment of the Company. However, the Company refuses to pay Francken for his earned vacation.

On May 8, 1962, the company replied to Francken's grievance as follows:

Grievance denied, as the employee did not pass through his anniversary date in accordance with Section 11 of the Contract. He has only met one requirement under the Contract. In order to be eligible an employee must meet two requirements—namely, he must pass through his anniversary date and must have worked during each of forty-one or more normal working weeks in the year succeeding his hiring date or anniversary date thereof.

The grievance eventually was submitted to arbitration.

BACKGROUND

The following provisions of the collective agreement between the company and the union became effective on February 19, 1962:

Vacations: Section 11. Each employee shall be entitled to a vacation on the following basis:

---

[1] All names disguised.

A. After one year of continuous service with the Company, one week vacation at his regular straight time hourly rate of pay.
B. After two years of continuous service with the Company, two weeks vacation at his regular straight time hourly rate of pay.
C. After twelve years or more of continuous service with the Company, three weeks vacation at his regular straight time hourly rate of pay.

An employee who has worked during each of forty-one or more normal working weeks in the year succeeding his hiring date or any anniversary thereof shall be considered to have a year of continuous service for the purpose of this section. An employee with more than one continuous year of service, i.e., 2, 3, etc., years, who worked less than forty-one weeks during the year preceeding his anniversary will be eligible when he returns to work for a pro rata share (based on fifty-two weeks) of the vacation benefits to which he would have been entitled if he had fulfilled the full vacation pay requirements. The vacation so earned, as previously described, shall be taken during the next regular vacation period, May 1st to September 1st after the employee has passed his anniversary.

No more than one vacation will be earned during any twelve months' period.

Pay for such vacations shall be paid in advance of the vacation, and shall be in accordance with rates paid the employee under this Agreement.

The period for vacations shall be mutually arranged between the individual and the Company with the understanding that older employees in seniority shall be considered in preference to younger employees where such determinations for a vacation period become necessary.

It is understood and agreed by both the Union and the Company that when the business of the Company is at an unusually high level, it may be impracticable for those employees who have three weeks vacation to take it all at one time. In such cases, it is understood and agreed that the Company will have the option of requesting the employee to take the third week of his vacation during a period of low business activity.

Under the former agreement (prior to February 19, 1962), an employee accumulated credit toward a vacation only by work performed after September 1 of each year, regardless of the date of employment, or anniversary thereof. A person employed after September 1 would not begin to accumulate credit toward a vacation until after the first day of the following September.

In negotiations leading to the new contract, the September 1 cutoff date was deleted in favor of the employee's date of employment, or an anniversary of that date. Thus, under provisions of the former contract, an employee was not eligible to receive a vacation until after he had been continuously employed for one year and had also been employed on September 1. Under the provisions of the 1962 contract, vacation credit was to be computed from the date of employment or an anniversary of that date.

POSITION OF THE COMPANY

The company contended that since Peter Francken was not in its employment on July 18, 1962, a full calendar year from the previous anniversary of his employment, he was not eligible for vacation pay at the time he resigned. The company relied exclusively upon this ground in the grievance meetings with the union. However, in the arbitration hearing, the company also contended that Francken had not actually worked during each of 41 normal working weeks from his last anniversary date, July 18, 1961, to the date of his resignation, April 27, 1962.

The company based this latter contention on the fact that of the 41 weeks between Francken's anniversary date and the date on which he quit, he was actually on vacation for 2 weeks. This two-week vacation was based upon service during the prior year. He had actually worked only 39 weeks, according to the company. Francken lacked 2 weeks of the 41-week requirement. Under Section 11 of the collective agreement, an employee must meet both requirements to be eligible for vacation credit.

POSITION OF THE UNION

The union objected to the introduction of a new argument into the arbitration proceedings and claimed that the company should be restricted to the position it asserted in the grievance negotiations conducted with the union during the previous steps of the grievance procedure.

The union also argued that since Francken had completed more than two years of continuous service with the company, he was entitled to 2 weeks vacation during each succeeding year upon completion of 41 normal working weeks in the year. After 12 years of continuous service, he would be entitled to a 3-week vacation upon completion of 41 normal working weeks of work in the year. Thus, the union held that Section 11 did not require that the employee pass through the next anniversary date to be eligible for vacation credit.

QUESTIONS

1. Should either a company or a union be permitted to introduce new facts at an arbitration hearing that have not been discussed in the grievance negotiations prior to the arbitration hearing?

2. Are the contract provisions governing this case situation in conflict? Are they somewhat ambiguous? As a general principle, in whose favor should this type of a situation generally be resolved?
3. Evaluate the conflicting positions of the company and the union. What are the key strengths of the positions of both parties in this case?

33. THE MOONLIGHTING WELDER

COMPANY: Ravens-Metal Products, Incorporated

UNION: Aluminum Workers International Union, Local Union No. 435

The Ravens-Metal Products Company calculated the value of the business which it believed it had lost to the Bentley Welding Shop during the first three months of 1962 as amounting to at least $9,000, and possibly as much as $11,600. The Bentley Welding Shop was owned and operated by Jack Bentley, a brother of Robert Bentley, who was an employee of Ravens-Metal Products, Incorporated.[1]

On March 28, 1962, the president of Ravens drove to the Welding Shop, where he observed an aluminum dump truck body on the premises and in the process of completion. He also observed Robert Bentley working on aluminum body sections inside the shop.

The company felt that it had no authority to restrict or discourage the competitive business of the Bentley Welding Shop. On the other hand, the participation in a competing enterprise by a highly skilled employee presented a conflict of interest which could adversely affect the competitive position of Ravens.

On March 29, Joseph Holtzman, vice president of manufacturing, called Robert Bentley to his office. He informed Bentley that his continued employment at the shop of his brother constituted a serious conflict of interest, and that he was discharged as of that date for violating posted "Shop Rules."[2]

Bentley filed a grievance, claiming that the facts did not establish just cause for discharge, that the action taken by the company was in violation of the collective agreement, that the company's behavior constituted an act of discrimination, and that he should be reinstated in his job with full reimbursement for lost earnings. The grievance eventually was taken to arbitration.

---

[1] The names of all persons have been disguised.
[2] See appendix following this case.

BACKGROUND

The company fabricates various types of aluminum bodies for trucks, including dump truck bodies, at its plant in Parkersburg, West Virginia.

Robert Bentley was hired on April 22, 1957, as a welder. He was considered to be a highly efficient and skilled employee; he frequently had been commended for the quality of his work performance. Prior to this case, he previously had not been the subject of either major criticism or disciplinary action on the part of management.

At the time of discharge, Robert Bentley held the job classification of master fabricator. The nature of his work was such that blueprints and designs of aluminum bodies were readily available to him. The information available to Bentley in the routine performance of his job included: confidential data pertaining to engineering techniques; calculations relating to load distribution; structural mechanical details; design techniques, including unique and unconventional fabricating processes; data relating to stress in frames, causes of cracks and metal fatigue, general shop techniques, gas mixtures for welding aluminum, cleaning agents used to guard against corrosion, and general repair procedures. In addition, Robert Bentley had access to all blueprints and design specifications.

Jack Bentley (Robert Bentley's brother) had worked for Ravens from April 21, 1957, to June 23, 1961, at which time he left to take over the operation of his father's business. This business operated under the family name of "Bentley Welding Shop," performing miscellaneous types of aluminum welding. The scope of the Bentley operations was indicated on a sign erected in front of the shop which read as follows:

BENTLEY WELDING SHOP
Open All Day Saturday

Heliarc   BOATS   MOTORS
CHAIN SAWS   LAWNMOWERS

Anything Aluminum
PORTABLE ALUMINUM WELDING
Truck Bodies   Tanks   Structural Aluminum

STEEL   *Portable   Anywhere*
Stainless Steel Cutting and Brazing

Part of the business of the Bentley Welding Shop included the building and fabricating of aluminum truck bodies, an activity which was similar to that performed by Ravens.

The Bentley Welding Shop employed no other full-time workers. Jack Bentley received occasional assistance from his father, and also some part-time help from Robert Bentley. Both Jack and Robert Bentley had acquired their skills and knowledge pertaining to the welding and fabrication of aluminum while employed at Ravens.

The aluminum dump truck body at issue in this case was fabricated for a customer who had previously inquired as to the cost, and who had received a quotation from a Ravens representative. The Bentley Welding Shop quoted a price of $2,600, which was $300 lower than the quotation of $2,900 offered by Ravens. Jack Bentley won the contract; he delivered the truck body four weeks later; it involved 80 man-hours of work. It was the first truck body fabricated by Bentley.

Labor–management relationships at Ravens had been excellent. This was the first grievance which had been carried to the arbitration stage.

POSITION OF THE COMPANY

The position of the company was that Robert Bentley had violated posted shop rules and had engaged in business and employment in direct competition with his employer. The company's shop rules, posted in March and July, 1961, were just and reasonable. Robert Bentley had knowingly and willfully chosen to violate these rules; therefore, his discharge should be upheld.

The company asserted that Bentley had violated a basic principle of the employer–employee relationship. Such conduct, together with his refusal to discontinue his activities, following a prior request to do so, presented just cause for discharge. While employees could engage in outside activities, such off-duty work should be confined to "unrelated fields." Whenever such work involved aluminum welding on products which normally were produced in the Ravens plant, it presented a conflict of interest.

Part-time association by employees with competitors would tend to make available to competitors valuable information pertaining to design and production techniques, including engineering and experimental work developed by the company at considerable expense and effort. The company feared that competitors could be enabled to "plagiarize its designs and know-how," resulting in undercutting of the company's established prices. Further, knowledge gained at Ravens could be used to contact customers in order to obtain orders.

The company pointed out that its production work was performed according to standards which had been negotiated with the union. This included rates of pay, fringe benefits, and working conditions. The company would be placed at a competitive disadvantage in the event the information and skills acquired at Ravens were made available to other companies not similarly obligated to its employees.

The company also regarded such part-time activities as being completely incompatible with shop rules, sound business conditions and standard business efforts. Employees should demonstrate their loyalty primarily to the company for whom they are working. They owe a corresponding responsibility to their job, and should refrain from conduct which would adversely affect the competitive position of the employer's business.

Finally, the company asserted that it had a right to take means to keep the fruits of its research and development program from becoming the property of its competition. The close association of Robert Bentley with his brother's business, which was considered to be a competing enterprise, placed the Bentley Welding Shop in a position where it could avail itself of information obtained at considerable expense by Ravens. Bentley could use the information to its own advantage and to the detriment of Ravens. The Bentley Welding Shop engaged in no research and development. It possessed no extensive knowledge of metallurgy or product design as a result of its own research activities. Inasmuch as employees at Ravens "had the run of the shop," the drawings, specifications, customer information, etc., could readily be made available to the Bentley shop through Robert Bentley.

POSITION OF THE UNION

The union's position was that the discharge of Robert Bentley was improper, and that his outside activities were not inconsistent with his duties and obligations to the company. The activities of Robert Bentley did not constitute "just cause" for discharge.

The Bentley Welding Shop was operated exclusively and solely by Jack Bentley. Robert Bentley was not a part-time employee, and he had performed no services which would be in conflict with his employment at Ravens.

The union acknowledged that Robert Bentley frequently visited his brother's shop after working hours. But the union claimed that Robert Bentley performed no major services in connection with this operation. On occasion he would assist in some routine physical activity, but his primary purpose in visiting on the Bentley shop premises was social—to visit his brother and his parents, who live on the adjacent premises.

Although Robert Bentley acknowledged performing small jobs about the shop, he denied that he had worked on any aluminum truck bodies, or that he had performed any other activities in competition with Ravens. He maintained that he received no compensation for the services which he rendered for his brother's business. The shop made no Social Security payments and maintained no employment records for either the elder Bentley or Robert. Finally, the union held that the company's shop rules were without merit. The union characterized them as "an arbitrary promulgation of rules by management which were inconsistent with the contract." The shop rules were not negotiated with the union, and the union neither accepted the rules nor acknowledged their validity. This case constituted the first incident of discharge of an employee for violation of the shop rules.

Since the evidence did not establish that Robert Bentley engaged in any direct competition with his employer, there was no just basis whatsoever for discipline. Robert Bentley should be reinstated and compensated for his lost earnings.

APPENDIX

Applicable Sections from the Shop Rules

1. From posted shop rules dated March 17, 1961:

Outside Work by Ravens Employees

A number of our employees have been engaging in part-time outside activities, and in some cases we have given assistance and help to these people in their part-time work. Frequently, however, several disadvantages arise from such jobs.

First of all, because of the excessive time and energy put on this outside work, employees can become overtired and unable to perform properly on their job at Ravens–Metal. This could hurt us all. These part-time activities can come into direct conflict with our company's products, by bidding low prices in competition to our truck bodies and other products. Because spare-time shops do not have to maintain large inventories, large sales forces, and overhead, and, because of nonunion facilities, such shops may be in a position to quote prices substantially lower than similar products made in union shops. Quite honestly, this can take the bread and butter from Ravens–Metal employees.

As a result of this, we are forced to lay down new shop rules concerning our employees.

First of all, we do not object to any small amount of outside work that our employees engage in; however, we must insist that their prime effort and prime loyalty be to Ravens–Metal Products as long as they are working here and are active members of our organization. Whenever their outside activities come to the point where the amount of time and energy spent in these activities starts to conflict with their work at our plant, they either reduce the outside activities or leave our operation. Furthermore, they must not compete directly with Ravens products. To do so will be considered a conflict of interest and will be just cause of severance of employment.

Outside activities, when undertaken, should preferably be in fields completely unrelated to those in which we are engaged. In other words, whenever the work involves considerable welding, particularly aluminum welding or work in aluminum products of the types that we normally make in our plant, this will be considered to be a conflict of interest and should only be undertaken with the knowledge and consent of management. Unless such knowledge and consent is given on a regular basis, it will be considered conflict of interest and may be cause for severance of employment.

I should like to point out that these are new rules and may affect three or four people in the plant. Consequently, I think it is desirable to give them several weeks in which to come into compliance with the new regulations.

No man can serve two masters: you either work for Ravens–Metal and boost its products and try to sell its products, or you don't: there is no halfway measure. It is completely incompatible to be quoting Ravens–Metal Products customers and potential customers for spare-time, nonunion work.

2. From shop rules posted July 26, 1961:

. . . Deliberate violation of the following rules will be considered cause for discharge: . . .

(8) Indulging in business which is competitive with the company's products.

Applicable Clauses of the Collective Agreement

Article I

Section 2. The Union recognizes that the management of the works and plants, the direction of the working force, including the right to hire, *suspend, or discharge for proper cause* (subject to the grievance procedure), and the right to relieve employees from duty because of lack of work, is vested in the employer. *The company agrees that it will not discriminate* against any employee on account of his or her union activity.

QUESTIONS

1. Was a serious conflict of interest present in this case, as charged by management of the Ravens company? Why, or why not?
2. Evaluate the company's arguments in support of its discharge action of Robert Bentley.
3. Evaluate the union's argument that the shop rules in the plant were not negotiated and therefore were not valid reasons for discharge of an employee.
4. What are the precedent implications in this case in regard to any part-time employment of an employee? In regard to other off-the-job activities of an employee?

34. FALSIFICATION OF PRODUCTION RECORDS

COMPANY: International Shoe Company, Searcy, Arkansas
UNION: United Shoe Workers of America, Local No. 179

BACKGROUND

Mrs. Jane Tyson[1] was employed by the company in 1955. On March 1, 1957, she was transferred to the operation of wetting or spraying uppers. The uppers of leather shoes are sprayed or dipped to make the leather more pliable. However, uppers made of velvet, satin, mesh, cloth or unlined straw are not normally dampened. Thus shoes of these materials normally bypass that part of the processing.

For accuracy of record keeping, the foremen regularly instruct the operators to be sure to record all cases of shoes on which they work. Payment of each operator is based upon the number of cases of shoes processed by the operator. According to Mrs. Tyson's testimony, about November 1959, foreman John Casper and his assistant, Mr. Art Keeling, instructed her to record all case numbers, whether they were sprayed or not. From that time on, she did just that, and collected pay for spraying all the shoes—those she actually sprayed or dipped and those which did not require this treatment. In his testimony, foreman Casper flatly denied this, insisting that Mrs. Tyson was never asked to record any but the cases on which she worked.

Regardless of whether or not there was an honest misunderstanding, Mrs. Tyson continued to collect pay for work not performed through December and January. After a routine check by company auditors in January, the company's industrial engineer, Mr. George Clovens, who was responsible for servicing plants in the Arkansas area, was instructed to investigate certain matters at the Searcy factory. He was asked to check the correctness of rates and the earnings of a number of operators, and specifically the earnings of Mrs.

---

[1] All names disguised.

Tyson. These instructions were received by Mr. Clovens about the first of February, and he began his check at Searcy on February 15.

Mr. Clovens found that for the week of February 14, 1960, Mrs. Tyson had recorded and had been credited with 365 cases which contained shoes which did not require wetting, and in fact had not been processed by Mrs. Tyson. This was brought to the attention of the plant superintendent, who had Mrs. Tyson, foreman Casper, and the local union president brought to the front office. When Mrs. Tyson was confronted with the industrial engineer's findings by the union president, she admitted what she had done and that she knew it was wrong. She further said that she had needed the money. With this admission, the plant superintendent discharged her.

Since this had been going on for two and a half months or more, both the assistant foreman, Mr. Keeling, and foreman Casper were revealed in an embarassing light. Shortly after this disclosure, the assistant foreman was discharged, and Mr. Casper was transferred to another factory in another state, where he was demoted to the position of assistant foreman.

The union filed a grievance which protested the discharge of Mrs. Tyson. The grievance was eventually carried to arbitration.

POSITION OF THE UNION

The union argued that the supervisors had told Mrs. Tyson to record the case numbers, regardless of whether or not she had sprayed or dipped the shoes. Mrs. Tyson was merely following the foreman's instructions; the discharge of one supervisor and the transfer and demotion of another indicated that these management representatives were responsible, in part at least, for what Mrs. Tyson did. The union claimed that Mrs. Tyson would have been disobeying orders had she not reported the number as she did.

Delbert Barnes, a swing operator who had worked part of his time on the spraying operation for the past two years, testified that he heard Mrs. Tyson get instructions to record all numbers; he further testified that at times operators were instructed to spray even the velvet shoes. According to Barnes, this was mostly experimental. He also insisted that at other times, when operators were behind, they were instructed to dip the shoes rather than spray them, so that they could catch up.

The union requested that Mrs. Tyson be restored to her job.

POSITION OF THE COMPANY

Foreman Casper denied that he had ever told Mrs. Tyson to record any case numbers other than those on which she performed work. However, the company conceded the possibility that Mrs. Tyson may have misconstrued the foreman's instructions "to be sure to record the numbers of all cases." It was possible that in telling the operators to record all case numbers, the foreman inadvertently may have omitted the last phrase, "on which you work," since it is quite generally understood that an operator is expected to record only the case numbers of those on which he or she performs the required operation.

Regardless of whether or not Mrs. Tyson did or did not honestly misunderstand her foreman's instructions, the facts of the case do not point to innocence on the part of Mrs. Tyson. Mrs. Tyson was well aware of the fact that she was cheating the company, that this was wrong, and that the matter might eventually be detected. Dishonesty of this kind is always cause for discharge. So, regardless of any knowledge or "connivance" on the part of the foreman and his assistant, Mrs. Tyson committed an act which gave the company cause to terminate her services.

The company claimed that the seriousness of Mrs. Tyson's actions justified the penalty of discharge, and it should be upheld by the arbitrator.

QUESTIONS

1. Who is guilty in this case? Are mitigating circumstances such that Mrs. Tyson should be absolved of basic responsibility for her action?
2. Are cheating or other dishonest acts just cause for discharge of an employee? Are these just cause for the discharge of Mrs. Tyson under the circumstances of this case?
3. Why is it difficult to arrive at the truth in a case situation of this sort?
4. What reasons could be suggested for the fact that the foremen were disciplined severely?

35. READING ON THE JOB

COMPANY: Menasco Manufacturing Company, Burbank, California

UNION: International Association of Machinists, Local Lodge 758

BACKGROUND

On October 30, 1961, the supervisor of the tool design group, George Carlson,[1] noticed employee Will Scott looking at something in the drawer of his drafting table. After a minute or two had elapsed, he walked to Scott's table. As he approached, Scott closed the drawer. According to the supervisor's testimony, the following exchange then took place.

The supervisor asked, "What are you looking at?"

Scott: "I'm looking up information."

Carlson: "What kind of information?"

Scott: "Just information."

At this point supervisor Carlson opened the drawer and saw an open book covered with a sheet of transparent plastic. Carlson accused Scott of reading private matter on company time.

Scott's reply, according to the supervisor's testimony, was, "So what?"

The supervisor went to his office and summoned a company representative, a union representative, and Scott for a review. During the meeting Scott was suspended for four and a half days.

Scott checked out about 11 a.m. on October 30, 1961, and on October 31 he filed the following grievance:

Management was in violation of contract by giving me a citation and suspension, based on false accusations and not true facts, which in turn constituted unjust cause for suspension. Request to discontinue violation of contract. Restore pay for any loss of time, due to unjust suspension and removal of citation from my record.

The matter was processed through the grievance procedure and was eventually taken to arbitration.

---

[1] All names disguised.

POSITION OF THE UNION

The position of the union was that "the company decided to move in on the grievant and used a collection of trivia as an excuse."

The contention of Scott was that he was looking up bushing sizes in a catalog in his brief case—which was in his drawer—and that he was also consulting a decimal conversion table pasted on the outside of the briefcase. Scott contended, in contradiction to company witnesses, that he needed these bushing sizes and decimal conversions for the job on which he was working. He accounted for some excessive time spent on the mill fixture design on which he was working by stating that he prepared an additional sheet, which he offered to show to management, but which he says was refused. He denied that he was reading private matter.

Scott and the union did not deny the statement of the supervisor that when he opened the drawer (which Scott had closed on the supervisor's approach) he saw an open book covered with a piece of transparent plastic material. Supervisor Carlson said the plastic was clear, but Scott said it was dark and that he kept it to put over glossy surfaces to reduce the glare. Scott claimed that he could not have been reading the book because of the dark plastic covering the book.

Finally, in his closing argument, counsel for the union stated that if the arbitrator ruled that Scott did violate a company rule by reading private material during business hours, the punishment imposed by the company was too severe. The suspension period should be reduced to one day at most.

POSITION OF THE COMPANY

The company contended that Scott was reading private material during working hours, but admitted that the evidence was circumstantial.

The position of the company was that Scott gave every appearance of reading a book lying open in his drawer and covered with a piece of transparent plastic. As for Scott's explanation that he was looking up bushing sizes and consulting a decimal conversion table, supervisor Carlson testified that when he first looked into the drawer he saw, in addition to the plastic-covered book, several catalogs but no briefcase. He testified also that after Scott checked out, he again looked into the drawer and this time saw the briefcase with a decimal conversion table fastened to the outside cover with "what appeared to be freshly applied masking tape."

Several company witnesses offered their opinions that it was not necessary for Scott either to look up bushing sizes in a catalog or to consult a conversion table. They contended that bushings should not be used for the job Scott was doing.

Further, they claimed that on this particular job, the dimensions "from the screw to each of the dowels" were not fixed on the blueprint but were discretionary with the toolmaker. So, even if Scott needed any dimensions (which was denied by the company witnesses), Scott would not get them from the blueprint but from the toolmaker after the part was made in the shop. Hence, the reason Scott gave for looking into his drawer was doubly spurious.

Article I, Section 9, Paragraph 1.91 of the contract stated as follows:

> The Company has and will retain the right and power to manage the plant and direct the working forces, including the right to suspend or discharge for just cause . . . its employees subject to the terms of this Agreement (i.e., Article III, Section 1, Paragraph 3.11, which deals with the grievance procedure).

The company witnesses maintained that in their judgment, employee Scott *was* reading private material during working hours. In the absence of proof to the contrary, management's judgment in this matter should be considered valid and the disciplinary suspension upheld.

QUESTIONS

1. When evidence in a case is circumstantial, how should an arbitrator resolve the basic problem of arriving at facts and their validity?
2. Was the company justified in suspending Scott for allegedly reading private material on the job? Was the action of the company too severe? Too lenient?
3. Should an employee's previous record be considered in a case of this nature? If Scott had been an exemplary employee, is it likely that his conduct would have led to this action by the company?

36. NO CHRISTMAS BONUS

COMPANY: White Baking Company

UNION: Bakery and Confectionery Workers International Union of America, Local 374

BACKGROUND

For many years, it was the practice of the company to distribute gifts of some sort to its employees at Christmas. Prior to the union's becoming the bargaining agent, the distribution typically consisted of merchandise orders. Since 1956, each year, immediately prior to Christmas, the company posted letters on the bulletin boards to the effect that the board of directors had decided to distribute Christmas checks and indicated the amount the employees were to receive. The amounts were determined by each employee's length of service. In 1960, the board of directors decided to make no Christmas distribution because of economic conditions and so notified the employees. Many employees complained to the company. Subsequent to these complaints, the board of directors voted to reverse its previous decision and to distribute Christmas checks for the current year. But the company included in its announcement to the employees a statement that any future distribution would continue to be at the discretion of the board of directors.

Prior to Christmas 1961, the company announced that the board of directors, because of economic conditions, would not make a Christmas distribution for that year. Following this action by the company, the union filed a grievance, which was subsequently carried to arbitration.

POSITION OF THE UNION

The union contended that it had been a long-established past practice of the company to make a Christmas distribution, even in the years prior to the union's becoming the bargaining agent. This past practice actually had become a part of and a condition of employment. Therefore, the company had violated the contract in failing to make a distribution of Christmas checks at Christmas, 1961. The company could not unilaterally abolish a Christmas bonus which was expected by the employees as a regular part of their employment compensation.

POSITION OF THE COMPANY

The company maintained that the Christmas bonus distribution had been a purely discretionary one with the company. Each year the company had posted the decision of the board of directors at Christmas time. Nothing in the contract required the company to pay such Christmas distributions. The company and the union had never bargained over the Christmas bonuses; therefore, the company was not in violation of the contract in failing to make a Christmas distribution in 1961.

QUESTIONS

1. Was the Christmas bonus a long-established past practice as claimed by the union, or was it a purely discretionary act on the part of the company? Evaluate the positon of both parties in regard to this issue.
2. At what point does a company custom or practice leave the area of management discretion and become a bargainable issue?
3. What are the precedent implications inherent in this case situation?

37. MANAGEMENT RIGHTS AND THE SUNDAY SHIFT

COMPANY: Mead Corporation, Kingsport Division, Kingsport, Tennessee

UNION: United Mine Workers of America, District 50, Local 12943

On August 23, 1965, the union filed the following grievance:

We, the undersigned, are aggrieved because the Company is contracting out the work of cutting chips to outside contractors. This action has resulted in affecting our working conditions and hours of work, by eliminating all Sunday work in this department.

We request that the Company make the proper adjustment in our working conditions, rates of pay and hours of work, which has resulted from the contracting out of the work of cutting chips to an outside contractor.

This grievance was signed by the employees of the wood-yard department of the Kingsport Division of the Mead Corporation.

The company throughout the steps of the grievance procedure denied any contract violation. Ultimately, the grievance was submitted for arbitration with the following question as the agreed-upon basic issue:

Did the Company's action in utilizing purchased wood chips and the resulting effect on Sunday work constitute a violation of the Labor Agreement?

BACKGROUND

The Mead Corporation is engaged in the manufacture and sale of products falling into four main groups; these are pulp, white paper, pasteboard, paper boxes and containers. At the Kingsport Division, located in Kingsport, Tennessee, the chief products are publishing and printing papers. Normal employment for plant operations at the Kingsport Division was slightly under 1200 at the time of this case.

On November 17, 1944, District 50, United Mine Workers of America, was certified as the bargaining agent for certain employees at the Kingsport Division. The first contract was negotiated on January 26, 1945, and subsequent agreements have been entered into since that date. The labor agreement currently in effect was dated to expire January 25, 1968.

The function of the wood-yard department is to furnish wood in chip form to the pulp mill operation where the chips are cooked, bleached, and otherwise processed in order to furnish wood pulp stock to the production facilities of the division. The pulp-using facilities consist of four paper machines and one dry pulp machine.

The wood-yard department normally operated on the same basis as other operating departments and had the same type of schedule. From the early 1950's until 1957, the department was scheduled mainly on a seven-day basis. During this time, the employees worked a total of 48 hours per week and were paid for a total of 56 pay hours, because Sunday is paid at the rate of double time.

In 1957, the company expanded its pulp producing facilities, and much of the equipment in the wood-yard department was automated. As a result, several employees were laid off and the number of Sunday time hours was reduced. The company generally needed to operate its pulp mill including the wood-yard department on only one shift on Sunday. In other words, when the pulp mill was scheduled to be down, the wood yard would be scheduled down. If the pulp mill operated one, two, or three shifts, the wood yard would operate one, two, or three shifts.

For several years prior to July 26, 1965, the wood-yard schedule was as follows:

	Mon.	Tues.	Wed.	Thurs.	Fri.	Sat.	Sun.
7-3 shift	X	Off	X	X	X	X	As needed
3-11 shift	X	X	X	Off	X	X	As needed
11-7 shift	X	X	X	X	X	Off	As needed

This schedule provided for manning 15 shifts per week with Sunday "as needed." As stated above, normally one shift would work each Sunday.

Nine employees per shift were involved in that part of the wood-yard operation associated with the conversion of logs to chips:

1 Crane Operator	1 Splitter Feeder
1 Barking Drum Operator	1 Chipper Operator
1 Barking Drum Helper	1 Chipper Feeder
1 Splitter Operator	2 Employees on bark disposal

However, for several years prior to 1963, the company also had told the union of its desire to obtain wood chips that already were chipped by sawmill operators in the local area. In negotiations of January 1963, the company again brought up the question, and told the union that the company planned in the near future to install a chip unloading operator at the plant and to contract out for enough chips to take care of wood that would be coming in by rail. The company estimated this would be about one third of the total chips that would be used. The union did not voice any strong objections to this plan because it realized, through its international union, that this was being done by many paper companies throughout the country as a conservation measure to save the wood supply, and that it was advocated by Department of Interior officials. The union informed the employees of this and told them that there would be a layoff of at least one shift and probably a relief shift.

The installation of the chip unloading and handling system began in late 1964. In January 1965, the company began receiving the first rail cars of chips. A new wood-yard classification of "chip unloader" was established at a pay rate set under procedures established in the contract. The number of cars received each month increased gradually, so that by July 1965, a substantial portion (20 percent) of wood receipts were in chip form.

On July 26, 1965, the schedule for the wood-yard department was changed by the company to be as follows:

	Mon.	Tues.	Wed.	Thurs.	Fri.	Sat.	Sun.
7–3 shift	X	Off	X	X	X	X	As needed
3–11 shift	X	X	X	X	X	X	As needed
11–7 shift	Off	X	Off	Off	Off	Off	As needed

This schedule provided for manning 12 shifts per week with Sunday "as needed." The net effect was to change the department from a three-shift operation with no relief crew to a two-shift operation with a relief crew. The wood-yard department work force correspondingly was decreased from 38 to 33 employees, but the five affected employees were placed on jobs in other departments throughout the plant. This schedule also resulted in a reduction of Sunday work for employees who remained in the wood-yard department. The pulp mill and digester department continued to operate on one shift each Sunday as previously, but the wood-yard department was not scheduled to operate the one shift as it had previously done.

The new schedule remained in effect except for the period from September 6, 1965, to November 8, 1965, during which time two shifts per day were scheduled with no relief crew. By November 8, 1965, production demand had increased and stabilized, and the relief crew was reinstated in the wood yard.

On August 23, 1965, the union filed a grievance protesting the company's action in utilizing purchased chips. The grievance was processed through the prescribed steps of the grievance procedure and was taken before an arbitrator for decision.

POSITION OF THE UNION

The union claimed that the company's practices of contracting out a part of the work of the chipping operation and purchasing wood chips deprived the wood-yard employees of a shift of Sunday work. The equipment and the normal way of operating the pulp mill remained the same. There was no change of method in any of the departments except for the use of chips that were shipped to the plant for use rather than logs. The contracting out of the work of chipping wood logs into chips, which resulted in depriving the wood-yard employees of Sunday work that they otherwise would have been permitted to work, was at the heart of the dispute in question in this case.

The union claimed that in the 1963 discussions over contracting out the cutting of chips, it only consented to the company practice of contracting to purchase about one third of its total use of chips. The union realized this would cause a corresponding reduction in the work force. The employees were informed through the union to this effect. There was no discussion concerning a reduction in hours of work on Sunday for the remaining employees. As far as the union was concerned, there would be no changes in hours of work, working conditions, or any other change, except the reduction of one third of the working force.

The union argued that if it saw fit to consent to contracting out the work of cutting pulp logs into chips by outsiders, and by so doing a reduction of one third of the crew, the company should not exploit this consent by reducing Sunday work of the remaining crews in the wood yard.

The pulp mill and digester department continued to operate on the same basis on Sunday as they did before the contracting out of cutting chips. The normal way of operating had been that if the pulp mill and digester department were scheduled down, the wood yard would be scheduled down; if the pulp mill and digester department operated one, two, or three shifts, the wood yard operated one, two, or three shifts. The pulp mill and digester department still operated on this basis, but the "need" for the Sunday operation of the wood yard was eliminated by the purchase of chips. The Sunday operations of the pulp mill and digester department were the same and required the same amount of chips, but the need was supplied by chips that were shipped in by an outside contractor, instead of being chipped by the employees at the plant's chipping operation.

The union noted that for years the company had always stated that Sunday work was predicated on the "need" for Sunday work. Should this principle be nullified by the contracting out of the cutting of chips and satisfying the "need" by this means? The union claimed that the company did not have the unilateral right to change the hours of work on Sunday—when there was a "need" for it—by contracting out the work of chipping pulp logs into chips, since the company had the employees, the facilities, and the pulp logs that could supply the needed chips.

The union stated that it was not trying to upset the entire contracting out of pulp logs into chips. The union felt it would be taking an unfair position to attack the entire practice of purchasing chips, because of its tacit consent during a negotiating session. However, the union believed that it would have had a good case in this regard, since (1) a unit and a department of a unit as established by the National Labor Relations Board was being somewhat obliterated, and (2) a unit is predicated on the work of the unit employees.

In summary, the union was only asking that the company do what it had said it was going to do—that is, contract for the purchase of one third of its total supply of chips and leave the rest at the status quo. Then the union would have no argument with the company. If the company wanted to do more, it should negotiate with the union, as provided in the labor agreement.

In this regard, the union claimed that it is a general proposition among NLRB officials and among arbitrators that a company cannot unilaterally contract out work that affects the hours of work or other conditions that affect unit employees. The union requested that the hours of work, and any other conditions that affected the wood-yard employees because of the company's contracting out the work of cutting chips, be returned to the former status.

POSITION OF THE COMPANY

The company basically claimed that: (*a*) it did have the right unilaterally to purchase the wood chips; and (*b*) its actions in regard to the Sunday work schedule were clearly within its management rights.

The company pointed to Article II of the contract, which had been revised during negotiations of January, 1963. Article II, the "Management Rights" provision, states as follows:

Article II–Management Rights

The Management of the Company and the direction of the working force including the right to plan, direct and control plant operations; to determine, alter, revise, change or eliminate any or all means, methods, processes, materials and schedules of production; to determine the number and size of crews; to determine the location of its plant; to establish production and work standards; to control the nature and specifications of all raw materials, semi-manufactured and finished goods whether or not they may be incorporated into the products manufactured; to temporarily transfer employees between jobs, shifts, and departments in order to maintain efficient and/or economical operations; and the right to hire employees are rights solely of the Company and are not abridged by any other provisions of this Agreement. All other rights not specifically nullified by this Agreement are retained by the Company.

In management's view, this provision clearly gave the company the right to contract out work by means of purchasing wood chips. It was no accident that most of the language of Article II had direct application to this case. One reason was that the issue concerned what to this (or any other) company was both a major and a basic management decision. Second, and perhaps more important, this was the type of problem which was lengthily and adequately covered in the negotiations of January 1963. Specifically, the subject of purchasing chips was covered and agreed upon in these negotiations.

In this grievance, as well as in discussions during the processing of this grievance, the Union's position had been that the use of purchased chips eliminated Sunday work in violation of the contract. Article VII, "Hours of Work and Overtime." provides in part:

This article is intended only to provide a basis for the calculation of overtime and none of its provisions shall be construed as a guarantee of hours of work. . . . An employee's regular work week shall be that number of hours which are not subject, as specified by law, to premium compensation.

The contract language of Article VII is clear and unambiguous—there is no guarantee of Sunday work. Further, over the years, the company repeatedly made its position clear—employees would be scheduled for Sunday work only on an "as needed" basis. Therefore, the company argued, the company had the right to change the wood-yard department Sunday work schedule in whatever manner it deemed appropriate to its operation.

Finally, the company asserted that its decision to utilize purchased chips was a major management decision. The total cost for equipment and installation of the new chip handling system was approximately $250,000. In addition, wood procurement personnel worked for several months negotiating long-term contracts with wood suppliers. The decision was not made capriciously or for the purpose of "hurting the union." The important factors leading to this decision were:

A. To Insure a Wood Supply.   This was a factor not because wood was not available in the immediate area, but rather a matter of a labor shortage, i.e., a scarcity of pulp wood cutters. During periods of high economic activity and high employment, timberland work is less attractive and people move to other steadier, easier jobs. Where company needs cannot be supplied locally, the only alternative is to go farther away, to the major rail wood suppliers. The company was certain that its operation could not be sustained using only local truck wood and "in close" rail wood suppliers.

B. Cost.   During 1965, 64,000 tons of chips were purchased, 20 percent of the usage. Had the company filled this need by utilizing rail round wood rather than chips, the increased manufacturing cost would have been approximately $47,000.

C. Competition.   Several of the company's competitors were contracting for chips in the wood areas that supplied the company's mills. The company felt that to wait until later to begin buying chips would mean that entry into the market would be both difficult and costly.

D. Conservation.   Purchased chips come from sawmill residue; heretofore most of this waste was burned. The use of these chips lessens the demand on standing timber.

The company's concluding statement was as follows:

The Company feels the decision to go to a purchased chip program was logical, and further, was well within the bounds of the Labor Agreement, particularly the provisions of Article II, Management Rights. Therefore, the Company requests that the grievance be denied.

QUESTIONS

1. Was the company required to negotiate with the union concerning the purchasing of wood chips from an outside contractor? Did the company violate its original agreement with the union on this point?
2. Evaluate the union statement that National Labor Relations Board officials have held that a company cannot unilaterally contract out work that affects the hours of work or other conditions that affect union employees. Why did the union insert this argument in an arbitration case hearing? Is it relevant to this case?
3. Were the arguments placed by the company in support of its purchase of wood chips appropriate to its position in this case? Even if the company was economically justified in purchasing wood chips, was this permitted under the contract and in terms of previous working relationships with the union?
4. Does a company have the unilateral right to change long-established work schedules? What are the limits of management rights in this regard?
5. Many arbitrators hold to the "residual management rights theory," which states that management retains all rights which have not been bargained away in a contract or otherwise surrendered. Is this theory valid in this case situation?

38. THE CASE OF THE CHALLENGED SUBCONTRACTING CLAUSE

COMPANIES: Selb Manufacturing Company, Division of Western, Incorporated; and Blades Manufacturing Company, St. Louis, Missouri

UNION: District 9, International Association of Machinists

BACKGROUND

Selb Manufacturing Company began business in 1952 in St. Louis, Missouri, operating as a job machine shop. In 1953, District 9, International Association of Machinists, AFL–CIO, organized the employees and was certified by the National Labor Relations Board. In May, 1955, the management of Selb purchased the Blades Manufacturing Corporation, which was also a machine shop located in St. Louis. Blades at this time was already organized and under contract with District 9. Since District 9's contracts with Selb and Blades expired at approximately the same time, the parties agreed to combine the two bargaining units into one multiplant unit and to write a single contract. On July 1, 1955, one contract was negotiated covering a multiplant unit consisting of the Blades and Selb plants; this multiplant bargaining has continued to the time of this case.

By 1960, the combined seniority list of the two plants was 269 employees, and there were 160 machines installed in the two plants.

In March, 1960, the company purchased an additional plant facility in Rector, Arkansas.

In late April, 1960, the company began shipping machinery from the two St. Louis plants to the Rector plant. Shortly thereafter, the company began to ship parts from the St. Louis plants to the Rector plant, where they were machined and, in most instances, returned to the St. Louis plants for further machine operations. On May 3, 1960, the company acquired another plant in Denver, Colorado, and on September 19 a plant at Walnut Ridge, Arkansas. With these new plants operating, parts were also shipped to these plants for various

248

machining operations and then in some instances returned to the St. Louis operations.

In May, 1960, the union filed a grievance protesting the removal of machines and parts from the St. Louis operations.

This grievance was processed through the second step, but it was dropped when management assured the union that no men would be laid off from St. Louis plants, and that the reason for the moving of machinery and jobs was because the company at that time was short of qualified personnel.

This was accepted by the union committee as satisfactory. However, machinery and work continued to leave the Selb and Blades plants at varying intervals.

On September 26, 1960, 35 St. Louis plant employees were laid off from their jobs. The union immediately filed a grievance to the effect that the company had violated the contract in that it:

Laid off list of employees dated September 26, because of runaway work— when machines and men were available to do said work.

The Union feels that the Company is unjustly treating these employees by moving work out of Selb and Blades and this area and laying off employees who were doing this work.

By November, 1960, the number of men laid off had increased to 56.

The union grievance eventually was carried to arbitration. The grievance carried a request that the company be ordered: (*a*) to return all machinery, equipment and work to the Selb and Blades plants which had been sent to Rector, Arkansas, Walnut Ridge, Arkansas, and Denver, Colorado; and (*b*) to recall all employees laid off from Selb and Blades since September 26, 1960, and reinstate them without any loss of seniority or loss of money as a result of the layoff.

Article XX—The Relevant Clause

Article XX of the contract had been in effect for several years prior to the events of this case. It stated:

Subcontract Work. The Companies will not, so long as equipment and personnel are available, subcontract work which is customarily performed by employees in the bargaining unit to any other company. When necessary to subcontract work, every effort shall be made to give the work to a contractor who employs members of the International Association of Machinists.

The parties began negotiations in June, 1960, for a new contract to replace the contract expiring June 30, 1960. A new contract was signed on July 8, 1960; it was made effective from July 1, 1960, to July 1, 1962.

During negotiations of the contract, a proposal was made by the company to delete Article XX, Subcontract Work. The union refused to agree to the deletion of this clause, and therefore the contract was signed by the company and the union with Article XX remaining in the agreement.

POSITION OF THE UNION

The union argued that the first paragraph of the contract specifically stated that the agreement was by and between Selb Manufacturing Company (Division of Western, Inc.), Blades Manufacturing Corporation, and District No. 9, International Association of Machinists.

If the employer intended the Arkansas or any other subsidiaries or operations to be party to the agreement, this result could only be achieved by making such subsidiaries parties to the contract. This was not done.

The union brief summarized the union's major contention as follows:

How the Management can contend when they ship work and equipment from Selb and Blades to any other plant that they are not violating Article XX, when they have trained personnel and equipment available, is beyond belief.

Further, the number of employees working in the other three plants is almost identical to the number of employees laid off at Selb and Blades. It should be plain to anyone that work sent to any other plant other than the Selb and Blades plants is subcontracted, and that the Company violated Article XX by subcontracting work which was customarily performed by employees in the bargaining unit. Also, this subcontracting of work caused employees to be laid off and created a violation of Article V, Seniority.

POSITION OF THE COMPANY

First of all, the company argued that their new plants were started because of insufficient space and other related problems in the St. Louis area; therefore by transferring the work to these other plants, management was only exercising its prerogative and right to distribute its work in the most efficient manner. This was an inherent management right, to apportion work where it could be most efficiently accomplished.

Second, the company argued that this was not subcontracting in violation of Article XX because there was no kind of contractual arrangement between the plants or with other third parties; management was simply rearranging its production operations. Management's right and prerogative to rearrange production operations could be limited only by extremely clear and express language, of which there was none in Article XX or other parts of the contract. The company representatives said that obviously equipment was not available at its St. Louis plants after it was moved to the other plants; therefore they were following the legal *letter* (if not the spirit) of Article XX.

In connection with the above, the company testified that the union had made no contention during the 1960 contract negotiations that the company was violating Article XX of the contract. Yet the evidence showed clearly that there had been, by this time, a substantial number of shipments of machines and parts from the St. Louis operations to the other operations of the company. The company stated it had no reason to believe at the time it negotiated the new contract that Article XX meant anything other than what the parties had already interpreted it to mean; namely, that it limited the company's right to subcontract to third parties.

Third, the company argued that under federal labor law, the company has a right to move its entire plant if such a move is not motivated by an intention to commit an unfair labor practice; and this can only be determined by the NLRB. If the company can move its entire plant, surely it can move parts thereof; this is what was done in this case.

Counsel for management stated as follows:

The absurdity of the Union's position becomes evident when its logic is carried to its ultimate conclusion. The Union claims that the Company is subcontracting when it moves part of its operations to other of its plants. The Union would have to concede that the Company could, without violating the contract, move its entire plant to another location, providing only that it was not discriminatorily motivated. Is the Union saying to the Company: "Don't move part of the plant, move it all?" It is hard to believe that the Union really intends this. The Company is trying to preserve part of its operations in St. Louis. It does not wish to move all its operations unless forced to do so by economic circumstances. In the interest of all parties, including the employees and the Union, this panel of arbitrators should not place such an absurd construction upon the clear language of this contract.

Finally, the company claimed that regardless of anything else, contract provisions like Article XX are illegal. Section 8 (e) of the

Labor-Management Relations Act as amended by the Landrum-Griffin amendments in 1959 states:

It shall be an unfair labor practice for any labor organization and any employer to enter into any contract or agreement, express or implied, whereby such employer ceases or refrains or agrees to cease or refrain from handling, using, selling, transporting or otherwise dealing in any other products of any other employer, or to cease doing business with *any other person*, and any contract or agreement entered into heretofore or hereafter containing such an agreement shall be to such extent unenforceable and void. [Emphasis added. The remainder of Section 8 (e) sets out certain exceptions permitting limitations on subcontracting in the construction and garment industries which do not apply in this case.]

The language of Article XX is:

The Companies will not, so long as equipment and personnel are available, subcontract work which is customarily performed by employees in the bargaining unit to any other company. When necessary to subcontract work, every effort shall be made to give the work to a contractor who employs members of the International Association of Machinists.

Article XX limits the company's freedom to do business with companies which do not employ members of District 9. Obviously, companies which do not employ members of District 9 are "any other person(s)." A contract clause such as Article XX clearly violates Section 8 (e) of the act and, by the terms of that section, is "unenforceable and void."

Counsel for management stated:

It is crystal clear that the parties should never have included Article XX in their new Contract, for by so doing they were entering into a Contract whereby the employer was agreeing to cease and refrain from doing business with other persons. For the [arbitration] panel to hold that the Company must comply with such illegal provision would be to compound the violation. . . . The National Labor Relations Board would not recognize any such award, for it would be clearly contrary to the statute. . . .

Article XX is void and unenforceable anyway and this panel should not try to enforce it.

In the interest of all parties, this grievance should be denied.

QUESTIONS

1. Did the company violate Article XX of the contract by removing machines and parts from the St. Louis operation and by laying off employees in the St. Louis plant?

2. Evaluate each of the company's arguments in support of its position in this case.
3. Was Article XX of the contract in violation of Section 8 (e) of the Labor-Management Relations Act as amended by the 1959 Landrum-Griffin Act? Should an arbitrator be permitted to rule upon the legality of Article XX in this case situation?
4. What are the precedent implications involved in this situation to any company which seeks to move all or part of its operations in order to obtain economic benefits, where a labor union has negotiated a contractual arrangement similar to Article XX at the Selb Company? What are the implications of this case in relationship to recent NLRB decisions concerning collective bargaining responsibilities?

39. WHO SHOULD OPEN THE STOREROOM DOORS?

COMPANY: The Nalpak Chemical Company [1]
UNION: The Independent Union of Chemical Workers

BACKGROUND

The Nalpak Chemical Company is a medium-sized firm which operates several plants in the central Midwest. The company manufactures chemical products for a variety of industries and consumers. The grievances which occurred in the two situations described in this case occurred in the company's St. Louis plant.

Both of the case grievances eventually were heard by an arbitrator at a single hearing. Each occurred in the early part of 1960 and focused upon a common issue. The issue was whether management violated the collective agreement by having, in one case, an electrician unlock the plant's clothing storeroom door; and in the other case, by having a guard open a materials storeroom door.

CASE A

On Saturday, March 19, 1960, four millwrights were called in to work on an "emergency" basis to service certain plant equipment which needed special attention. They arrived at the plant after the 12-to-8 shift custodian had gone off duty. Since no custodian was scheduled to work on the Saturday day shift, the maintenance department foreman instructed a guard to unlock the clothing storage room door. The millwrights then obtained their work clothing from the storage room.

Under normal circumstances, no inventory is kept of the contents of the clothing storage room. Even when a custodian is present, he normally lays out clothing in size groups so that employees may serve themselves. The actual issuance of clothing

---

[1] All names disguised.

is only a small part of the custodian's job. The custodian primarily is responsible for the policing and maintenance of the entire plant locker room.

Position of the Union

The union contended that a custodian should have been called in at the same time that the millwrights were called in. The union argued that since a guard opened the clothing storage room door, there was a violation of job classifications. According to the contract, a custodian should receive the agreed-upon call-in pay. The union cited Article III, Section 7 of the contract:

Employees called in for emergency work any time after ringing out their time cards except for lunch time, shall be paid a minimum of four (4) hours pay in accord with the following schedule:
A. Monday through Saturday—One and one-half times rate.

Position of the Company

Company management contended that no real extra plant custodial work had been associated with the emergency call-in of the four millwrights. The entire task for a custodian to open the clothing storage room door would only take a few minutes at most. Besides, the clothing storage room was partially operated on a self-service basis, and no inventory records were kept. Therefore, there was no need to call in a custodian for this minor task. The grievance should be dismissed.

CASE B

On Sunday, May 1, 1960, an electrician, with the aid of a guard, unlocked the materials storeroom door for the purpose of getting necessary supplies. A storekeeper was not called in.

The company maintains, both dollar- and item-wise, an accurate inventory of the contents of the materials storeroom. As a general rule, if work is to be done on a Sunday, personnel are instructed to withdraw all necessary supplies on the previous regular work day. However, it sometimes happens that additional materials may be needed which have not been anticipated.

In this situation, the electrician needed to get certain supplies from the materials storeroom. The electrician first called the maintenance foreman at home. The maintenance foreman then in turn attempted to contact the foreman and assistant foreman in charge of the storeroom in order to have a storekeeper called in. However, the maintenance foreman was not successful in contacting anyone who had a direct supervisory responsibility for the storeroom. Therefore, he instructed the electrician at the plant to have a guard help him unlock the storeroom, so that they could get whatever supplies were needed.

Position of the Union

The union acknowledged that management did make an effort, although unsuccessfully, to locate a supervisor of the storeroom so as to have a storekeeper called in. However, the union claimed that this did not excuse management from the duty of calling in a store-keeper to perform his function. Management's failure to make the necessary contacts was a failure within management's liaison and not a failure to reach a qualified storekeeper on the overtime list. As in Case A, the company violated job classifications by instructing the guard to open the materials storeroom door.

The fact that management recognized that a storekeeper should be called in is indication that if a storeroom foreman could have been reached, there was an overtime opportunity for a storekeeper. A storekeeper should be awarded four hours' call-in pay in accordance with the contract (see Case A).

Position of the Company

The company admitted that if no effort had been made to contact storeroom supervision or to have a storekeeper called in, then the storekeeper who headed the list for overtime assignments would be entitled to payment. However, the company stated that the maintenance foreman had made a reasonable effort to locate a storeroom supervisor. Under the circumstances, this should have been enough for such a minor problem; therefore, it was proper that a guard be instructed to open the storeroom door for this few minutes' work.

Management admitted that in order to keep and have an accurate inventory, a storekeeping system was necessary. A failure to have a storekeeper called in might result in some inaccuracies in inventory. However, this was a risk management accepted under these circumstances. In this situation, no actual work was performed by a store-keeper. The necessary supplies withdrawn from the storeroom were noted by the electrician, and this information was turned over to the storekeeper on the next regular working day in order to have the proper records made out.

The union grievance should be dismissed.

QUESTIONS

1. Why were these cases heard by the same arbitrator at the same time? Could this have been in an effort to have an arbitrator "split the difference" in these two cases focusing upon a common issue?
2. Are these trivial cases to be heard by an arbitrator? Is there a basic objective at stake which the union is trying to force?
3. Did the company violate the contract by not calling in a custodian (Case A) and a storekeeper (Case B) in the two situations involved? From an economic standpoint, were management actions understandable and/or justifiable?
4. How much effort must a company exert under these circumstances in order to be relieved of its responsibility under the contract provisions to call in bargaining unit employees to perform work?

40. WAS THE DESKMAN DERELICT IN HIS WORK PERFORMANCE?

COMPANY: United Independent Telephone Company, Luebbering, Missouri [1]

UNION: Local 12, United Communication Workers of America

The parties agreed that the issue of this case was summarized in the following question: Did the company violate Article XII of the 1959 agreement when it transferred Mr. Tracy McNeil from his position as deskman to that of exchange repairman? Since the pay rate for both jobs was equal, the union asked for restoration of Mr. McNeil to the deskman's job.

Article XII stated:

Section 1. Length of service shall be taken into account in the treatment of employees covered by this Agreement insofar as the conditions of the business and the abilities of the employees permit.

Section 2. The Company shall decide the necessity for and shall determine the extent of force adjustments.

BACKGROUND

Prior to the grievance in this case, Tracy McNeil worked as a deskman at the telephone exchange office in Luebbering, Missouri. A deskman is a craft position which is rated equal in pay to that of an exchange repairman in the United Independent Telephone Company. A deskman works in an inside office and is responsible for testing lines and central office equipment when trouble reports are received from customers.

If a deskman determines the trouble to be in the outside plant, he assigns the work order to an outside exchange repairman. The exchange repairman calls in to the deskman upon finishing an order and to receive a new assignment of work from the deskman.

---

[1] All names disguised.

Mr. McNeil first came to work for the United Independent Telephone in 1937. He held a variety of jobs during the ensuing years, and was assigned to the test desk at Luebbering in 1946. With minor exceptions, brought about at his own request, he worked as a deskman from his initial assignment to that job until he was transferred to the job of exchange repairman, effective April 20, 1959.

On April 20th, the company transferred McNeil off the deskman's job because, in the company's terms, "of his refusal to accept the responsibility of properly dispatching, or assigning work orders, or of such an indifference to such dispatching as to equate to a refusal, or even a defiance."

POSITION OF THE COMPANY

The company contended that Mr. McNeil was transferred from the deskman's job "for refusal, or willful failure, to dispatch work orders as the company required."

Part of the evidence against McNeil was gathered by Plant Superintendent George Roberts through his use of an observation circuit.

Observation circuits permit management officials to listen to business conducted over the deskman's line. Roberts had an observation circuit in his office, and he claimed that on several occasions he heard McNeil permit repairmen to accept or reject work orders (which McNeil had assigned them) according to the repairmen's desires. This action ignored the system of priorities which company supervisors often set up on such orders. Mr. Roberts claimed that he spoke to McNeil's supervisor, Milt Harrigan, about this, and he felt that Harrigan had talked to McNeil about it.

One direct conversation with McNeil which Mr. Roberts related was the result of what he called the "elevator incident." On that occasion, Roberts and McNeil were in the same elevator, and McNeil made some remarks in jest which Roberts considered inappropriate. Roberts, therefore, made it a point to stop off at McNeil's floor and reprimand him for the remarks. At the same time, he mentioned to McNeil his unsatisfactory handling of orders on the deskman's job.

Supervisory service foreman Wesley Ables was directly responsible for the exchange repairmen, and he often would visit the test desk to review and help assign orders. On the afternoon of April 20, 1959, he noted that one of the repair orders seemed particularly urgent. Because of this fact, he asked several deskmen, including McNeil, to assign it to the next exchange repairman who called in. It so happened that the next call came in on McNeil's line. The repairman objected to the order in question, so McNeil let him get away without taking it and assigned him a different order. Ables overheard this conversation and immediately asked McNeil what the responsibilities of the deskmen were in terms of assigning orders to repairmen. McNeil took the position that it was not part of his responsibility to distinguish between orders, and that he had no obligation to report repairmen who were in the same bargaining unit who refused to take orders as they were assigned, since a deskman was not a management supervisor over the repairmen.

A serious discussion then ensued in which Ables made it clear that he felt McNeil was wrong. However, since McNeil was not under Ables' direct supervision, Ables felt that it was not his obligation to take disciplinary action himself. Ables reported the incident to Roberts and also to Milt Harrigan, who was McNeil's immediate supervisor. Ables said, "My reports were conversational, and I didn't expect anything in particular, although I wanted the matter straightened out."

However, when Mr. Roberts and Mr. Ables discussed the incident, they decided that in view of McNeil's long service with the company and his "indifferent attitude towards his responsibilities," he should no longer be a deskman in the central office. Ables believed that McNeil could handle the position of exchange repairman, and he agreed with Mr. Roberts that McNeil should be transferred from the test desk to work as an exchange repairman under his (Ables') supervision.

In summary, since McNeil had refused to carry out a legitimate work order, the company claimed that its lateral transfer disciplinary action against McNeil was just and reasonable, and that the union grievance should be dismissed.

POSITION OF THE UNION

The union claimed that at most the company's "evidence" showed that McNeil was not issuing repair orders from the test desk in the priority which had been assigned to them, and that he was permitting repairmen to refuse one order in favor of another. Perhaps this called for disciplinary action. Nevertheless, the union did not consider this to be a refusal or willful failure to issue orders in compliance with company procedures. A refusal or willful failure implies more than a mere violation of a procedure; it indicates that the dereliction has been called to the employee's attention, that contrary orders had been issued, and that the employee persisted in his previous conduct.

The union claimed that it was at this point that the company's evidence failed. The logical person to talk to McNeil would be his direct supervisor. Roberts stated that he believed that Harrigan had talked to McNeil previously, but Harrigan did not testify. The union alleged that actually Mr. Harrigan would testify that he thought McNeil's work was satisfactory. Roberts himself talked to McNeil about his handling of orders only accidentally, since the meeting resulted from an elevator incident which had nothing specifically to do with McNeil's prior handling of orders on the desk. Ables conceded that he had not issued any direct orders to McNeil, because the latter was not under his supervision. Who, then, ever did tell McNeil to correct his ways? The union claimed that the record was barren of any proof that anyone did. Certainly, McNeil was never warned that continued noncompliance would result in removal from his job.

The union did not question the company's right to discipline employees who refused to comply with reasonable operating rules established by the company. But this very prerogative of management carried with it certain responsibilities. If an employee was found who was not following the rules, the dereliction should be called to his attention, to be sure there could be no mistake about it in the future. Here the dereliction was called to McNeil's attention only in such a roundabout fashion that it is impossible to conclude that he was ever given a fair and clear warning.

In summary, the union claimed that since McNeil had not been given a clear warning, he should be restored to his position as deskman, and that he should be made whole for any lost overtime or other types of benefits which he might have received on the test desk (while he was working as an exchange repairman) due to the company's arbitrary and unjust action.

QUESTIONS

1. Should a deskman be made responsible for assigning work orders to another employee who is in the same bargaining unit as is the deskman? Does this place the deskman in a "pseudo-management" position, i.e., having responsibility but not commensurate authority?

2. Does the evidence indicate that McNeil had refused to carry out a legitimate work order of the company, and therefore was subject to disciplinary action? Why, or why not?

3. Evaluate the argument of the union in this case. What is the key element upon which the union case rests?
4. From a management standpoint, how might case situations such as this be avoided? What are its implications to management training, follow-up action, and disciplinary technique?

41. THE HOT-HEADED PHARMACIST

COMPANY: Bartell Drug Company, Inc., Seattle, Washington
UNION: Retail Clerks Union, Local 330

INTRODUCTION

Howard Eaton,[1] chief pharmacist of Store No. 16 located in downtown Seattle, was discharged after two years employment at the Bartell Drug Company. The company's reason for discharging Eaton was that he could not get along with either customers or his fellow employees.

The Bartell Drug Company operates several retail drug stores in the Seattle area. Howard Eaton had been a licensed pharmacist for 19 years. His duties with Bartell consisted of filling prescriptions and waiting on customers.

On March 4, 1971, eight days after Eaton's discharge, the union sent the company a letter which read in part as follows:

In accordance with the terms and provisions of the collective bargaining agreement in force and effect between Bartell Drug and Local 330, R.C.I.A., we hereby protest and submit as a grievance, that the discharge of Howard Eaton was not proper, just, or for reasonable cause, and judgment of management in reaching a decision to terminate Eaton was not fairly and reasonably exercised.

The union requested that Eaton be reinstated to his former position with full back pay and with restoration of all rights and benefits.

POSITION OF THE COMPANY

The company pointed out that the retail drug industry was highly competitive. If it was to compete successfully, company employees must not only be highly qualified but also possess the ability and desire to get along with both customers and fellow employees.

---

[1] Names disguised.

The company recognized that Eaton was a qualified and able pharmacist, a fact which he demonstrated by his accurate and rapid filling of prescriptions. However, by Eaton's own admission, he possessed a very quick temper and easily became angry. In fact, his quick temper caused him on several previous occasions to lose jobs with other companies.

The company stated that it was aware of Eaton's quick temper and previous discharges at the time it hired him about two years previously. At the time Eaton was hired, both the manager of store number 16 and the operations manager of the parent company spoke with Eaton about his past behavior and pointed out that he would have to change both his attitude and actions toward customers.

The manager of store number 16 testified that he received the first customer complaint about Eaton's behavior about two months after he had been hired. Thereafter, he received a major complaint almost every week, and minor complaints from both customers and other Bartell employees almost every day. The manager stated that the company counseled with Eaton and did not discharge him immediately in the hope that his behavior might change. Eaton possessed excellent technical skills, which enabled him to fill prescriptions both quickly and accurately.

The operations manager stated that the company conscientiously attempted to work with Eaton. He and the store manager attempted to smooth over the difficult situations with customers.

The company stated, in response to inquiries by the union, that it did not record the names and addresses of complaining customers, because it was not good for customer relations to check on the complaints of angry customers or to indicate to them that they might be called upon to testify against an offending employee. Two of Eaton's fellow employees working in the same department with him cited several instances of his rude behavior both toward customers and toward them. They testified that they had heard him make sarcastic remarks to customers, use offensive language toward then and argue with them. One of the employees testified that, in a fit of anger, Eaton had struck her on the head with a writing pad and had grasped and twisted her arm. Both employees were members of Local 330, to which Eaton belonged, and both testified under oath against him.

The company admitted that it decided to discharge Eaton early in February 1971, but delayed action for two or three weeks in order to find another pharmacist to replace him.

All four company witnesses testified that they believed that Eaton disliked older customers and people on welfare. Many of the customers with whom he had difficulties fell into these two categories.

The company held that it possessed the right to discharge Howard Eaton under Section 22.1 of the collective agreement which read as follows:

The employer shall be the judge as to the competency of his employees and continuity of employment shall be based upon the Employer's judgement of the merit and ability of the individual employee, provided that such judgement shall be fairly and reasonably exercised.

Further, management representatives stated that Eaton violated Section 2b of *Company Rules and Policies* which read as follows:

Never argue with a customer even though you may be entirely correct. The customer is our Boss and comes first.

The company stated that this policy statement was well-known to all employees. Eaton was reminded of it on many occasions. It was a reasonable policy, and it reflected the spirit and philosophy of Bartell Drug Company.

The company cited several prior arbitration cases in which arbitrators upheld discharges of employees who were guilty of emotional outbursts and the use of bad language within the hearing of customers. The company also cited a case in which an arbitrator held that an arbitrator should not substitute his personal judgment for that of the company, if the company has acted in good faith after a proper and fair investigation. In view of the precedents cited and the evidence presented, the company asked that Eaton's grievance protesting his discharge should be denied.

POSITION OF THE UNION

The union contended that Eaton's behavior was not as bad as the company had alleged, since the company had retained him in its employ for approximately two years. The union also argued that, during this time, Eaton was promoted to chief pharmacist of store number 16.

Eaton admitted that his temper did have "a short fuse", but he stated that there was usually a just and good reason for his anger. Consequently, under oath, he testified that many of the instances which the company cited did not actually occur. He also admitted that he had occasional arguments with customers, but he also contended that he cheerfully had helped many customers who needed it. Although some customers complained when the arguments occurred, Eaton believed that no customer had ever asked that the company discharge him. When complaints about his behavior were lodged, he did not know about them immediately nor did he realize that his job with the company was in jeopardy. Eaton emphatically denied the charge that he disliked old people or people who were on welfare. Eaton admitted that he grasped a fellow employee and twisted her arm, but only because she had refused to say "hello" to him. However, he quickly apologized to her, and he also apologized to customers when there was an appropriate reason or an opportunity to do so. Eaton insisted that he got along well with his co-workers, including those who testified against him.

The union pointed out that if this dismissal were upheld, Eaton probably would not be able to find another job in the retail drug industry.

The union further attested that there may have been another reason for Eaton's dismissal. Under Washington state law, certain drugs, called exempt drugs, could be purchased without a prescription, depending upon the judgment of the pharmacist. Eaton often had refused to sell exempt drugs to some people, and he felt that the manager of the store wanted him "to look the other way" when such a sale could be made. Three other pharmacists had been dismissed in the past by the company, and the union argued that they had felt at the time that their refusal to sell exempt drug items against their better judgment was the reason for their dismissal.

The union objected strenuously to the testimony of company witnesses that Eaton did not get along well with customers. The union requested that the company provide the names of the alleged complaining customers in order that they might be cross-examined. Since the company claimed that it was unable to furnish such a list, the union claimed that Eaton's alleged poor relations with customers were only rumors and not fact. The union argued that the company's refusal or inability to furnish such a list constituted an unfair labor practice under the Taft-Hartley Act. Further, the union claimed that the company's refusal to supply the names of complaining customers violated Section 17.4 of the collective bargaining agreement which stated:

The Employer and the Union agree to make available to the other such pertinent data as each may deem necessary for the examination of all circumstances surrounding a grievance. The arbitrator shall be empowered to effect compliance with this provision by requiring the production of documents and other evidence.

The union also contended that, before the hearing, the company did not include poor fellow employee relations as a reason for dismissing Eaton and to do so now was late and unfair. The company should not be allowed to rely on one set of reasons in the first three steps of the grievance procedure and then add another set when arguing its position before the arbitrator. Consequently, only poor customer relations should be considered by the arbitrator, and testimony concerning poor employee relations should be stricken from the record.

In support of its case, the union cited several NLRB cases. One case concerned the Metropolitan Life Insurance Company in which failure on the part of the company to provide the names of complaining policy holders indicated that there was no just cause for discharge of three of the company's agents. Also, the union contended that in cases where names of accusers are withheld, discharge is too severe a penalty for an alleged display of poor attitude on the part of the employee. Therefore, the union argued that much of the Bartell Drug Company's case was based on inadmissable and unsubstantiated evidence. The union claimed that Howard Eaton should be reinstated to his job with full back pay.

QUESTIONS

1. Was employee Howard Eaton's behavior serious enough to justify discharge under provisions of the collective agreement? Why, or why not?
2. Evaluate the company's position citing an arbitrator who held that, "an arbitrator should not substitute his personal judgment for that of the company, if the company has acted in good faith after a proper and fair investigation."
3. Evaluate the union's argument that the company should provide the names of alleged complaining customers in order to cross-examine them. Should the arbitrator rule upon this issue in relationship to the company's duty to bargain under the Labor-Management Relations (Taft-Hartley) Act?
4. Is it permissible for the company to include "poor fellow employee relations" as a reason for dismissing Eaton if, as the union alleges, this was not originally a reason for dismissing Eaton during the first three steps of the grievance procedure? Discuss.

42. THE DISPUTED MEMORIAL DAY HOLIDAY

COMPANY: Highway Products, Inc., Kent, Ohio

UNION: United Automobile, Aerospace and Agricultural Implement Workers of America, Local 1137

BACKGROUND

The company fabricates and produces camping trailers and other camping equipment and supplies. In 1970, Memorial Day (May 30) occurred on a Saturday. Ten days prior to Memorial Day, the company posted the following notice:

May 20, 1970

To: All Highway Products Employees

Subject: Memorial Day Weekend

Under the terms of our Labor-Management Agreement, Memorial Day Holiday will be Friday, May 29, 1970.

Pay for Friday May 29, will be made to all those who are eligible in accordance with the terms of this agreement.

The company will cease all operations at the conclusion of the second shift Thursday May 28, 1970, and resume operations Monday morning, June 1, 1970.

No productive operations are anticipated for this weekend. However, if the need should arise to schedule work, the employees effected will be notified by their respective supervisor.

The company extends its best wishes for a safe and pleasant Holiday weekend to all employees and their families.

One week later, on May 27, the company posted a notice that certain departments would have to work on Friday, May 29, 1970. The notice, in part was as follows:

NOTICE

The Company regrets the fact that we must schedule the Fabrication Dept. and Loft and Template Dept. for work on Friday, May 29, 1970. Our decision was based on the following:

268

1. Bus Line shortages of fabricated parts have just about shut down the line and have already caused some layoffs.
2. Cortez is also dependent on our fabricated parts supply and is also threatened with a severe production cut-back. We hope our efforts can correct this situation.

Work Schedule: The Fabrication Dept. #100 is scheduled to work two 8-hour shifts on Friday, May 29. The Loft and Template Dept. #840 is scheduled to work one 8-hour shift on Friday, May 29. All employees will be paid straight time for Friday's work. All employees entitled to Holiday Pay for Memorial Day will be given an additional day's pay.

Shortly thereafter, the union filed a grievance, which read as follows:

On May 20, 1970 the company posted a notice which states that the plant will observe Memorial Day holiday as Friday, May 29, 1970. On May 27 at approx. 5:00 P.M. the company posted a notice that some Departments would be scheduled to work two 8 hr. shifts on Fri. May 29. The Union requests that all employees who worked on Fri. May 29, 1970 be paid the 3 times their straight hourly rate, as provided in the Agreement Article XV, Section 3.[1]

The grievance ultimately was carried to arbitration.

POSITION OF THE UNION

The union submitted that the company had the right, under Article XV, Section 6, to designate May 29 as the official Memorial Day holiday. But after declaring May 29 as the Memorial Day holiday, the company never rescinded this nor posted any notice revoking the designation. Further, when some fifty employees were required to work in the Fabrication department and the Loft and Template department on May 29, they were working on Memorial Day as designated by the company. Therefore, under Section 3 of Article XV, any employee who works on a holiday should be paid at the rate of three times the straight-time hourly rate. Since these employees had to work on a holiday, they should be paid the triple rate. The grievance should be allowed.

POSITION OF THE COMPANY

Representatives of the company claimed that the company could not legally change an official holiday from May 30 to May 29. Since Memorial Day in 1970 fell on a Saturday, the company had the right,

---

[1] See appendix for applicable contractual clauses.

under Section 6 of Article XV, to declare the preceding work day, May 29, as a "day to be observed as a holiday." This is all the company could do under the agreement. Memorial Day itself did not change by the May 20 notice of the company.

The company further testified that the notice posted on May 27 was necessitated by a shortage of parts referred to therein. Under the agreement, the company had the right to revoke, as it did by the notice of May 27, the designation of May 29 as a Memorial Day holiday for certain employees. The employees who worked on May 29 received their regular rate of pay and, in addition, the holiday pay. All other employees (who did not work on May 29) were paid for that date as provided for under the company's first notice.

The company stated that it did not try to deprive anyone of holiday pay for Saturday, May 30, to which they were entitled under Section 6 of Article XV. Some employees worked four days and others five days during that week, but all received holiday pay. No employees worked on Saturday, May 30, the only day legally defined Memorial Day.

Therefore, no employees were entitled to triple pay for working on May 29. The company claimed that the union was trying to take advantage of a unique situation which would be unfair to the large majority of about a hundred employees who did not work on May 29. The union grievance should be denied.

APPENDIX

Applicable Provisions from the Agreement

Provisions for holidays are set forth under Article XV of the Agreement, the pertinent sections of which are as follows:

Section 1.   For the purpose of this Article, New Year's Day, Memorial Day, July Fourth, Labor Day, Thanksgiving Day, Day after Thanksgiving, Day before Christmas and Christmas Day shall be considered as holidays. One additional floating Holiday beginning in 1968, notification to be given by the Company at ratification the first year and not later than January 31st, in the second and third years.

Section 3.   Any employee who works on any of said holidays shall be paid at the rate of three (3) times his straight time hourly rate.

Section 6.   If any of the above holidays fall on Saturday, the employees will, at the option of the Company, either be paid for the holiday or given the preceding work day or the next succeeding day as a holiday.

The management rights are set forth in Article XVII as follows:

Section 1.   Except as herein expressly qualified, the Company retains the exclusive right to manage its business, operations and affairs and to direct the working force. Prominent among such unqualified rights, although by no means a wholly inclusive list thereof, are the following: to introduce new or improved products, methods, equipment or facilities, and to alter or discontinue any operation or product; to select suppliers and to determine whether to "make or buy" to maintain order and efficiency in its plant and operation; to determine processes, production methods, quality standards, degree of workmanship required, the size of the working force.

Section 2.   The Company not exercising rights reserved to it or its exercising them in a particular way shall not be deemed a waiver of said rights or of its rights to exercise them in some other way not in conflict with the terms of this Agreement.

QUESTIONS

1. Evaluate the conflicting arguments concerning whether May 29 was, as the union claimed, the "official Memorial Day holiday," or as management claimed only a "day to be observed as a holiday." Why is this a crucial difference in the positions of the parties?
2. Why does the company feel that the union is trying to take advantage of a unique situation which "would be unfair to the large majority of about a hundred employees who did not work on May 29"?
3. What are the precedent implications of this case in relation to clauses such as Section 3 and Section 6 of the agreement in the case?

43. LEAVE FOR RELIGIOUS FESTIVAL

COMPANY: Armstrong Rubber Company, Southern Division, Natchez, Miss.

UNION: United Rubber Cork, Linoleum and Plastic Workers of America, Local 303

BACKGROUND

The Armstrong Rubber Company discharged William R. Mallone[1] on October 20, 1971, because he had "violated Plant Rule 29." This rule included the following grounds for discharge of an employee:

Being absent from work three consecutive working days and either (a) not reporting absence or advancing a reasonable excuse for not reporting absence; or (b) having no reasonable excuse for being absent; or (c) falsifying the reason for being absent or not reporting the absence. Penalty for first violation: discharge.

William Mallone was hired into the Natchez, Mississippi, plant of Armstrong Rubber Company in September, 1968, as an assistant machine operator in the color mix department. He was an excellent employee, and one year later was promoted to machine operator.

In early 1970, Mallone became a member of the Worldwide Church of God. This religious organization teaches absolute adherence to certain "holy days" and requires each member to observe these days as well as to attend certain religious festival meetings. One such period of holy days extends for a span of one week and is designated as the "Feast of Tabernacles and Last Great Days." Mr. Mallone considered his presence at these religious meetings to be a commandment from God. In 1971, this period of holy days extended from October 4 to October 11. Mr. Mallone was absent from work without leave from October 4 through October 13, 1971, to attend the various religious festival meetings of his church. It was the first occasion on which Mr. Mallone had been absent without authorization during his three years with the company.

---

[1] All names disguised.

Mallone previously had followed required procedures stated in Rule 29 in requesting a leave of absence. He made three requests for a leave of absence for this period. On the first occasion, September 24, Mallone asked his immediate supervisor, Joseph Lorne, for a two-week leave of absence for "personal reasons." Lorne denied this request, telling Mallone that due to a backlog of work he was needed on the job. On September 30, Mallone then took his request for a two-week leave "to attend an important religious festival" to the plant's Assistant Industrial Relations Manager, Robert Botts. Botts checked with Mallone's department and found that a heavy backlog of work had accumulated in that department. Mallone's request was again denied, but Botts told Mallone that a two-day leave perhaps could be arranged. Mallone informed Botts that he needed an eight-day leave and that his attendance at these religious meetings was "a must." Subsequently, on October 1, Mallone made one final request for this leave, which again was denied by Lorne who stated that he was needed on the job.

Mallone did not report for work from October 4 through October 13, and he could not be reached by telephone at his home during that time. After he returned to work, a conference including company and union officials as well as Mallone was arranged to discuss this situation. On October 20, Mallone was discharged by the company for violating Rule 29. On Mallone's behalf, the union subsequently filed a grievance which eventually was carried to arbitration.

POSITION OF THE UNION

The union contended that the company engaged in religious discrimination in refusing to grant Mallone a leave of absence to attend a required religious activity of his church. According to Mallone's testimony, he was required by his church to attend the church's October 4-11 celebration of the "Feast of Tabernacles and Last Great Days." In support of this contention, the union produced as evidence an affidavit by a church official that Mallone's denomination "teaches absolute adherence to the annual holy days, and that it is the duty of each member to observe these days in order to maintain his status in this church."

The union also argued that Mr. Mallone had made a request for leave as required by Rule 29. In fact, he made repeated requests for leave because he did not wish to place his church and job in conflict with each other.

Mr. Mallone's absence was for a good reason, as also required by Rule 29. The union pointed out that the company recognized required religious activities as constituting a valid reason for absence. For example, employees who requested so in advance were excused on Good Friday, and no one worked on Christmas Day.

Finally, the union argued that Mallone was an excellent employee. He had always been regular in his attendance, had never been late, and always had met or exceeded production standards. Consequently, the union requested that the grievant, Mallone, be reinstated to his job with all seniority and back pay.

POSITION OF THE COMPANY

The company maintained that it had the right to discharge William Mallone for being absent without leave from his job from October 4-13. The company pointed out that it properly denied Mallone's request for leave due to a heavy backlog of work, which required Mallone to be on the job. High production was important during the months of September, October and November when new lines and designs were being produced to stock distributors' warehouses. Although the color mix department was small, it was critical for continued operation of the plant. Inexperienced operators thus could not be assigned to the department.

The company denied that it engaged in religious discrimination and claimed that it always had granted religious leaves whenever possible. In this situation, however, Mr. Mallone's request came at a time when he could not be spared, especially for the long period requested. The company could not afford to excuse Mallone's absence from work without permission.

The company stressed that nothing in the contract required the company to grant Mallone a leave to attend a religious function. Therefore, the company was well within its rights to deny Mallone's request for leave. Since Mallone deliberately chose to be absent from work, the company was completely justified in discharging him as provided for in Plant Rule 29.

The company requested that the grievance be denied, and that Mallone's discharge for cause be upheld by the arbitrator.

QUESTIONS

1. Must the company recognize attendance at religious activities as constituting a valid reason for absence from work by an employee? Discuss.

2. Did employee William Mallone meet the requirements for requesting leave under Plant Rule 29?
3. Could the company properly deny Mallone's request for a leave due to a heavy backlog of work, since nothing in the contract specifically required the company to grant Mallone a leave to attend a religious function? Discuss.
4. Why does a case such as this pose a difficult problem to company management both from the standpoints of employee policy and public relations?

44. THE STOCK MARKET DROP AND THE PROFIT SHARING PAYMENTS

COMPANY: ITT Canteen Corporation

UNION: Teamsters' Local Union No. 688, St. Louis, Mo. Affiliated with International Brotherhood of Teamsters, Chauffeurs, Warehousemen, and Helpers of America

THE ISSUE

The issue as stated by the union in its grievance dated October 26, 1970, was that the company was in "violation of Article XXXIV, Section 4[1] of its agreement" with ITT Canteen Corporation. This agreement was in effect from March 16, 1970 to March 15, 1973. The union complaint on the grievance form was signed in the name of Alphonse Garnatz,[2] chief shop steward in the maintenance department. However, the complaint was made on behalf of all Division A employees defined in the agreement as Exhibit A, page 37. The union settlement requested was that the company should pay termination payments from the company profit sharing plan on calculated figures to be based as of the end of March, 1970. The grievance eventually was submitted to arbitration.

In their testimony, company representatives agreed to the union's basic statement of the issue, subject to the clarification that the company itself did not have direct control over disbursements of its profit sharing trust fund, since the company profit sharing trust fund is administered independently of the company itself. Counsel for the company stated his position that the sole issue rested upon the interpretation of Article XXXIV, Section 4 of the agreement. As a result of the hearing, the arbitrator ruled that the issue could be restated as follows: "Did the company violate the agreement when it arranged to terminate membership in the ITT Canteen profit sharing

---

[1] See Appendix for all applicable contract provisions. At the time of this case, approximately sixty employees were classified as Division A employees.

[2] All names disguised.

plan for Division A employees effective May 2, 1970, with termination payments based upon an evaluation of employee member accounts as of the end of May, 1970?"

BACKGROUND

Although the prior agreement had expired on March 15, 1970, negotiations between the parties continued throughout March and April, and it was not until the weekend of May 1-3, 1970, that agreement on the new contract was reached. Negotiations had included a reverse type of ratification procedure in which a list of demands was presented to the company as part of a "package" which the union membership said it would accept. Included in the list of demands presented to the company was a change which would bring Division A employees under the Teamsters' negotiated pension plan during the third year of the contract. These employees had been covered under a company profit sharing plan which included both employee and company contributions.[3]   The change, which also would require these employees to be removed from the company profit sharing plan, was acceptable to the company. However, a misunderstanding concerning this issue arose when the membership of the bargaining unit subsequently voted that it wanted to be covered under the Teamsters' pension plan for the entire period of the new three-year agreement. Negotiations continued between Mr. Arthur Rudolph, representing the company, and Mr. Daniel Bolle, representing the union, in order to resolve the pension plan issue. The parties found it necessary to reconsider different items within the total settlement, since the prior "package" offer had been based upon the premise that the Division A employees would not enter the Teamsters' pension plan until the third year of the agreement. In order to bring Division A employees into the Teamsters' pension plan for the entire three years of the agreement, a number of "fringe" items were bargained lower, and special terms for the company's contributions for Division A employees in the Teamsters' pension plan were negotiated. Mr. Bolle and Mr. Rudolph determined that in order for Division A members to be covered during the three years of the agreement, the company contribution would be reduced from the "normal" $2 per week per employee to $1 per week per

---

[3]Employee contributions to the company profit sharing plan are made by payroll deduction; the company contribution is based upon a periodic evaluation of company earnings.

employed member. This figure was included in Article XXXIV, Section 3 of the agreement as follows:

> Effective May 4, 1970, the Employer shall contribute for and on behalf of its employees covered by this Agreement, except Mobile Catering and Vending Attendants, to said Pension Plan and shall pay to said Trustees and Trust Fund established in Exhibit "B," the sum of One ($1.00) Dollar per week for each said employee.

Both the company and the union have policies prohibiting "dual coverage," i.e., simultaneous participation of bargaining unit employees in both a company profit sharing and a union pension plan. But during negotiations, there was no real consideration given to the question of the effective date of termination of Division A employee accounts in the company profit sharing plan. Both union and company representatives testified that the question of an effective date of termination of employees from the company profit sharing plan never really was discussed specifically. The parties did agree that the company would begin its contributions to the Teamsters' pension plan effective May 4, 1970, at the rate of $1 per week per employee, which coincided approximately with the weekend when the negotiations concluded.

According to the union, the May 4 date was requested by the company in order to save a certain amount of money in contributions to the Teamsters' pension plan, and the union agreed to this in the bargaining sessions. Mr. Bolle testified that his implied understanding was that the effective date for the coverage of the Teamsters' pension plan and the termination of the profit sharing plan would be March 16, 1970, since all other items in the agreement were retroactive to that beginning date. According to testimony by Mr. Rudolph, however, the May 4 date was significant to insure that there would be no dual coverage of employees in both the company profit sharing and union pension plan. Mr. Rudolph stated that, "We agreed that when the pension plan would come in, the profit sharing would go out. Although we never really discussed a termination date, my feeling was that profit sharing termination could not be retroactive to the March 16 date, because we never knew for sure whether it would be part of the final settlement."

When final settlement was reached, Mr. Rudolph instructed a letter to be written to the national office of the ITT Canteen Corporation requesting that Division A employees should be removed from company profit sharing coverage. This letter, dated May 4, 1970, was written by Mr. Peter Chruden of the St. Louis office to

Mr. Sherman Witney in the national office. Since employee contributions to the company profit sharing plan had continued automatically during the entire negotiating period, the letter directed that payroll deductions to the profit sharing plan should be stopped for Division A employees with the pay period ending Saturday, May 2, 1970, and that accounts for these employees should be processed accordingly. The union did not participate in formulating and sending this letter, and the union did not receive a copy of this letter.

This matter did not become an issue until about fall, 1970, when Division A employees began receiving checks as their payments for being withdrawn from the company profit sharing plan. The checks paid to these employees were considerably less than the employees had expected due to a significant drop in stock market evaluation of their accounts which had occurred during the period from March through May, 1970.[4] The market value of investments held by the company profit sharing trust fund had dropped some 20 to 25% during the period March to May, 1970, and this drop was reflected in the termination checks paid to Division A employees. At this point, the issue of the proper evaluation date for termination of employees' accounts from the company profit sharing plan was raised and formalized in the union complaint heard in arbitration. As testified by both parties, this was the first time that the termination date actually became a significant issue in the minds of either the company or union representatives.

POSITION OF THE UNION

In his testimony, Mr. Bolle stated that, although the date for termination of Division A employees in the company profit sharing plan had never really been considered directly, he had simply assumed that it was March 16, 1970, to maintain the continuity and retroactivity of all the benefits from the old to the new agreement. The union representatives pointed out that the exact wording of Article XXXIV, Section 4 of the agreement stated:

Effective March 16, 1970, when the Teamsters Negotiated Pension Plan becomes effective for Employees in Division "A," the Canteen Profit Sharing Plan will cease for such employees.

---

[4] These checks varied considerably depending upon each individual employee's share in the company plan. The union testified that the checks ranged in amounts from "under fifty dollars to several thousand dollars." The company profit sharing fund is administered by an independent board of trustees. All withdrawls or termination checks from the fund to individual employees are based upon an evaluation of the "fair market value" of an account at the end of the month during which the withdrawal or termination takes place.

This clause clearly states that March 16, 1970 was the effective date for the beginning of coverage in the Teamsters' plan and the termination of coverage in the company plan for Division A employees. The May 4 date in Section 3 of the agreement merely states when the company was to begin its contributions to the Teamsters plan on behalf of Division A employees.

Based upon this clause the union contended that the proper date for termination and evaluation of the employees' accounts should have been based upon a March 16, 1970, date of withdrawal from the company profit sharing plan. The union requested (a) that the company should be directed to request the administrators of its profit sharing plan to determine an appropriate additional termination compensation to be paid to Division A employees based upon the March 16, 1970, date; and (b) that these employees also should have refunded to them the amount of their contributions to the company plan which had been improperly deducted from payroll checks during the period March 16 - May 2, 1970. The union assumed that such a request as awarded in arbitration would be honored accordingly by trustees of the profit sharing plan.

POSITION OF THE COMPANY

In his testimony, Mr. Rudolph stated that, in his mind, the May 4, 1970, date to begin the company contributions to the Teamsters' pension plan was correspondingly the end of the Division A employees' participation in the company profit sharing plan. Mr. Rudolph testified that he was instrumental in having Article XXXIV, Section 4 placed in the agreement to be certain that there would be no duplication in membership of employees in both the profit and pension sharing plans. Upon cross-examination by the arbitrator as to why different dates were included in Article XXXIV, Section 3 and Article XXXIV, Section 4, Mr. Rudolph replied that he "honestly did not know." But he declared there was no intention in his mind to have retroactivity extended back to the March 16 date. Mr. Rudolph stated that an exact date for termination in the company profit sharing plan never was discussed, and he explained this as follows: "We were primarily interested only in determining when the one plan would come in, the other plan would go out. It wasn't until members received their termination checks from the profit sharing plan that the exact withdrawal date came up in anybody's mind. The drop in the stock market during this period was just one of those unfortunate coincidental things."

Mr. Rudolph further testified that his "blanket" request for withdrawing Division A employees from the company profit sharing plan was made by him because of the negotiated change of the status of these employees, and that to his knowledge there were no individual requests to withdraw. Normally, employees make individual requests for withdrawal, or they are terminated if they leave the company. Under the provisions of the ITT Canteen Corporation profit sharing trust fund, the termination or withdrawl payout checks normally are based upon an evaluation of each individual's account at the "fair market value" of the account at the end of the month of withdrawal or termination. Because of this negotiated situation, the "blanket" request for withdrawal was made by the company unilaterally.

Finally, Mr. Rudolph testified concerning the apparent confusion surrounding the date included in Article XXXIV, Section 4 of the agreement. He stated, "Why the March 16 date is there, I don't know. I saw that date there when I signed the contract, but it didn't make any impression on me then. I do know, however, that our mutual intention was to avoid double coverage in both the company and union plans. The March 16 date mentioned in the agreement obviously should have been May 4."

In this context, counsel for the company argued that Article XXXIV, Section 4 should be interpreted to mean May 4 rather than March 16, because otherwise there would be a gap in coverage of employees under the Teamsters' pension plan during these dates. With this proper interpretation of the intention of the agreement, the May date used for terminating Division A employees from the company profit sharing plan was therefore appropriate, and the union grievance should be denied.

APPENDIX

Applicable Contract Provisions

Article XXXIV – Teamsters' Negotiated Pension Plan

The Employer agrees to participate in and to contribute to the Teamsters' Negotiated Pension Plan on the following terms and conditions:

1. Said Pension Plan shall be administered by a Board of Trustees under the uses and trusts as set forth in that certain Trust Agreement[6] attached hereto as Exhibit "B" and whose terms and conditions are herein incorporated by reference.

---

[6] This refers to the trust agreement which governs the Teamsters Negotiated Pension Plan. This trust agreement was attached to the contract as Exhibit B.

2.The Employer does hereby agree to be bound by and does hereby assent to all of the terms of said Trust Agreement, including the Trustees therein named; the Employer further agrees to execute such other and further documents and papers (including said Trust Agreement) as shall be necessary or appropriate to evidence that it assents and subscribes to the terms thereof and accepts the Trustees therein named.

3. Effective May 4th, 1970, the Employer shall contribute for and on behalf of its employees covered by this Agreement, except Mobile Catering and Vending Attendants, to said Pension Plan and shall pay to said Trustees and Trust Fund established in Exhibit "B," the sum of One ($1.00) Dollar per week for each said employee.

4. Acceptance of the Employer as a contributing Employer hereunder shall be in writing by the Board of Trustees referred to in said Exhibit "B."

The Canteen Profit Sharing Plan will remain in effect for all employees in Division "B."

Effective March 16th, 1970, when the Teamsters Negotiated Pension Plan becomes effective for Employees in Division "A," the Canteen Profit Sharing Plan will cease for such employees.

EXHIBIT "A" (pp. 37-38 of agreement)

DIVISION "A"
EMPLOYEES

SCHEDULE OF NEGOTIATED HOURLY WAGE RATES

	3/16/70	3/16/71	3/16/72
MAINTENANCE	$4.25	$4.55	$4.80
SERVICEMAN	4.20	4.50	4.75
STOCKROOM	3.70	4.00	4.25
GENERAL LABOR	3.25	3.55	3.80
DELIVERY	4.20	4.50	4.75
INSTALLATION	4.03	4.33	4.58
ASST. INSTALLATION	3.63	3.93	4.18
CASUAL	3.00	3.25	3.50

HIRING RATES FOR NEW EMPLOYEES LISTED ABOVE:

NEW HIRES	75¢ UNDER BASE RATE
AFTER SIXTY (60) DAYS	60¢ UNDER BASE RATE
AFTER SIX (6) MONTHS	45¢ UNDER BASE RATE
AFTER TWELVE (12) MONTHS	30¢ UNDER BASE RATE
AFTER EIGHTEEN (18) MONTHS	15¢ UNDER BASE RATE
BASE RATE AFTER TWO (2) YEARS	

MOBILE CATERING   *SALESMEN'S WAGES*

The Wage Scale for Route Salesmen shall be as follows:

EFFECTIVE 3/16/70 — $91.50 on their first $300.00 sales, plus 11½% commission on all sales they make on their respective routes over $300.00.

EFFECTIVE 3/16/71 — $95.50 on their first $300.00 sales, plus 11½% commission on all sales they make on their respective routes over $300.00.

EFFECTIVE 3/16/72 — $99.50 on their first $300.00 sales, plus 11½% commission on all sales they make on their respective routes over $300.00.

EXHIBIT "A" (*continued*)

DIVISION "B"			
EMPLOYEES:	*SCHEDULE OF NEGOTIATED HOURLY WAGE RATES*		
	3/16/70	*3/16/71*	*3/16/72*
VENDING ATTENDANTS	$2.30	$2.60	$2.85

HIRING RATES FOR NEW EMPLOYEES LISTED ABOVE.

NEW HIRE	40¢ UNDER BASE RATE
AFTER SIX (6) MONTHS	20¢ UNDER BASE RATE
BASE RATE AFTER ONE (1) YEAR	

QUESTIONS

1. Why does the crucial issue in this case center upon the question of the date that the company profit sharing plan was to terminate and coverage under the Teamsters' pension plan was to begin for the Division A employees?
2. Is there any basic conflict in the dates included in Article XXXIV, Section 3, and Article XXXIV, Section 4?
3. Evaluate the company's argument that "Article XXXIV, Section 4 should be interpreted to mean May 4 rather than March 16, because otherwise there would be a gap in coverage of employees under the Teamsters' pension plan during these dates."
4. Is equity to the employees' interest at issue in this case? Discuss.
5. Would this issue have occurred if during the period March to May, 1970 the stock market would have risen substantially resulting in an increased termination payoff to Division A employees?

45. MUST THE MACHINISTS PURCHASE THEIR OWN TOOLS?

COMPANY: Stoody Company, Los Angeles, California

UNION: Local 803, International Union Allied Industrial Workers

BACKGROUND

The Stoody Company is a major supplier for the Department of Defense, United States Government. In the fall of 1970, the company was subject to a quality control inspection and report by a Naval Nuclear Quality Control team. The inspection team was composed of representatives of major manufacturers, with staff help from governmental employees. In a report dated October 8, 1970, the Department of Defense recommended procedures for strengthening the company's quality control system. One recommendation was to "establish a calibration system meeting the requirements of MIL-C-45662[1] for the calibration and control of measuring and testing equipment." In discussing this recommendation, the report noted that the calibration on a number of the tools was improperly accomplished and that "no system exists to insure that defective personal micrometers are removed from service."

However, the report contained no recommendation that individual machinists own or buy their own tools.

Company management became concerned over the October 8 report and began to fear that its Defense Department contracts were in jeopardy. Consequently, management initiated a series of meetings with union representatives to determine which tools should be required of all machinists. It also established procedures for testing all machinists' tools, whether company-owned or employee-owned.

Prior to this time, the company had assumed that all of its machinists possessed the required tools of the machinists' trade. It was only after the inspection began that the company learned that a

---

[1] This is a code identification number for a Department of Defense regulation pertaining to this area.

considerable number of its machinists didn't own a basic set of tools.

Growing out of these inspections and several meetings and discussions with union representatives, the company, on December 16, 1970, issued a bulletin to "all machinists, turret lathe operators, and engine lathe operators" stating that effective March 19, 1971, all of these employees would be required to "possess a prescribed basic set of tools" consisting of items costing $256. The memorandum stated that required tools, if repairable, would be repaired by the company at no charge; if a tool was damaged beyond reasonable repair costs, an individual employee would be responsible for "replacing that tool at his own expense."

In the December 16 bulletin, the company described this list of tools as only "a basic set of tools to meet precision standards in work in various departments as well as tools needed to make necessary adjustments on the machines." The company had taken into consideration the frequency with which particular instruments were required. Many of the company's more than 50 machinists had all the tools on the list; some had more. However, the company had in its "tool crib," prior to December, each tool on the list in varying quantities. The machinists had had full access to the use of the various tools in the company tool crib.

At this time, the company had in existence a tool purchase payroll deduction plan. Under the plan individual employees could purchase up to $100 in tools and have deducted from their weekly pay, $10. The plan was available to any machinist or machine tool operator holding his present classification for more than 90 days. Also in the December 16 bulletin, the company modified its tool purchase plan; effective December 17, 1970, the maximum purchase amount was increased to $200 and the minimum weekly payroll deduction reduced to $5.

The March deadline was extended at the union's request. Further meetings were held. On April 7, 1971, the company issued a second bulletin to the machinists, engine lathe operators and turret lathe operators stating that company inspection of individual tool sets had been rescheduled for May, and that certain tools designated as required in the December list had been removed from the required classification. The total cost of the required tools on the revised list was $226.50.

In a meeting with union representatives on May 13th, the company again brought up the subject of required tools and asked whether the union agreed to the list. The union president stated it was his position that the list represented a fair amount of tools, but he did not agree that the company had the right to require the tools be purchased prior to a union vote on the proposal.

A few days before a scheduled union meeting at which the issue was to be raised, the company presented the union president with a letter dated May 19, 1971, stating that "all concerned employees (machinists, engine lathe operators and turret lathe operators) must possess the required basic machine tool set as itemized on the attached list," effective May 21, 1971. The company asked the union president to indicate his approval on the letter. The union president said he agreed that the tools represented a fair amount of individually owned tools, but that it was not his intent to make this binding on the machinists generally. The union president did sign the letter. There was also a signature line on the May 19th letter for the chairman of the union's bargaining committee. Subsequently, the company proposal was rejected at a union membership meeting. The bargaining committee chairman did not sign the letter. He, too, informed the company that the union believed the company did not have a right to require employees to buy tools, but that the union membership did not say that the list was unjust. He personally felt the list was reasonable and had obtained his own tools in December.

The Employee Disciplinary Actions

Karl Ford[2] had been a machinist for 40 years; he had been with the company 12½ years. Ford had some of his own tools, but he had been relying on using tools from the company tool crib. When he was hired, Ford was asked whether he owned his own tools, including a micrometer up to two inches; the company did not specify that he should own any particular tools other than the micrometer. After working for Stoody, Ford had disposed of some of his tools, since the company had furnished them and he saw no need for his own. In May, 1971, his supervisor asked to see his tools. Ford told him that he could look at his tools to see if he had something he should not have, but not to see whether or not he had all the tools on the list. Previously, in March, 1971, one of Ford's own micrometers had been submitted for inspection, and he was given a memorandum declaring that the "spindle is worn out of tolerance" and that the repair costs would exceed 60 percent of the value of a new tool. In May, Ford stated that he had taken his micrometers home, and he was using company-owned micrometers when their use was necessary.

[2] All names disguised.

On June 2, 1971, the Company issued a notice to Ford that:

As per the notice of December 16, 1970, and succeeding notices, the Company has requested that you make your tool set available for inspection. You have refused to do so.

You, of course, have been given substantial notice of the requirement that you produce your tool set for inspection. Since you cannot properly perform your responsibilities as an employee of the Company without tools which meet Company inspection requirements, this will advise you that effective June 7, 1971, you will be suspended, for cause, from your employment with the Company until you have submitted your tool set for Company inspection.

The Company reserves the right to terminate you, for cause, at any time subsequent to 30 days from the date of this notice if you have not brought yourself into compliance with Company policy with respect to your tools.

On the same date, the company issued notices to employees Virgil Gibson and Wesley Busch that they did not have certain required tools. They were advised that they would be suspended effective June 7, 1971 until they had submitted satisfactory evidence that they had the designated tools. The company further reserved the right to terminate them for cause, if the tools were not purchased within 30 days from the date of the notice.

Gibson, a turret lathe operator trainee, was suspended on June 15th, but he was reinstated four weeks later after he had purchased the additional tools required by the company. Gibson claimed that at the time he was hired on the trainee program, he owned no tools. From December, 1970, to April, 1971, he had purchased some of the tools needed for the job. Gibson acknowledged that he knew he would need some tools, but he felt that as a trainee he did not need all the tools on the company list.

Under protest, Wesley Busch bought the tools and was never suspended. However, Karl Ford steadfastly refused to buy the tools "as a matter of principle." Ford was kept on the job until June 16th, when he was suspended. He was terminated on August 6, 1971.

The union filed a grievance protesting the disciplinary actions of the company and the rule of the company which required the machinists to purchase the list of tools. The grievance eventually was carried to arbitration.

POSITION OF THE UNION

The union argued that the company had no right to adopt a new rule forcing employees to own their own tools "mid-term of the contract". Under Article XXII, Section I of the agreement[3]

---
[3] See Appendix for applicable contract provisions.

governing past practice, the company can not unilaterally change a long-standing rule or practice as was done by the company in this case. Further, the employees acted reasonably; even if the company's right to change the rule concerning the ownership of tools would be upheld, the disciplinary measures against the employees were not warranted and should be rescinded.

The union stated that the company had offered no evidence to show that it had been forced by the government or by any company customers to adopt the rule compelling employees to furnish their own tools. On the contrary, inspection of the calibration of precision tools could better be accomplished by maintaining tools in the tool crib rather than in each employee's possession. The company had furnished tools for many years. Because of this, a number of the employees, including Ford, sold or otherwise disposed of their tools, which was a reasonable reliance on company practice. The company's furnishing of tools over a period of years rose to the "dignity of a past practice." This was especially true when the employees, relying on the past practice, had sold or otherwise disposed of personal tools.

In addition to a normal past practice, the company, by furnishing tools, gave employees an additional benefit which should not be changed mid-term of the contract, because it affected the economic advantages of the working force. In this connection, the union cited other arbitration awards allegedly holding that benefits which had become, in effect, a form of wages could not be changed or withdrawn during the period of the contract. The union cited Article I, Section 1 of the contract which recognized the union as the sole bargaining representative of the employees for the purpose of collective bargaining in respect to "condition of employment." The company was therefore obligated to bargain with the union concerning the issue of the purchase of the tools.

Finally, the union argued that the company acted hastily in disciplining the grievants, who acted reasonably. Once the tools were purchased, they would have had no recourse against the company. Therefore, by refusing to purchase the tools, they reacted in the only possible way they could. Ford, as a matter of principle, refused to capitulate to the company's one-sided edict.

In this case, refusal by employees to purchase the tools caused no immediate problem, since tools were available in the tool crib. Work was not disrupted, nor was the efficiency of the employees affected by their refusal to purchase tools. Ford, in particular, was a valued employee of the company. Ford would have continued to be an excellent employee if it had not been for the company's unfair action requiring him to purchase tools.

In summary, the union asked: (a) that the arbitrator require the company to bargain with the union over the matter of personal ownership of the required tools; and (b) that the disciplinary actions against Ford and Gibson be rescinded and these employees be made whole for any loss of earnings during their periods of suspension and termination.

POSITION OF THE COMPANY

The company argued that it had the right under the agreement to adopt the rule requiring purchase of the required list of machinists' tools, and that the company was justified in disciplining the employees who refused to comply with the rule.

The company offered testimony concerning practices of other area employers who required employees to own their own tools. One company witness testified that the list required by the company was less than is typically required by most major defense manufacturers in the Los Angeles area. Another company witness who interviewed prospective machinists testified that as a matter of practice he asked prospective employees which tools they personally owned.

The company always had had the right to require the machinists to own the basic tools of their craft. When the calibration problem arose and the company learned for the first time that a number of machinists did not own a basic set of tools, the company moved to correct this situation. The company claimed that even though enforcement of its policy requiring employees to own a basic set of tools was left earlier to the good faith of the parties, nevertheless the employees knew of the company's policy generally. When the company became subject to Department of Defense criticism concerning the calibration of tools, it had no choice but to require ownership and inspection of personal tools. The consequent establishment by the company of more formal rules and regulations, after consultation with the bargaining committee, was reasonable.

Further, Article XXII Section 1 supported the company's position. As outlined above, the company clearly had a long-standing policy that machinists own their own tools. Article XXII Section 1 only required that "due consideration be given to employees' interests before changes were made" in past practice. The company's attempts to negotiate with the union a satisfactory list met the requirements of Article XXII.

The company pointed out that its machinists had purchased their own tools for a number of years prior to the new requirements issued for 1971. For the year 1971, up to May 13th, 14 of the 54 machinists had purchased tools through the company plan costing a total of $2,011. These purchases ranged from a low of $23 for one employee to a high of approximately $190. The plan was used in 1970 by 9 employees, who purchased $1,416 worth of tools, and in 1969 by 12 employees, who purchased approximately $2,200 worth of tools.

All but three of the 54 machinists obtained the required tools. The remaining three, though not bound if the company had violated the contract, nevertheless were, in effect, told by the great majority of their co-workers that they felt the company's position was proper under the contract. It is impossible to believe that the machinists would have used the plan over a period of at least three years unless they understood that the company had a policy requiring that they personally own certain tools.

Finally, the company felt it had no recourse other than to suspend the three employees who refused to comply with the new rule. Ford, because of his adamant refusal, in effect terminated himself from employment with Stoody Company.

The company urged that the grievance be denied.

APPENDIX

Relevant Contractual Provisions

1. Article XVIII Section 1 provides that employees will not be discharged "without just and sufficient cause."

2. Article XXII Section 1 provides in part:

Certain methods, customs and practices, through long usage, have tended to become standardized. It is the Company's right to make any changes which do not violate this Agreement. However, the Company affirms that its policy will continue to be to respect tradition and precedence and that due consideration will be given to employees' interests before changes are made.

3. Article XXII Section 4 provides in part:

Both the Union and the Company recognize that all jobs provided by the Company are made possible only by selling the Company's products and that in order to sell its products, the Company must use such materials, processes and services as will result in costs low enough to be competitive.

The Company policy has been, and is, to constantly seek additional work which it is qualified to do and to increase both its facilities and its work force. Its intention is to continue diligent efforts to promote sound growth and expansion of all its activities, with continuous consideration being given to the preservation of existing jobs and the creation of new ones.

QUESTIONS

1. Did the company have the right to require employees to purchase their own tools? Why, or why not?
2. Was the company obligated under the agreement to bargain with the union concerning the issue of the purchase of the tools? Discuss. Could the union have filed unfair labor practice charges with the NLRB concerning the issue of the company's not bargaining about the tool purchases as a condition of employment under the Labor-Management Relations Act? Discuss.
3. Discuss the union's argument that furnishing of tools to employees over a period of years had risen to "the dignity of a past practice."
4. Did the company's actions in this case fulfill the requirements of Article XXII, Section 1? Discuss.
5. Should it have any bearing on the arbitrator's decision that all but three of the 54 machinists had acquired the required tools?
6. Should the arbitrator be influenced by the fact that employee Ford was a long-term employee who in this case was resisting the company edict at least partially as a matter of principle? Discuss.

46. THE "BUSTED RADIATOR"

COMPANY: *Veteran's Administration Center, Martinsburg, W. Va.*

UNION: *Local R4-78, National Association of Government Employees (N.A.G.E.)*

BACKGROUND

On July 6, 1971, Mr. James B. Biggs,[1] a nursing assistant, was due to work the day shift at the Veteran's Administration Center. The day shift began at 7:30 a.m. Shortly after 7 a.m., Biggs telephoned the nursing supervisor's office and spoke to Miss Rose Hamilton, the night supervisor. Biggs told Miss Hamilton that his car had broken down between Harper's Ferry, where Biggs lived, and Charlestown, which is on the way to Martinsburg. Biggs requested that he be permitted to take the day off on an emergency basis, as part of his annual leave, and he told Miss Hamilton that he could not come to work on account of a "busted radiator" in his car. However, Miss Hamilton was reluctant to grant this request; she told Biggs "to come in as soon as he could."

Shortly before Biggs called, another nursing assistant, Mr. Tom Short, had called in sick and was granted sick leave. Both Biggs and Short worked in the same ward. As a result of the absence of these two nursing assistants, this ward was shorthanded. Another nursing assistant was shifted from another assignment to fill the void. The situation was further complicated because Biggs' ward was in a state of transition and was very crowded. Consequently, both Miss Hamilton and Mrs. Dorothy Garrison, the day shift supervisor, were very anxious to have Biggs at work on July 6.

However, Biggs never made it to work that day. There was no public transportation or taxi service between the point where Biggs' car broke down and the hospital. Further, very few VA Center employees lived in the Harper's Ferry area. After a fruitless attempt to continue toward Martinsburg by hitchhiking, Biggs returned to the

---

[1] All names have been disguised.

repair shop in the vicinity of Harper's Ferry, where he had left his car. Biggs' car was not repaired until 2 p.m. at which time he felt it was too late for him to drive 20 miles from Harper's Ferry to Martinsburg to work on a shift that ended at 4 p.m.

The VA Center is staffed continuously. July 6 was Bigg's scheduled day off, but because of the work load at the Center, Biggs had been assigned to work on that day. If he had not experienced difficulty with his car and had he worked on July 6, he would have received double time for hours worked on that day. However, after reviewing the facts, the hospital officials decided to suspend Biggs for ten days for failing to report to work.

The union filed a grievance on behalf of Biggs which was ultimately carried to arbitration.

POSITION OF THE UNION

The union's arguments consisted mainly of Biggs' testimony and the circumstances surrounding his absence on July 6.

Biggs testified that his car had broken down between Harper's Ferry and Martinsburg. Since there was no public transportation or taxi service between Harper's Ferry and Martinsburg, and since very few VA Center employees lived in the Harper's Ferry area, Biggs' lack of success at hitchhiking was understandable.

The union argued that two prior disciplinary actions against Biggs by the VA Center were not related to this instance. Biggs had been reprimanded on two earlier occasions during the previous year for being tardy. These incidents should have no bearing in this case because on July 6 Biggs made a genuine effort to get to work. The union supplied receipts and affidavits from the garage owner indicating that he had towed Biggs' automobile to its premises, that the car was inoperable, and that while waiting for repairs Biggs made several attempts to get to work, including attempts to hitchhike a ride and to rent a car.

The facts revealed that if Biggs had gone to work that day, he would have received double his normal day's pay since this day was considered a "holiday" for him. Therefore, Biggs had considerable incentive to make every effort to report to work.

The union noted that records revealed that sick leave was readily granted to VA employees, as evidenced by the granting of sick leave to Biggs' fellow employee, Tom Short. Knowing this, Biggs easily could have called in sick instead of reporting honestly that his car had broken down. The union suggested that it could logically be concluded that Biggs' car indeed had broken down, and that he had no means of transportation to get to work.

In light of the above testimony and circumstances surrounding this case, the union requested that this grievance be sustained, and that Biggs be reimbursed for the wages he lost due to the ten-day disciplinary suspension.

POSITION OF THE VA CENTER HOSPITAL

VA management argued that Biggs had an absolute duty to report to work on July 6, and that his excuse about his car breaking down was not sufficient to warrant his absence from work. Biggs had been told by Miss Hamilton to come to work as soon as possible. The center maintained that Biggs should have found another method of getting to work if his regular means had failed.

Management pointed to Article XIX, Section 2, of the contract[2] provisions and called special attention to the second sentence of this section which specified that annual leave "for emergency reasons will be considered on an individual basis and generally granted when conditions warrant." But since Biggs' ward was in a state of transition and overcrowded as well as being short-handed, the center argued that it was within its rights not to grant Biggs' request.

Finally, center officials cited two previous disciplinary actions that preceded this suspension. The first occurred about a year earlier when Biggs received a warning for arriving to work late. Biggs claimed that on that occasion he was late as a result of a minor accident on a icy highway while driving to work. The second warning occurred about six months earlier when Biggs said he had overslept as a result of his being weak and tired after being ill with the flu. In management's opinion, these prior warnings should have impressed on Biggs that he was expected to report to work on time and as scheduled. As a result of these circumstances, the center requested that the arbitrator dismiss the grievance.

APPENDIX

Relevant Contract Provisions

Article XIX–Annual Leave

Section 1. Full and part-time employees shall earn annual leave in accordance with applicable statutes.

---

[2]See Appendix to case.

Section 2. Approval of an employee's request to take annual leave shall be granted when he has given his supervisor reasonable notice and can be spared. Approval of annual leave for emergency reasons will be considered on an individual case basis and generally granted when conditions warrant.

QUESTIONS

1. Did employee James Biggs have an "absolute duty to report to work" on July 6th, as argued by VA management? If so, was his excuse sufficient to warrant his absence from work? Discuss.
2. Was the VA Center within its rights not to grant employee Biggs a day of annual leave to compensate him for the day in dispute? Why, or why not?
3. Should the previous disciplinary actions involving employee Biggs have any bearing on this particular case? Why, or why not?

47. DISCHARGE FOR HYPERTENSION

COMPANY: San Francisco Retailers' Council representing Macy's Department Store

UNION: Department Store Employees, Local 1100

BACKGROUND

Mary Hartzke[1] applied for employment at Macy's, a large department store in San Francisco, on August 15, 1969. She filled out the standard application form, "Macy's Application for Employment." On the application form Ms. Hartzke indicated that she was born November 9, 1914, that her height was 5'7", and that her weight was 165 pounds. In response to the statement "Describe State of Health," she wrote "Good"; in response to "List Physical Defects," she wrote "None." The application blank also contained under the heading "Employment Agreement," the following statement:

"I agree, upon request, to submit to a physical examination by a doctor designated by the employer at times specified by the employer, and further agree that failure to pass such physical examination will be grounds for terminating my employment."

Following an interview with the personnel manager of the store, Mary Hartzke was employed by Macy's on August 19, 1969, in the nonselling classification of "merchandise marker." Ms. Hartzke was assigned to work in Macy's warehouse. Her duties involved affixing price tags to garments and other merchandise. She was not required to lift or move the items she tagged. Her work did not require any heavy physical or mental effort or stress. Ms. Hartzke worked only on an intermittent "on call" basis, and she had only worked a total of 62 working days by July 20, 1970. She was never laid off during this period for reasons of health. Her supervisor had reported that her work performance was acceptable and her conduct was exemplary.

Nevertheless, since the company probationary period for new employees was 65 working days (as stipulated in the agreement with

---

[1] All names have been disguised.

the union),[2] the company asked Ms. Hartzke to submit to a physical examination to be administered by the company physician. The examination took place on July 20, 1970, and the company physician prepared a written "Macy's Medical Department Examination of Applicant" report (dated July 20, 1970) which showed as normal:

temperature 98.2, pulse 70, vision R.20/30 L20/30, near test 13.13. color sense, hearing R70/70, development, personal hygiene, eyes, pupils react, ears, teeth, perforated septum, tonsils, thyroid, skin, bones, and joints, feet, varicose veins, hernia, reflexes, genitals, heart, lungs, abdomen, emotional stability, scars, deformities, etc., urinalysis and other tests Abil. O Sugar O Sedt. O.

The report, however, included the following additional entries:

B.P. 190/140[3]
Remarks: Hypertension
Rating: Accept   Restrict (how)
                        Reject (X)

Upon receipt of this medical report, the personnel manager called Ms. Hartzke to inform her that she was being terminated immediately because of her condition of hypertension. Ms. Hartzke protested, and she said to the personnel manager, "My blood has never been that high." She furnished the personnel manager with the name of her personal physician and requested that he be consulted. The personnel manager declined her request and proceeded to discharge her.

The union immediately filed a grievance on behalf of Ms. Hartzke and sought her reinstatement with full back pay and restoration of all rights and benefits unimpaired. The grievance eventually went to arbitration. Both the company and the union agreed that the issue was as follows: Was Mary Hartzke discharged for just cause? If not, what should the remedy be?

POSITION OF THE COMPANY

The company argued that the application form filled out by Mary Hartzke had been in use for approximately 15 years. It was clear and unambiguous in its wording. The form asked direct questions concerning the state of health and physical defects of applicants. Ms. Hartzke never indicated that she did not understand the language of

---

[2] See Appendix for relevant provisions of the agreement.
[3] Blood pressure.

the form. Her responses to the questions were untruthful and incorrect. Ms. Hartzke actually had had a long history of hypertension. She was obligated to report this on the application form. If she had reported her illness, the company initially would have rejected her application for employment, or would have at least required a physical examination prior to employment. By virtue of the fact that Ms. Hartzke tried to deceive the company concerning her physical condition, she deserved to be discharged. This was particularly true since Ms. Hartzke still was only a probationary employee at the time of the examination which revealed her true physical condition.

The company further pointed out that the union was aware of the physical examination procedure employed by the company and had consented to and ratified the procedure through long acceptance and practice.

Finally, the company contended that the medical testimony in this case was contradictory, and therefore the opinion of the company physician should be accepted. It was in Ms. Hartzke's own best interest as well as the company's that she not be permitted to continue working in her unsatisfactory physical condition. The grievance should be denied.

POSITION OF THE UNION

The union first of all denied that its failure to challenge the administration of a physical examination in the past constituted approval or ratification of the company's policy.

However, the union primarily argued that the company placed undue reliance upon its own medical report in terminating Mary Hartzke. The company failed to take into consideration such matters as the physical and mental demands of the job, other medical opinion, and the work record of the individual.

The union offered in evidence two letters written to the union by Ms. Hartzke's personal physician. On July 30, 1970, Ms. Hartzke's physician wrote a letter which stated in part:

Mary Hartzke has been under my care since 1953. She has been treated for moderate hypertension with good results. There have been times when her b/p has been more elevated than others, but never to what we have considered a dangerous level.

Her most recent readings have been quite satisfactory, and there has been no evidence of any significant cardiorespiratory disease. I feel that Ms. Hartzke is in no way incapacitated and should have no difficulty in working in a normal manner.

Just prior to the arbitration hearing, the physician wrote the union again on April 28, 1971, as follows:

I reported to Mr. Kelley of the Retail Clerks Union on July 30, 1970 about Ms. Hartzke in which I stated that she had been treated for moderate hypertension with excellent results. I have been seeing her at routine intervals since then, and she has remained in good health. Her blood pressure has remained moderately elevated but of no great significance. She is taking small doses of anti-hypertension drugs.

At no time have I found it necessary to in any way restrict her activities.

The union claimed that Ms. Hartzke's physician was in a better position to evaluate her true physical condition for work. The union claimed that the discharge action therefore was unjustified, and the union urged that the arbitrator reinstate Mary Hartzke with full back pay and with full restoration of full benefits.

APPENDIX

Relevant sections of the collective agreement are as follows:

Section 8. Probationary Period (to May 31, 1972). Any person hereafter entering employment of the employer shall be required to serve a probationary period of 65 working days and his employment may be terminated by the employer (except for union membership or activity) within the probationary period. Except for employees who have been employed for 45 working days or less, the right to appeal from such termination of employment, as provided by Section 36 (Processing of Complaints and Disputes) hereof, shall not be impaired by this subdivision.

Section 26. Fidelity Bond Premiums and Physical Examinations. A. The employer shall pay all premiums for fidelity bonds required by the employer and shall pay for all charges for physical examination required by the employer.

B. The employer shall compensate the employee at his straight time rate for time spent undergoing any physical examination required by the employer.[4]

Section 19. Discharge of Employees. A. The employer shall have the right to discharge any employee for just cause. Any employee feeling he has been unjustly discharged shall have the right to appeal such discharge . . . .

QUESTIONS

1. Was employee Mary Hartzke discharged for just cause, that is, for giving responses to questions on the application form that "were untruthful and incorrect"? Discuss.

---

[4] Note: Ms. Hartzke underwent the physical examination required by the company on July 20, 1970 and she was paid for that day, officially her 62nd working day.

2. Evaluate the company argument that since medical testimony in the case was contradictory, that the opinion of the company physician should be accepted.
3. Evaluate the union argument that the company was placing undue reliance upon the medical report concerning Ms. Hartzke, and that the company had not taken into consideration various job factors, other medical opinion, and the employee's own statement.
4. Was the fact that Mary Hartzke was depending on medication to control her hypertension a justification for termination of her employment under provisions of the agreement? Discuss.

48. SICK LEAVE PAY DURING A STRIKE

COMPANY: *Reliance Universal, Inc., Louisville Plant, Louis-ville, Kentucky*

UNION: *Local 604, International Chemical Workers Union*

BACKGROUND

Employees Art Wilson and Marvin Hill[1] were quite ill with the flu and other related ailments, and they were unable to report to work on Thursday, December 4, 1969. On this same day, another union in the plant, the Teamsters, went out on a legal strike at the end of its contract period and set up a picket line around the plant.

Both Wilson and Hill medically were able to return to work on Monday, December 15, but because of the Teamsters' strike and picket line, they refused to do so. Both employees did not return to work until December 26, 1969, the date which coincided with the termination of the Teamsters' strike.

Upon return to work, Wilson and Hill turned in a claim for sick pay and insurance reimbursement for the seven working days of their illness, during the period December 4-15, as provided in Article XXIV[2] of the agreement.

The company rejected the claims of Wilson and Hill on grounds that because of the Teamsters' picket line and their reluctance to cross it, they would not have reported to work anyway on the days involved in their claim. The company's insurance carrier, Connecticut General, explained the rejection thus:

Our Cincinnati Claim Office has had an opportunity to review the disability claims of employees Wilson and Hill.

The Active Service requirement in your contract with Connecticut General precludes any consideration of this claim and future claims, if any, during the work stoppage at your plant. In other words, the employees who have chosen to refuse to cross the picket line are not considered as active employees performing the customary duties of their employment.

---

[1] All names disguised.
[2] See Appendix for applicable contract provisions.

301

The union filed a grievance on behalf of Wilson and Hill which eventually went to arbitration.

POSITION OF THE UNION

The union contended that Wilson and Hill met every single requirement of paragraph 24.7 of the agreement in that they were "regular employees" and had the requisite "earned credits" for the benefits. They were also on a "regularly scheduled work day," had "no duplication of earnings," and had supplied the requisite medical report of their illnesses. Both were, by stipulation, so ill that they could not have reported to work under any circumstances; each had carefully telephoned the plant on each of the seven claimed days to report their illness. Therefore, asserted the union, the only conceivable reason why their claims were being denied was because subsequent to their illnesses they refused to cross a picket line as was their right under the agreement, Article V.

The union urged that Wilson and Hill should be reimbursed for the appropriate amounts, which were rightfully theirs under the sick pay and sick insurance provisions of the agreement.

POSITION OF THE COMPANY

The company contended that the real reason that Wilson and Hill were absent was their refusal to cross the Teamsters' picket line. This was self-evident since they did not return to work following their illnesses. The purpose of disability and sickness insurance, said the company, was to replace lost income. Since it is plain that the grievants would not have worked anyway, the company claimed that they could not be reimbursed regardless of how ill they may have been (and the company did not dispute the fact of their illnesses). The company pointed out that its insurance carrier, Connecticut General, stated in its letter of December 24, 1970, that the grievants did not meet the "active service" requirement if they refused to cross the picket line, and therefore they could not be considered active employees performing the customary duties of their employment. In this context, the company pointed out that during the strike, the company had maintained its usual schedules including those of the grievants, and it sought in every way possible to encourage employees to report for duty.

In summary, the company claimed that regardless of whether or not they were ill, Wilson and Hill would not have worked during the period of December 4-15 because of the Teamsters' strike and picket line. Under these circumstances, reimbursement under the sick pay and insurance provisions was inappropriate. The grievance should be denied.

APPENDIX

Pertinent Contract Provisions

Article V–Strikes and Lockouts

Section 5.2. Picket Line. This Article shall in no way restrict the individual's right to cross or refuse to cross a legal picket line at premises, authorized by the recognized collective bargaining representative of employees at such premises in its capacity as such bargaining agent, nor shall refusal to cross such a picket line be cause for discharge or disciplinary action.

Article XXIV–Miscellaneous

Section 24.7. Sick Pay. (1) Regular employees shall accrue paid sick leave, not to exceed five (5) days of paid sick leave per calendar year, at the rate of one (1) day of paid sick leave upon completion of each (2) months of active full time employment during such calendar year.

(2) Sick pay benefits accruing during any calendar year shall become available as of January 1 of the succeeding calendar year, must be used within such succeeding calendar year, and will not accumulate from year to year. For absence because of illness on days when the employee would otherwise have been regularly scheduled to work, sick pay will be paid beginning with the first (1st) full day of such absence and may continue until accrued sick pay available to the employee has been exhausted. Sick pay for any such full day's absence shall be equal to eight (8) hours straight time pay at the employee's regular base rate, excluding shift differential or other premium.

Section 24.9. Insurance. During the term of this Agreement (provided such coverages continue to be available): . . .

Memorandum for Agreement

It is understood that the Sickness and Accident Insurance provided for in Section 24.9 will be payable first day of injury, third day of sickness, for a maximum of fifty-two (52) weeks, and the weekly benefit will be seventy percent (70%) of the employee's forty (40) hours straight time base rate, not to exceed Sixty-Five Dollars ($65.00).

QUESTIONS

1. Aside from the money involved, why would the company and its insurance carrier be reluctant to pay the medical benefits to employees Wilson and Hill in this case?

2. Discuss the argument of the company and its insurance carrier that the grievants "did not meet the active service requirement if they refused to cross the picket line, and therefore they could not be considered active employees performing the customary duties of their employment."
3. Why does the arbitrator's decision in this case hinge upon the question of whether the absences of the grievants were primarily a result of their sicknesses, or of the picket line placed around the plant? Discuss.

49. CAUGHT WITH POT

COMPANY: Vulcan Materials Company, Geismar, La.

UNION: Oil, Chemical and Atomic Workers International Union, Local 4-620

BACKGROUND

In November, 1968, the Vulcan Materials Company opened a new plant in Geismar, Louisiana. This was the newest plant in a group of eight chemical plants located in Geismar. The plant produces a group of chlorinated hydrocarbons. The continuous process involves the manufacture of several potentially hazardous chemicals; production employees work rotating shifts to provide continuous staffing. The plant is highly automated; at the time of this case, it was operated by 45 production workers, who were members of Local 4-620, plus a small managerial and technical staff. Most of the employees live in four small surrounding communities.

On May 12, 1969, the Company hired Robert Mead,[1] 22 years old, as a process technician. However, an incident concerning the possession of marijuana caused the company to discharge him on November 13, 1970 as an "undesirable employee." Mr. Mead and the union filed a grievance protesting that there was no just cause for dismissing him. They asked that Mead be reinstated with full seniority rights, and that he be reimbursed with full back pay, and all benefits, including overtime, shift differentials, and holiday pay. The grievance was eventually submitted to arbitration.

The incident leading to Mead's discharge occurred, in early October, 1970, when approximately 30 persons were arrested in Ascension Parish, Louisiana, for possession of marijuana. One of those arrested, a friend of Robert Mead's, agreed to cooperate with the authorities in determining the source of the marijuana.

On October 9, 1970, Robert Mead, in order to help his friend, voluntarily surrendered to Sheriff Pierre Boisseau and admitted that

---

[1] Names disguised.

he was the one who had supplied the marijuana. The authorities possessed no evidence indicating that Mead had supplied the marijuana; nevertheless, Mead admitted his involvement. He stated, however, that he was not a "pusher" and that he was not in the business of peddling marijuana, or any other drug. Mead was arrested following his admission to Louisiana state authorities that "he had supplied marijuana to 38 persons in Ascension Parish, Louisiana." After his release, and prior to court trial, Mead returned to his job and reported his arrest to his foreman.

On Monday morning, November 9, 1970, Mead requested a two-day leave of absence from his shift supervisor, Matt Jacobson. Mead stated that it was necessary for him to appear in court the following day. Later, at approximately 10 a.m., Mead was summoned to a meeting with three supervisors, including Superintendent Jack Horton. In this meeting, Mead informed the three supervisors that he was planning to plead guilty to the charge of possession of marijuana, and that the state authorities were going to fine him $500 as well as place him on supervised probation for two years. Superintendent Horton informed Mead that if anything like this happened again, he would be dismissed or severely disciplined by the company. Superintendent Horton then asked Mead to sign a written statement confirming Mead's understanding of the company's action. Mead requested permission to consult his union steward, Harold Wellborn, who advised him not to sign such a statement. Mead signed anyway and was then granted his two-day leave of absence. Neither the union nor Mead received a copy of this signed statement.

On Friday, November 13, 1970, four days after the meeting, the company telephoned Mead at his home to summon him and union steward, Harold Wellborn, to a meeting in the office of the Plant Manager, Henry Billings. Among those present at the meeting was Director for Administration, Paul Drummond. At this meeting, Mr. Billings asked Mead what had transpired in his appearance at court on November 10. Mead stated that he had pleaded guilty to the charge; that he was fined $500, which he had to earn himself; and that he was placed on supervised probation for two years. In addition, Mead and Mr. Wellborn informed Mr. Billings of the events on November 9 concerning his meeting with the three supervisors. The company officials requested that Mead and Wellborn leave the meeting while they discussed the matter among themselves. Mead and Wellborn were subsequently called back into the meeting. Mead was asked by the company to either resign or be discharged. Mead refused to resign, and therefore he was discharged on November 13, 1970 by the company as an "undesirable employee."

POSITION OF THE COMPANY

The company presented the following arguments and evidence in defense of discharging Robert Mead:

1. The company stated that it was essential for it to maintain close and harmonious relations with other companies of the area and with the people in the neighboring communities. Widespread publicity concerning Mead's conviction of possessing marijuana would prove detrimental to the image of the company as a good corporate citizen, if it did not discharge him.

2. The company had established high employment standards. It carefully screened applicants, including an investigation for possible conviction of serious crimes, before hiring in order to avoid hiring undesirables. The company expected that employees, as a condition of continued employment, would behave themselves both on and off the job. The conduct of employees should reflect favorably upon the company.

3. The company stated that it considered its relationships with its employees to be a very important part of its personnel management program. The continued employment of Mead would have a very adverse effect upon company-employee relations. Further, his continued employment would place him in a position to encourage other employees to use marijuana.

4. Process technicians are responsible for the operation of a very sophisticated and complex plant worth almost 30 million dollars. They must be alert and attentive to duty at all times in order to operate the plant safely and efficiently. Emergency situations occur frequently; marijuana slows reaction time and impairs judgment. The consequences could be serious to fellow employees if Mead, or some other employee, were under the influence of marijuana.

5. The company argued that its decision was not hasty, capricious, or arbitrary. It made a careful and extensive investigation following Mead's conviction and only then took formal action against him.

6. The company attested that any discipline short of discharge would have been inappropriate, for the possession of marijuana is such a serious offense that it flouts the principles of corrective discipline. In the interests of employee safety and welfare, and

community relations, the company could not tolerate off-the-job conduct of this nature on the part of any employee.

7. The statement which Mead signed on November 9 did not constitute a formal warning and had no bearing on any disciplinary action subsequently taken. It was intended only as a memorandum of consultation or counseling for Supervisor Jacobson's file, and it was never made a part of Mead's personnel record. The company pointed out that it did not pressure Mead to sign the statement, and that he did so in the presence of and over the objection of his union steward.

8. Finally, the company maintained that Mead admitted his guilt, and he was tried and convicted of an admittedly serious crime involving moral turpitude. It could not continue Mead's employment "without courting disaster."

POSITION OF THE UNION

The union presented eight arguments to support its position that Mead should be restored to his job with full back pay, restoration of all seniority rights and privileges, and compensation for all other benefits and monies lost as a result of the company's action:

1. The company did not show just cause for discharging Mead, since his behavior away from company premises affected neither his attendance nor his work performance. Article 16 of the agreement[2] specifically states that disciplinary action is to be used by the company for the sole "purpose of impressing the employee that it is necessary to correct some undesirable work related problem . . . ." The company offered no evidence that Mead's offense was in any way work-related or that any subsequent work-related problems resulted from his activity or conviction. The company agreed that Mead's work performance was satisfactory both before and after his arrest and conviction.

2. The company offered no evidence that the performance of any employee was in any way influenced by Mead's conduct, arrest or conviction. In fact, none of his associates at the plant knew of these activities until his arrest, at which time several of his associates, including his foreman, volunteered to serve as character witnesses.

3. Sheriff Boisseau, the arresting officer to whom Mead voluntarily surrendered, testified strongly in Mead's behalf to the effect that he was convinced that Mead was merely an experimenter and not a hard-core pusher or user.

---

[2] See Appendix for full text.

4. The sheriff also testified on a major legal change enacted by the Louisiana Legislature in 1970 to the effect that a first offense for possession of marijuana is no longer a felony with a mandatory minimum sentence of five years in prison. The new "Uniform Controlled Dangerous Substances Law" (Act 457 of 1970)[3] distinguishes marijuana from "narcotic drugs" and changes a first offense for possession of marijuana to a misdemeanor.

5. Section 977.1 of the 1970 Louisiana law cited above allows the court considerable latitude in handling cases such as this. The court may, as it did in the case of Mead and all others convicted with him, fine the offender and place him under supervised probation. In this case, Mead and all others over the age of 21 were fined $500 and placed on probation under terms which closely regulated their conduct.

6. The new law allows the court, as it did in Mead's case, to hold in abeyance a finding of guilt on a first offense and specifies that it be erased upon satisfactory completion of probation. The intent of the provision for the erasure, after a satisfactory probation, of any record of the offense is clearly to avoid branding a first offender as a convicted criminal, which the company had erroneously chosen to do.

7. The union pointed out that the company had no firm policy for dismissing all men convicted of misdemeanors, even for drunken driving or battery. In this context, the union quoted the testimony of Director for Administration, Paul Drummond. Drummond testified that it was not company policy to discharge employees automatically for any and all criminal convictions, and that a determination as to whether a conviction without a jail sentence would result in discharge would depend on the offense and surrounding circumstances. He also testified: (a) that if the company knew of off-premises possession of marijuana but that no court action resulted, it would "probably not" discharge the employee; (b) that the company would consider a conviction more serious if it remained on the record than if it were expunged after successful completion of a probationary period; (c) that he was not aware, at the time the company decided to discharge Mead, that the offense would be removed from the record after completion of the probationary period and payment of the fine.

8. Finally, the union claimed that the company violated the contractual requirement for progressive corrective discipline both in its discharge of Mead for this offense and in its placing him in double

---

[3] See Appendix for full text.

jeopardy by discharging him after having settled the issue through a written warning on November 9. The recollections of Mead and of steward Wellborn clearly established that this November 9 memorandum was really a written warning, in spite of the fact that the company did not provide the union with a copy as required by the agreement. The union alleged that the company had steadfastly refused to produce the written warning or to offer the testimony of any of the three supervisors who signed it. The union further contended that after Superintendent Horton had obtained all the facts on the nature of the court proceeding and the penalty which had been imposed, he informed Mead and steward Wellborn that this warning would be the extent of the disciplinary action. It was with this understanding that Mead signed it against the counsel of his steward.

APPENDIX

Relevant Articles and Laws

Article 5—Management

5.1 Except as explicitly limited by a specific provision of this agreement, the Company shall continue to have the exclusive right to take any action it deems appropriate to the management of its operations and direction of the work force in accordance with its judgment. All inherent and common-law management functions and rights which the Company has not expressly modified or restricted by a specific provision of this Agreement are retained and vested exclusively in the Company.

5.2 Examples of this right include, but are not limited to, responsibility and authority for the following . . . relieving employees from duty when necessary due to lack of work or other legitimate reasons; . . . and taking action required in promoting, transferring, suspending, demoting, granting leaves of absence, and disciplining employees, including but not limited to discharge for cause.

5.3 The Company's not exercising any function hereby reserved to it, or its exercising any such function in a particular way, shall not be deemed a waiver of its right to exercise such function or preclude the Company from exercising the same in some other way not in conflict with the express provisions of this Agreement.

Article 16—Discipline and Discharge

16.1 When it is necessary for the Company to take disciplinary action against any employee for the purpose of impressing the employee that it is necessary to correct some undesirable work related problem, the recognized principles of progressive corrective discipline will be followed. In the event discipline or discharge is necessary following an investigation and development of facts, and employee may elect to have his steward present at the time the action is taken. The employee involved and the Union will be furnished a copy of any record prepared relative to any disciplinary action taken against the employee.

16.2 The Company will not discharge or discipline an employee without just cause . . . .

16.3 When an employee is discharged for just cause, the Union will be advised as to the reasons for such discharge prior to the Company's taking such action. In the event a discharge is determined to be without just cause, the employee involved will be reinstated with full seniority.

Uniform Controlled Dangerous Substances Law Act 457 of 1970, State of Louisiana

Section 977.1—Conditional Discharge for Possession as First Offense. Whenever any person who has not previously been convicted of any offense under this subpart relating to the unlawful use, possession, production, manufacture, distribution or dispensation of any narcotic drugs, marijuana, or stimulant, depressant, or hallucinogenic drugs, pleads guilty to or is found guilty of possession of a controlled dangerous substance under Subsection 971 (c), the court may, without entering a judgment of guilt and with the consent of such person, defer further proceedings and place him on probation upon such reasonable terms and conditions as it may require. Upon violation of a term of any of such conditions, the court may enter an adjudication of guilt and reimpose upon such person the sentence of the court as originally imposed. Upon fulfillment of the terms and conditions, the court shall discharge such person and dismiss the proceedings against him. Discharge and dismissal under this Section shall be without court adjudication of guilt and shall not be deemed a conviction for purposes of disqualifications or disabilities imposed by law upon conviction of a crime including the additional penalties imposed for second or subsequent convictions under Section 978 of this Title. Discharge and dismissal under this Section may occur only once with respect to any person.

QUESTIONS

1. Evaluate each of the company arguments in support of its discharge action of Robert Mead.
2. Evaluate each of the union arguments in support of its position that Mead's discharge should be rescinded.
3. Was Robert Mead discharged for just cause as required under the provisions of the agreement? Why is this difficult to determine when the issue involves

conduct of an employee that occurred off the company premises and was not directly work related?

4. From a management standpoint, is it desirable for a company to develop policies for dealing with situations of this sort involving employee behavior off the job? Would it be desirable to negotiate clauses into the agreement to cover these types of situations? Discuss.

50. GUN OR BOTTLE?

COMPANY: *Corhart Refractories Company, Incorporated, Louisville, Kentucky*

UNION: *International Union of District 50, Allied & Technical Workers of United States and Canada, Local 14084*

INTRODUCTION

On June 3, 1970, the union filed the following grievance on behalf of Robert Billings[1], who had been discharged the previous day for violation of the company rule against bringing firearms on company premises on May 29, 1970.

Please be advised that this communication is to be considered as a grievance processed in behalf of, requested by, and with the consent and knowledge of the grievant, Billings, in accordance with the current labor agreement, Article 30, titled, "Suspension and Discharge Cases." Specific attention is directed to Section 3 of such Article, permitting and making necessary that all such grievances pertaining thereto are to commence at Step 3 of the grievance procedure.

GRIEVANCE: The discharge of Robert Billings by the Company on June 2, 1970, alleging 'Possession of firearms on company property' was and is unwarranted, unfair, unjust, unreasonable, biased and completely without justification.

SETTLEMENT REQUESTED: That the Grievant, Billings, be made whole by receiving all compensation due as a result of such discharge, restored to full seniority rights and any records of any employee contact relating to this discharge be removed from grievant's file.

Further, the Union requests a copy of the statement offered as evidence at the meeting of Company and Union on the subject case, any previous employee contacts, together with all information as pertains to any verbal warning issued heretofore against this grievant, same to contain dates, reasons, etc.

BACKGROUND

On May 29, 1970, Robert Billings worked as a machine operator

---

[1] All names have been disguised.

on the 3 to 11 p.m. shift. After the 5 p.m. break, Foreman Horace Buder noticed that Billings and another employee, Richard Rawlings, had overextended their break time about 15 or 20 minutes. As a result, foreman Buder called both men, along with their union steward, into the office and told them that the company would not tolerate such behavior. However, no formal disciplinary action was issued to either employee at that time.

At about 9:15 p.m. on the same shift, Foreman George Logan, while walking through the mold storage section, noticed that Billings and Rawlings had not yet returned fron their regular scheduled 9:00 p.m. break, whereupon he made a search in the departmental area and searched the lunch room. Logan found Billings at approximately 10:00 p.m. in the rear of the locker room; Logan instructed Billings to return to work. He later also found Rawlings in the rear corner of the locker room. Logan subsequently instructed both men to come to his office. He also telephoned the union steward, Jim O'Brien, asking him to attend the meeting; steward O'Brien arranged to be present. Billings was told to wait outside Logan's office while Logan talked with Rawlings and O'Brien. However, while Logan was talking with these men, Billings came into the office and interrupted the meeting. Since both Billings and Rawlings appeared to have been drinking, Logan decided to order both of them to leave the plant. At this point both employees started shouting profane language at Logan. Logan charged both Billings and Rawlings with insubordination and again ordered them to leave the plant. However, the two employees did not leave, and they told Logan that he and the plant guard together could not make them leave. Logan then called Foreman John Sheldon from the Furnace department to witness subsequent events. When Sheldon arrived, both Billings and Rawlings still refused to leave and challenged both of the foremen to come outside the plant and fight. Logan then called Lester Cotton, the plant guard, who was finally successful in persuading Billings and Rawlings to leave, and who then escorted the two employees out of plant.

Immediately after escorting the two men out of the plant, Cotton noticed that both men were standing on the sidewalk making threatening remarks concerning foreman Logan. Cotton heard Billings threaten that, "I would like to meet Logan in the parking lot and beat the hell out of him."

A few minutes later, Billings approached plant guard Cotton and requested permission to reenter plant property to obtain an item from his locker. Cotton gave Billings his permission to return to the locker room, which was located behind the guard shack, about eight to ten feet from the main gate. Cotton accompanied Billings to the locker room. He observed Billings remove something from his locker which he thought was a revolver, place it in his belt, and then pull his shirt over it.

As Billings left the plant premises at about 11 p.m., Cotton stopped him and told him that he had seen him "remove a gun from his locker." Cotton told Billings that he was required to make a report about this to the guard foreman, John Stennis. Cotton told Billings, "You are placing me in the middle by doing this." Billings told Cotton that he "didn't have to report it if he didn't want to." Cotton was a member of UAW Local 1336, which was the bargaining agent for the plant guards. He told Billings that he, too, was a loyal union member, and he was very reluctant to file a report on Billings as a fellow union member, although he was a member of a different union.

On June 2, 1970, with several of his own union representatives and Billings present at a meeting, the company discharged Billings. On June 3, 1970, the union filed a grievance with the company, on Billings' behalf. The grievance was eventually carried to arbitration.

POSITION OF THE UNION

The union contended that the company did not have just cause to discharge Robert Billings. Such a discharge was unwarranted, unfair, and unreasonable.

The union argued that the issue of the case rested upon who was telling the truth, the plant guard, Cotton, or the grievant, Billings. The union claimed that the following questions had to be answered in order for the arbitrator to determine who was telling the truth: (a) Did security guard Cotton tell the truth at the hearing? (b) Was he honestly mistaken in what he thought he saw? (c) Had his credibility been impugned?

The union contended that if the alleged gun incident had not occurred, Billings would only have been given a five-day suspension from work, the same penalty which the company gave Richard Rawlings, the other employee involved. Billings testified that he took a bottle of whiskey, not a gun, from his locker. According to Billings, Cotton mistakenly thought the bottle of whiskey was a gun.

The union pointed out that Cotton did not enter the locker room while Billings was there, and that he had only observed Billings from a small window in the locker room. There was no light in the locker room and visibility was poor.

The union contended that Cotton was reluctant to report to management that he thought he had seen Billings remove a gun from his locker. Testimony revealed that Cotton had first tried to meet with the president of Local 14084, Billings' union, to discuss the problem with him. The President, Peter Thompson, refused to see him, and Cotton became irritated, thinking that Thompson did not "want to become involved." Only then did Cotton report the incident to his supervisor. In the union's view, Cotton did so not because he was sure that Billings had removed a gun from his locker room, but rather because he felt slighted by the union president.

The union also argued that Cotton knew that Billings had carried a gun into the plant on previous occasions, but Cotton had neither commented nor reported it prior to this incident. However, in this situation Cotton was mistaken, as it was a whiskey bottle, not a gun, which Billings had in his locker. To support this argument, the union produced a letter dated October 16, 1970, from "Stan's Pawnshop." The letter stated that Robert Billings had pawned a .38 calibre revolver on February 29, 1970. The letter was signed by the owner Stanley Ross.

To whom it may concern:

On February 20, 1970 Mr. Robert Billings who lives at 7024 S. 16th pawned a nickel plated Rossi Revolver serial no. 994717. The gun showed up stolen from Pete McCoy. I held the gun in my possession at my store until the trial was over Sept. 16, 1970.

The union claimed that this clearly indicated that Billings' gun was in the possession of the pawnbroker at the time Billings was supposed to have had it in his possession at the plant.

Finally the union asserted that Billings' past good work record of several years had proven him to be a well-qualified worker, and that he should be given the benefit of the doubt in this case.

Consequently, the union requested that the arbitrator sustain the grievance.

POSITION OF THE COMPANY

The company maintained that it had just cause to discharge Robert Billings on June 2, 1970. The company contended that the issue in question rested solely upon whether or not Billings had brought a gun onto company premises. Although Billings had denied this charge, the company stated that plant security guard, Lester Cotton, saw Billings remove a gun from his locker and put it into his belt. According to Cotton's testimony, he had told Billings about seeing him take the gun from his locker. Cotton had said to Billings "You are placing me in the middle," and Billings had then replied to Cotton that he did not have to report it. Consequently, the company agreed with the union that this was essentially a question of who was to be believed, Cotton or Billings.

The company argued that by bringing a gun onto company property, Billings had violated Article 41, 4A (4) of the agreement, and Plant Rule No. 9,[2] which was clearly a dischargeable offense. The company stated that, before the arbitration hearing, Billings had not denied this charge against him and he had not indicated that he would deny the charge. Consequently, the company asserted that the arbitrator should not consider whatever evidence Billings submitted in the arbitration hearing.

The company called attention to the fact that Billings was obviously under the influence of alcohol when foreman Logan talked with him; this also violated Article 41, 4A (1), regarding drinking on company premises. A violation of this article was also a dischargeable offense. The company pointed out that Billings had consistently maintained that the drinking rule was the only rule he violated. The company noted that Billings was aware of both of these rules and the penalties associated with these rules. In this regard, the company noted that it had only recently in March of 1970 issued and posted a bulletin notice concerning Plant Rule 9 which was consistent with Article 41, 4A (4) of the collective agreement.

The company went on to state that it would be unreasonable to believe Billings' denial as opposed to the plant guard's testimony, because the plant guard had nothing to gain by lying whereas Billings' testimony was entirely self-serving. In fact, the company maintained that plant guard Cotton at first refused to tell his supervisor the name of the employee involved. Cotton's testimony revealed that he was something of a reluctant witness, because when Mr. Russell Stinson, Cotton's supervisor arrived at the plant, Cotton only told him that "one of the employees" had a gun. When Mr. Stinson asked Cotton for the name of the employee, Cotton at first refused to give it because he did not want to involve a fellow union

---

[2] See Appendix to case.

member, even a member of another union. Under duress, Cotton finally identified Billings as the employee involved.

Finally, the company reminded the arbitrator that he should not substitute his judgment for that of management when, as in this case, there was a clear violation of company rules. Consequently, the company requested the arbitrator to dismiss the grievance and uphold Billings' discharge.

APPENDIX

Pertinent Contract Provisions

Article 5—Management

1. The management of the work, the supervision, direction and control of the work force, the right to hire and the right to discharge or discipline for just cause are vested exclusively in the Company and the Union shall not abridge this right. Nothing in this agreement shall be construed to in any way, restrict the installation, use, or application of labor saving device or equipment.

. . . .

5. In no case shall the exercise of the above prerogatives of Management be in derogation of any of the terms and conditions of the collective bargaining agreement between the parties.

Article 30—Suspension and Discharge Cases

1. In the event an employee is discharged or suspended by the Company, such employee and the Union shall be given a written memorandum of the cause of his discharge or suspension, and if he believes he has been unjustly dealt with, such discharge or suspension may constitute a case arising under the method of adjusting grievances herein provided. In the event that the Union may prove that grounds for discharge or suspension are unfounded and that thereby injustice has been done, the Company shall reinstate such employee with back pay for the time lost based on the employee's day rate of pay at the time of discharge or suspension times forty (40) hours per scheduled week or eight (8) hours per day that the employee lost.

2. Any complaint arising under this Article must be appealed to the Company in writing within forty-eight (48) hours exclusive of Saturdays, Sundays, Holidays, and off days (including vacations or shut-down for repairs) after such discharge or suspension or the particular case will be considered closed.

3. If timely written appeal is taken, the matter may be processed as a grievance, commencing with Step 3 under the grievance procedure of the contract, within seven (7) days of receipt of the appeal following the discipline.

Article 41—Discipline

1. General—In a company where people work together as in a society where people live together, rules and regulations must be established and obeyed for

the benefit of the group. When rules are not complied with, it becomes necessary to take positive action to insure that such infractions will not be repeated. When lesser penalties fail to impress upon employees that certain actions cannot be tolerated, separation of employment may become necessary.

2. The Company shall have the right to make and after proper publication thereof, to enforce any reasonable factory rule. Should the Union consider any such rule unreasonable, it shall be a matter for joint consideration as a grievance by the representatives of the Union and those of the Company under this Agreement, commencing at Step 3 of grievance procedure.

3. Disciplinary Action—In most cases, when severe and/or willful infractions are not involved, the five step disciplinary procedure listed below will apply.

1st Offense—The employee will be warned that such action is contrary to company policy and advised that subsequent violations will result in further disciplinary action.

2nd Offense—The employee will be given a written warning that such action cannot be tolerated, and that another violation will result in suspension.

3rd Offense—Suspension for three (3) working days.

4th Offense—Suspension for five (5) working days with a warning that the next offense will result in discharge.

5th Offense—Discharge.

4. Handling Severe/Willful Rule Infractions.

A. Violations subjecting an employee to discharge.

(1) Drinking on company premises

(2) Fighting on company premises

(3) Willful destruction or theft of company property

(4) Bringing or carrying firearms or explosives on company premises.

B. Violations subjecting an employee to five (5) days suspension with second offense being discharge.

(1) Falsifying company records

(2) Insubordination—towards supervisor or Management Representatives

(3) Sleeping during working hours

(4) Willfully hindering or limiting production

(5) Reporting to work under influence of alcohol

(6) Gambling on company premises

(7) Possession of intoxicating liquors on company premises.

5. Time Lapses Between Infractions—If, after having been cited for a violation, an employee goes for a period of one year without subsequent violations, the disciplinary action to be invoked in the event of another violation will be the same as previously taken.

After a period of two (2) years, with no subsequent violations, the disciplinary record will be removed from the employee's file.

6. Comments—The procedure outlined above represents the basic policy in seeking to discourage the breaking of company rules and regulations. Deviations in this procedure may be necessary according to the circumstances of each case.

Penalties for offenses unlike in nature will not be pyramided. If an employee continually breaks company rules so as to indicate unreliability, discharge will result.

7. The Company shall furnish the Union a copy of all written contracts, suspensions and discharges as referred to in Section 3 of this Article. If more than a notation of verbal warning is necessary, the Union will receive a copy.

Relevant Plant Rules and Bulletins

General Plant Rules adopted June 18, 1965 and thereafter posted on the bulletin board read in part as follows:

The Company must of necessity enforce reasonable plant rules. Rules forbidding the following offenses are presently in force. Violations by any employee will result in disciplinary action.

. . . .

9. Bringing in, carrying, or possessing firearms on Company premises.

. . . .

Company bulletin on the subject of firearms under date of March 5, 1970, which was duly posted, read:

To: All Employees
Subject: Firearms
Attention is directed to General Plant Rule No. 9 in regard to Firearms. Firearms on company premises are strictly prohibited. This includes pistols, shotguns, rifles, or teargas guns.

No employee shall possess any type firearm on company premises on either his person, in his locker, or hidden anywhere on plant property.

No employee shall engage in the sale, transfer, or delivery of any type firearm on these premises.

It is a criminal offense in the State of Kentucky to carry concealed weapons and the punishment is from one to five years confinement in the penitentiary.

Any violations of the above Firearm Regulation will result in discharge.

Company notice to all employees dated February 27, 1970 regarding enforcement of General Plant Rule No. 9 reads as follows:

NOTICE

To: All Employees
Bringing in, carrying, or possessing firearms on Company premises is strictly prohibited (General Plant Rule No. 9).

Attention is directed to this rule in view of recent reported incidents. All employees are cautioned that anyone found in violation of the Firearms Rule will be subject *to severe disciplinary action to the extent of discharge.*

QUESTIONS

1. Why is it difficult to ascertain the truth of what happened in this case given the circumstances involved?
2. If, as both the company and union contend, a major issue of the case depends upon who was telling the truth, how can the arbitrator utilize circumstances and facts presented in the case to judge the credibility of statements by plant guard Cotton and the grievant Billings?
3. Evaluate the company's argument that the arbitrator should not substitute his judgment for that of management in a situation involving a clear violation of company rules.
4. Discuss the detailed list of infractions and penalties included under Article 41—Discipline in the contract. Is it desirable to spell out these types of infractions and penalties in this much detail in an agreement? Why, or why not?

51. A DRINK "TO CUT THE DUST"

COMPANY: *Packaging Corporation of America, St. Louis Container Plant*

UNION: *International Brotherhood of Pulp, Sulphite and Paper Mill Workers, Local 535*

BACKGROUND

Philip D. Blendon[1] had worked since 1958 at the Packaging Corporation of America as a ZA Auto-Taper operator.[2] On March 26, 1969, the company hired Miss Sally Rollins as a feeder. Both employees worked at the Saint Louis, Missouri, plant, which manufactures corrugated shipping containers.

On September 18, 1970, both Blendon and Miss Rollins were assigned to work on a band saw on the first shift. On this same day, Production Manager Jerry Dillings handed out paychecks in the plant. At 9:20 a.m., Dillings walked toward the band saw and noticed that it was not running. Since the morning break for the first shift ended at 9:10 a.m., Dillings knew that the band saw should have been operating. As he approached the band saw, he noticed that there were three loads of material pushed around the machine. Dillings looked around the three loads and noticed that Blendon and Miss Rollins were kneeling down. He observed that Blendon took a drink from a whiskey bottle, then handed it over to Miss Rollins who put the cap back on and placed the bottle of whiskey in her purse. At this time, Dillings approached them and said: "Come on. Let's go to the office." All three went to the office where Frank Harder, the plant manager, and Donald Crowell, the chief union steward, joined them. Blendon and Rollins admitted to what Dillings had observed. They were immediately discharged by the company for violating Rule 2 of the company's Rules of Conduct.

Both Rollins and Blendon filed grievances which protested their discharge. The company denied these grievances, and the case eventually was submitted to arbitration.

---

[1] All names have been disguised.

[2] The ZA Auto-Taper applies a paper or fabric tape to the side seam of corrugated paper cartons.

POSITION OF THE COMPANY

The company maintained that Philip Blendon and Sally Rollins, by bringing and drinking alcoholic beverages in the plant, had violated long-established work rules placed in effect for the safety and convenience of all employees.[3] The company pointed out that eleven months before the discharge of Blendon and Rollins, two other employees, Sam Gieger and Ed Kirk, had been discharged for similar offenses concerning the possession and drinking of alcoholic beverages. The company stated that on October 7, 1969, Production Manager Dillings had found almost a full can of beer belonging to Gieger, and the company promptly discharged him. Also, on July 31, 1970, the company discharged employee Ed Kirk, because Dillings had observed that Kirk was in no condition to continue working after the company physician had confirmed that Kirk had been drinking alcoholic beverages. The company stressed that neither the two employees nor the union had filed a grievance concerning these two incidents.

Moreover, the company pointed out that on February 9, 1970, Dillings held a meeting with all employees to discuss this problem of drinking alcoholic beverages in the plant; Dillings had warned the employees that the company would take action if this drinking continued. The company pointed out that both Blendon and Rollins were at the meeting.

The company further maintained that it had been trying seriously to reduce accidents in the plant as well as to improve the plant safety record. Company efforts in this direction would be in vain if employees continued to bring intoxicating liquor into the plant.

Finally, the company emphasized that both Blendon and Rollins should have been working instead of drinking at the time they were caught, since the company's morning break period lasted only until 9:10 a.m.

For all of these reasons, the company concluded that Blendon and Rollins were properly discharged for cause. The company requested that the grievances be denied.

POSITION OF THE UNION

The union recognized that Philip Blendon and Sally Rollins violated Rule 2 and that they sould be penalized. However, the penalty of discharge was too severe.

---

[3] See Appendix to this case.

The union asserted that Blendon was a good worker, and that his work attendance had been good. Before this incident occurred, Blendon had been reprimanded previously on only one occasion by the company and that was for taking excessive smoking breaks. This reprimand was meted out by a plant foreman, and it subsequently was rescinded and removed from Blendon's file in the course of the grievance procedure. The union pointed out that Plant Manager Frank Harder did not remember Blendon ever having been disciplined during the five years he had been plant manager. Production Manager Dillings had admitted that, prior to this incident, he had found no cause whatsoever to discipline Blendon. Further, the union submitted that the company should have taken into account the fact that Blendon had taken only one drink, and that he had never done anything of this nature during his 12 years with the company.

Blendon argued that certain other extenuating circumstances should have been considered by the company. On the day of the incident in question, the ventilation around the band saw was very poor, and he had gone twice to the water fountain to obtain a drink of water. When he returned from the water fountain the second time, he made a remark to Sally Rollins about the dust; specifically he told her that he would like to have something stronger than water "to cut the dust." Miss Rollins then replied that, just by chance, she had some whiskey in her purse. Miss Rollins offered it to him, and he then took a single drink.

Blendon added that he was not intoxicated. His mental and physical faculties were not impaired, nor was his judgment affected by only one drink.

The union pointed out that Blendon had had an excellent work record during his 12 years of employment, and that his behavior, other than for this offense, had been outstanding.

Concerning Miss Rollins, the union pointed out that she never had been disciplined previously by the company; to discharge her for a first offense would be too severe a penalty. The union conceded that Miss Rollins was wrong in offering Blendon a drink of whiskey and the union did not object to a penalty for her. But the union argued that something less than discharge was justified.

Miss Rollins testified that certain mitigating circumstances were relevant to her case. She testified that, on the night preceding her discharge, she was at a party. She took several friends home in her automobile. When they got out of her car, they left a small bottle containing about two inches of whiskey in the car. She noticed the bottle when she arrived home and placed it in her purse, since she did not want to leave it in the car. She stated that she was in a hurry the next morning (the day of her discharge) and forgot about the bottle until she took a kleenex tissue from her purse shortly after 9:00 a.m. She testified that when Blendon said he could use a drink (or words to that effect)—that only then did she offer him the bottle. The union claimed that Miss Rollins brought the bottle into the plant without any intent to violate Rule 2, and that her violation of the rule occurred when she offered Blendon a drink.

The union argued that the case differed in several respects from that of former employees Gieger and Kirk, both of whom had been discharged. Gieger had knowingly brought a can of beer into the plant, whereas Rollins unknowingly brought the bottle of whiskey on company property. Kirk was under the influence of alcohol at the time he was discharged, whereas Blendon had only a single drink and had full possession of all his faculties. Finally, neither Gieger nor Kirk had come to their union steward seeking to file a grievance. The fact that both Gieger and Kirk decided, for reasons known only to them, not to file a grievance should not influence the arbitrator's decision in this instance.

Both Blendon and Rollins admitted to their offense and stated that they regretted their behavior. They were asking to be given another chance. The union requested that the discharge actions of the company be rescinded, and that Blendon and Rollins be returned to their jobs.

APPENDIX

Pertinent Provisions of the Agreement

Article I—Management Rights

It is recognized and agreed that the management and operation of the plant and the direction of the work forces are the sole and exclusive rights of the Company and that in the fulfillment and accomplishment of these functions, the Company has and retains all of the rights, powers, and authorities it would have in the absence of this agreement; provided, however, that nothing herein shall supersede any other provisions of this Agreement. The subjects and matters contained in the various articles of this Agreement shall be subject to the grievance and arbitration procedure.

Pertinent Provisions of the Plant Rules and Safety Instructions

Rules of Conduct

The following list of offenses, practices and actions may subject an employee to disciplinary action including immediate suspension or final dismissal without notice: . . .

2. Introducing, possessing or using on the property of the Company intoxicating liquors . . . or reporting for duty under the influence of such liquors . . .

QUESTIONS

1. Did the company have the right under the agreement to discharge the two employees for taking a drink on company premises? Are there any limitations to the rights of management to enforce its rules in this situation?
2. Should the fact that employees Blendon and Rollins had relatively long and good employment records influence the arbitrator in his decision? Why, or why not?
3. Evaluate the testimony of Miss Rollins concerning the mitigating circumstances which contributed to her bringing the whiskey on plant premises.
4. What are the precedent implications involved in a case of this sort, particularly in reference to enforcement of plant rules and safety considerations?

52. SEX DISCRIMINATION IN THE FOOD PROCESSING PLANT

COMPANY: Canton Provision Company, Canton, Ohio
UNION: Meatcutters Local 17

BACKGROUND

At the time of this case, the Canton Provision Company, located in Ohio, employed approximately 200 persons in 8 departments. The company handles and processes a wide variety of food products, including bologna, sausage and other specialty meats.

On January 20, 1969, Helen Golden,[1] employed as a laborer, filed the following grievance:

According to Paragraph 13, page 7 of the contract, I am not getting the right to exercise my plant-wide seniority.
Settlement Requested: Equal right to exercise my plant-wide seniority.

Both the company and the union agreed, however, that this grievance was part of a larger issue which they stated to be:

Has the Company violated the contract by its practice of laying off the grievant (senior women) while retaining junior men on the job?

The company had, on numerous occasions, placed long-service female employees on layoff while continuing to work shorter service male employees. This practice had caused considerable grumbling and bitterness among the female employees. The women complained that they lost wages, and that they sometimes lost all or part of their vacations because they could not work a sufficient number of hours and days to qualify for a longer vacation period.

Helen Golden was classified as a laborer, as were all the other female workers with an interest in this grievance. Laborers perform a wide variety of tasks. An employee may perform the same work during an entire shift, or she may be assigned several different tasks during the shift.

The grievance was carried to arbitration.

---
[1] Name disguised.

POSITION OF THE UNION

The union contended that women in the plant had performed very heavy work in the past and had lifted weights in excess of 25 pounds. They had performed all of the jobs at one time or another as assigned, and they were qualified to perform all tasks.

The union posed the situation to be as follows:

In the event of a departmental production slowdown, the company instead of laying off the employees from that department, will lay off female employees from various other departments, and then slot more senior employees from the primary department into the then vacant positions in the various departments.

The union argued that the labor agreement was clear in stating that seniority governed layoffs and recalls. Furthermore, the rights of the women were protected by federal legislation which provides that there shall be no discrimination because of sex.

Helen Golden asserted that she could perform the various jobs in the plant. While the full spectrum of the work performed in the plant was not reviewed by the parties, she stated that she could do and had done the jobs of "Bologna packing, washing pans, sanitation, and Cry-O-Vac."[2] Yet junior men had been assigned to perform these tasks, while she and other qualified senior women were laid off. In addition, junior men frequently were recalled to work before senior women; this, too, was a violation of the provisions of the contract.

Helen Golden indicated that she was willing to lift heavy weights, and she even testified that, "I would lift 100 pounds to hold my job."

The union took exception to a company assertion that "females must be laid off because the company may have work that only a man could perform." The union argued that the company had the right to move the laborers temporarily from job to job to avoid layoffs, but that the company must respect seniority. Thus, if the future possibility of having to perform certain work were a valid reason for layoff, then no women could ever work at the plant, for this possibility always existed.

The union agreed that job content had changed somewhat recently, but argued that the work was still "closely similar" and that the changes had not made the work inappropriate for women. The union pointed out that junior men recently performed 15 hours of bologna packing, a job that had been done on former occasions by

---

[2] A process for vacuum packing bologna, wieners and other sausages.

women in a satisfactory manner. The union further argued that it was an insufficient excuse that the company had elected to have only male employees do further heavy work on the pretext that the work was unsuitable for females.

The union agreed that the company might encounter some scheduling problems, but contended that the hardship did not justify ignoring Helen Golden's seniority rights.

POSITION OF THE COMPANY

The company relied upon an Ohio law, Revised Code Section 4107.43, to support its action. This law prohibits women from "frequent or repeated lifting of weights over twenty-five pounds." The company stated that it had been allowing women to perform all the work permitted by this law; yet under paragraph 10 of the collective agreement, the company was not required to take any actions which would be in violation of this state law.

Women had packed bologna until two years ago. They were taken off this work because a new segment of the job required lifting heavy weights. However, the company did admit that women had lifted weights greater than 25 pounds in the past, and that they probably would continue to do so, but only from time to time.

The company responded to the union's contention that junior men performed bologna packing which should have been performed by senior women by pointing out that the jobs now required heavy lifting. For example, male workers in the Sausage department moved 480-pound "trees," pushed 1,500-pound trucks, lifted 75-pound boxes, and lifted 100-pound racks.

The company argued that the real problem was the nature of the work. A great deal of flexibility must exist. That is, an employee may only perform one job on a shift, or may perform one job for a short time and then move on to another. Sometimes there was weight lifting and sometimes there was not.

In conclusion, the company argued that it was not required to create:

... easier portions of existing jobs in order to accommodate women whose jobs otherwise would be in contravention of state law. To do so, of course, would be discriminatory to the rights of men who perform the entire job in all of its aspects.

The grievance should be denied.

APPENDIX

Contract Provisions

Par. 10. Non-violation of Laws.   Nothing contained in this agreement shall require the Employer or the Union to take any action which shall be in violation of any law of the United States or the State of Ohio, or of any order or regulation issued pursuant to such law.

Par. 12. Non-discrimination.   Employment shall not be denied, in classifications covered by this contract, to any individual by reasons of race, creed, sex, color, national origin or ancestry.

Par. 13. (a) Seniority rights shall prevail in reduction, restoration and increases of forces; when two or more employees are hired on the same day, seniority shall commence from the time of hiring.

Par. 15. (a) In the event of a reduction of the workforce within a particular department, the employees having the least seniority within that department will be required to exercise their plant-wide seniority in order to avoid a lay-off but shall not have the right to select the jobs to which they were transferred.

Par. 26. (f) Where women supplant men or are otherwise accomplishing the same work with equal efficiency, they shall receive equal compensation. Female employees shall not be required to handle heavy products or equipment.

Equal Employment Opportunity: Sex Discrimination

Following is the text of the Equal Employment Opportunity Commission's guidelines on discrimination based on sex, issued November 24, 1965, and last amended on August 19, 1969:

1604.1 Sex as a bona fide occupational qualification.   (a) The Commission believes that the bona fide occupational qualifications exception as to sex should be interpreted narrowly. Labels—"Men's jobs" and "Women's jobs"—tend to deny employment opportunities unnecessarily to one sex or the other.

(1) The Commission will find that the following situations do not warrant the application of the bona fide occupational qualification exception:

(i) The refusal to hire a woman because of her sex, based on assumptions of the comparative employment characteristics of women in general. For example, the assumption that the turnover rate among women is higher than among men.

(ii) The refusal to hire an individual based on sterotyped characterizations of the sexes. Such sterotypes include, for example, that men are less capable of assembling intricate equipment; that women are less capable of aggressive salesmanship. The principle of non-discrimination requires that individuals be considered on the basis of individual capacities and not on the basis of any characteristics generally attributed to the group.

(iii) The refusal to hire an individual because of the preferences of coworker, the employer, clients or customers except as covered specifically in subparagraph (2) of this paragraph.

(iv) The fact that the employer may have to provide separate facilities for a person of the opposite sex will not justify discrimination under the bona fide occupational qualification exception unless the expense would be clearly unreasonable.

(2) Where it is necessary for the purpose of authenticity or genuineness, the Commission will consider sex to be a bona fide occupational qualification, e.g. an actor or actress.

(b) (1) Many States have enacted laws or promulgated administrative regulations with respect to the employment of females. Among these laws are those which prohibit or limit the employment of females, e.g., the employment of females in certain occupations, in jobs requiring the lifting or carrying of weights exceeding certain prescribed limits, during certain hours of the night, or for more than a specified number of hours per day or per week.

(2) The Commission believes that such State laws and regulations, although originally promulgated for the purpose of protecting females, have ceased to be relevant to our technology or to the expanding role of the female worker in our economy. The Commission has found that such laws and regulations do not take into account the capacities, preferences, and abilities of individual females and tend to discriminate rather than protect. Accordingly, the Commission has concluded that such laws and regulations conflict with Title VII of the Civil Rights Act of 1964 and will not be considered a defense to an otherwise established unlawful employment practice or as a basis for the application of the bona fide occupational exception.

1604.2 Separate lines of progression and seniority systems. (a) It is an unlawful employment practice to classify a job as "male" or to maintain separate lines of progression or separate seniority lists based on sex as a bona fide occupational qualification for that job. Accordingly, employment practices are unlawful which arbitrarily classify jobs so that:

(1) A female is prohibited from applying for a job labeled "male," or for a job in a "male" line of progression; and vice versa.

(2) A male scheduled for layoff is prohibited from displacing a less senior female on a "female" seniority list; and vice versa.

(b) A seniority system or line of progression which distinguishes between "light" and "heavy" jobs constitutes an unlawful employment practice if it operates as a disguised form of classification by sex, or creates unreasonable obstacles to the advancement by members of either sex into jobs which members of that sex would reasonably be expected to perform.

QUESTIONS

1. Should this case have been submitted under the grievance procedure mechanism, or should it have been filed directly with the Equal Employment

Opportunity Commission as a matter of sexual discrimination in violation of the law? Discuss.

2. Evaluate paragraphs 10, 12, 13, 15 and 26 of the agreement as included in the Appendix. Are these various provisions in conflict with each other and in possible conflict with the Civil Rights Act as amended?

3. Why does this type of situation pose a difficult dilemma for the union in its efforts to protect the rights of both male and female employees, both legally and under the agreement?

4. Evaluate the company's argument that it was not required to create special jobs for women which would be "discriminatory to the rights of men who perform the entire job in all of its aspects."

53. THE CONTROVERSIAL BUS DRIVER

COMPANY: Baltimore Transit Company

UNION: Amalgamated Transit Union, Division 1300

BACKGROUND

A news item in the Friday, November 5, 1965, newspapers in Baltimore, Maryland, revealed that Wally George,[1] an employee of the Baltimore Transit Company, was the Acting Grand Dragon of the recently activated Ku Klux Klan. George announced to the press that the Klan intended to institute a membership drive in Maryland and "let people know what the Klan stands for and give them an opportunity to join." A rally was held on Saturday, November 6, at the Rising Sun, a rural area of Maryland near Baltimore. The rally attracted 2,000 persons for what the newspapers described as "an evening of race baiting and cross burning by Ku Klux Klansmen." The press reported excerpts from the speech delivered by George at the rally: "We will not entice violence, but we won't walk away from it either . . . Forward the white race. Segregation forever!"

Wally George, age 36, had been employed by the Baltimore Transit Company for 13 years. The company is a public utility operating passenger buses in the city of Baltimore and adjacent areas in Baltimore county. At the time of the case, approximately 540 of the 1200 company bus operators were black. About 44 percent of the population of Baltimore were black and about 50 percent of the patrons of the bus line were also black.

As soon as Wally George had been publicly identified as a bus operator for the company and as Grand Dragon for the Klan, the company received numerous complaints and telephone calls. At about the time that his identity had been disclosed, Wally George went to the office of John Ray, Manager, Eastern Division of the company, where Wally George's connection with the Klan was discussed. Mr. Ray spoke to Wally George as follows: "The company

---

[1] All names disguised.

has no objections to anybody belonging to any organization as long as it doesn't affect their job or that they conduct the business of the organization on the company property."

George's statement concerning his plans to revive the Klan in the Baltimore area had stirred up considerable local interest. He was interviewed by television, radio and newspaper reporters, and the news media gave the event extensive coverage.

At first the company took no official position in regard to the matter, apparently hoping that the publicity storm would subside. However, the company immediately began to receive numerous telephone complaints which extended over the weekend and into the following week.

On Thursday, November 11, the company received a telegram from the NAACP, and later that day the secretary of that organization telephoned the office of the company's president to report that the NAACP had been receiving numerous protest calls. Numerous citizens were urging that an economic boycott among patrons of the company should be organized to protest Wally George's activities. The NAACP executive also confirmed the company's information that a wildcat strike among black bus operators appeared to be imminent. This information triggered action by the company. Management officials held a staff meeting during the afternoon of November 11. They decided to terminate the employment of Wally George. After the decision was made at the staff meeting, Mr. Ray and Jack E. Waring, Assistant Division Manager, were directed by company officers to remove Wally George from the bus he was operating. At about 4:40 p.m., on November 11, a substitute driver was placed on the bus, although Wally George was scheduled to finish his work shift at 5:18 p.m. that day. November 12, 1965 was supposed to be Wally George's last scheduled day before his vacation was to have commenced on November 14, 1965. Wally George was not suspended, as was customary, but was immediately discharged.

The union filed a grievance on behalf of Wally George. The grievance contended that the company's action was not justified and demanded that Wally George be reinstated. The grievance eventually was submitted to arbitration.

POSITION OF THE COMPANY

The company maintained that George was discharged for just cause. Although admitting that the manner of discharge without first suspending George was irregular, the company contended that the urgency of the situation justified the variance from normal procedure. The company stated that the discharge was based not on membership in any organization, but on Wally George's widely publicized activities in carrying out Klan objectives. As Acting Grand Dragon of the Klan, one of George's functions was to recruit new members, and he was required to make public speeches inciting racial and religious bigotry which spreads hatred in the community. The company regarded this conduct as highly inflammatory to the general public and in particular to the black community which constituted one-half of the patrons of the company's busline.

Bus operators do not work at a place where their activities can be constantly supervised by management personnel. A bus operator is in direct contact with the public during his entire working day, and he is obligated to maintain order on his bus. When the public learned that Wally George was pledged to support Klan objectives, suspicion was aroused which involved both black and white bus operators. The indignation of those who opposed Wally George's stated objectives could lead to incidents of violence. Even George had admitted that, after his official position of leadership in the Klan had been publicized, he had received several threats of bodily violence from various parties. Due to all of the circumstances involved, including the possibilities of a wildcat strike and an economic boycott of the company by its patrons, it was in the overall best interests of the company, its employees, and the community to terminate Wally George's services. The company requested that the discharge be upheld.

POSITION OF THE UNION

The union argued that George's discharge was not justified under the labor-management agreement. The union stated that, "Wally George's activities and beliefs, as obnoxious and abhorrent as they are to the great majority, are neither illegal nor are they job-connected. This case does not involve any misconduct on the part of the grievant. . . .All company witnesses concede that Wally George did his job in a satisfactory manner and that the discharge was not based upon job performance."

The union maintained that the principal issue in this case was whether or not a man should be discharged because he takes certain positions which are unpopular to a substantial segment of the population. The union admitted that the Klan was a very controversial and unpopular organization among large segments of the population. However, the union asserted that Wally George had a legal right to join the Klan and a right to take leadership in the Klan until some court decided that the organization was illegal. The union feared that anyone who belonged to an organization unpopular in the community might face discharge or other company discipline.

Further, the union argued that the manner of discharge violated the agreement, and that George was improperly deprived of his vacation in violation of the contract. The union requested that he be reinstated to his former position as bus operator with full back pay.

APPENDIX

Excerpts from Wally George's Testimony at the Arbitration Proceedings

Q: There is no question, is there, that you are a member of the Ku Klux Klan?
A: There is no question about that.
Q: And there is no question that you are the Grand Dragon of the Ku Klux Klan in Maryland?
A: At that time I was.
Q: Do you still hold that office?
A: No answer.
Q: Do you refuse to answer?
A: Right.

After Wally George admitted that he was a member and a leader of the Klan he was asked:

Q: What is the function of the Grand Dragon of the Klan in Maryland?
A: The Grand Dragons in any state, not only Maryland, are to have control of the membership.

When questioned with regard to violence by the Klan, Wally George was evasive at first but finally stated:

Q: Well, with your knowledge of the Klan or your contact with it, you don't deny that they have been involved in violence throughout the country do you?
A: From what I have seen in the paper, that is right.
Q: They have been involved?
A: I have seen it in the papers. That is true. I wouldn't deny it. That is right.

With regard to the question of racial intolerance, he testified:

Q: Would you deny that the Klan basicly—and I am talking about your Klan—that one of the basic tenets of your Klan is white supremacy?

A: That is right . . . .

Q: The point is that, insofar as your organization is concerned, white supremacy is one of the guiding principles of your Klan?

A: It has always been that. That is true.

Later, Wally George was asked: "Is the Klan still anti-Negro?" He replied, "Yes."

With regard to the Civil Rights Laws, as they existed at that time in the United States, Wally George was questioned and made the following response:

Q: Let's just assume that, whatever it is, a large percentage of the citizens of this State are Negro. Now, when you say that the Klan is basically anti-Negro, do you feel that this in any way conflicts with the opinions of the Supreme Court which has held in essence that everyone in the country is entitled to equal rights irrespective of their race? Do you believe that those two concepts are in conflict?

A: I didn't agree with the Supreme Court's decision . . . .

He was equivocal with regard to whether the Klan was anti-Semitic and testified as follows:

Q: Is the tenet of anti-Judaism part of the Klan's tenets?

A: Like I said a while ago, in one respect, yes; and in another one, no.

With regard to anti-Catholicism, he testified as follows:

Q: Is anti-Catholicism a part of your Klan?

A: Well, in one respect, yes; and, in another, no. I can't wholeheartedly say that it is 100 per cent.

Applicable Contract Provisions

Article (4)–Hire, Promote and Discharge

Section (2). The Association[2] further recognizes that the power of discipline is vested exclusively in the Company. The Company agrees that discharge will be for just cause. Where disciplinary action is contemplated, the following procedure shall be adhered to:

(a) In the event disciplinary action is to be taken against an employee, which may result in suspension or discharge, final action will be withheld until such time as the Association office has been notified in writing and given an opportunity to determine whether or not it desires that a hearing be held for such employee.

(b) It shall be incumbent upon the Company to serve this written notice to the Association office within one (1) day (except Saturdays, Sundays and

---

[2] Amalgamated Transit Union, Division 1300.

Holidays) after the employee has been interviewed on the infraction which causes the need for contemplated discipline.

(c) If the incident is one of a more serious nature which may result in the discharge of the employee, the employee may be withheld from active service pending a hearing and final action, payment or non-payment for the lost time to be part of the final determination.

Section (3). The Association covenants that its members shall render faithful service in their respective positions and shall cooperate with the management in the effective operation of the business; foster friendly relations between the Company and the general public; that they shall be courteous to passengers and to others with whom they come in official contact; that they shall at all times seek to protect the property of the Company from injury at their own hands or at the hands of others . . . .

Applicable Statutory Law

The Company had a duty under Article 78, Section 26, of the Code of Maryland not to:

. . . discriminate or cause any undue or unreasonable prejudice to any person.

QUESTIONS

1. Was Wally George discharged for just cause under the provisions of the collective agreement? Discuss.
2. Does it make any difference in this case that employee Wally George's activities and statements could reflect upon his employer as a public utility? If the company was not a public utility, would it make any difference? Discuss.
3. Evaluate the union's argument that Wally George's activities and beliefs were "neither illegal nor are they job-connected."
4. Are there any limits upon the right of an employee to join an outside organization which might adversely reflect upon the image or position of his employer? Discuss.

54. THE BOMB THREAT

COMPANY: *Goodyear Tire and Rubber Company, Dallas, Texas*

UNION: *Dallas General Drivers, Warehousemen and Helpers, International Brotherhood of Teamsters, Local 745*

BACKGROUND

At about 12:45 p.m. on July 8, 1970, the telephone operator at the Dallas plant of Goodyear Tire and Rubber Company received a bomb threat from an anonymous caller. The police were notified immediately, and arrived at about 1:20 p.m.

After conferring with the police and executives at company headquarters, management decided to evacuate all personnel before 2:30 p.m., the time the caller indicated that the bomb would detonate. Everyone was out of the plant by 2:00 p.m., and work was suspended for the day.

Subsequently, the company decided that the 50 warehouse employees who were covered by the contract with the union[1] should be paid for this day until 2:15 p.m. These employees had begun work at 8:00 a.m. and received pay for 5-3/4 hours. Four warehouse employees who had started work at 10:00 a.m. were paid for 3-3/4 hours. However, the 175 office employees who were not in the union were paid for the full day. The union filed a grievance alleging that the company had discriminated against the warehouse employees in paying them for only 5-3/4 hours (and 3-3/4 hours), rather than the full 8 hours on that day. The union also alleged that the company had discriminated against the warehouse employees, because the office employees were notified and evacuated somewhat earlier (about 20 minutes) than the warehouse employees. The union requested that the arbitrator require the company to pay the warehouse employees for the full 8 hours on July 8.

---

[1] See Appendix for pertinent contract provisions.

POSITION OF THE UNION

The union stated that no one at the Dallas plant could ever remember having been sent home early without receiving pay for the full day. The union argued that since office workers were paid for the full day, the company was acting discriminatorily in not also paying warehouse workers for the full eight hours.

The union further argued that the men were available and ready for work and that they were deprived of the opportunity to work through no fault of their own. The company voluntarily closed the plant. In fact, the union pointed out that the company had received a similar bomb threat a few days later but did not send the employees home. Finally, the union contended that the contract specifies "major mechanical breakdown, fire, flood, or similar conditions" as cause for nonpayment, but that it nowhere mentions voluntary closing of the plant by the company.

POSITION OF THE COMPANY

The company agreed that office personnel were evacuated from the plant somewhat sooner than warehouse personnel. However, the reason for this was not a result of dereliction or discrimination by the company, since supervisors of both groups began notifying their people at about the same time. Police and management agreed that it would be inadvisable to notify personnel by means of the public address system. It was feared that use of the public address system might create panic conditions and that it would probably fail to reach everyone, especially the warehouse workers. The office occupies about 10,000 square feet, while the warehouse occupies about 200,000 square feet. The delay in contacting some warehousemen was caused by the much greater physical space involved and the time required to contact everyone personally.

The company stated that the warehousemen were not paid eight hours pay for the day, because it followed the provisions of the contract which did not require them to do so. A telephone bomb threat by an anonymous caller is clearly a condition "beyond the control of the company"; hence it was not obliged to pay for the time not worked. Therefore, the grievance should be denied.

APPENDIX

Relevant portions of the agreement between the parties, signed 4 April 1969 follows:

Article IX, Section 2 (c).   Unless notified otherwise, an employee reporting for work on his regular scheduled shift will be given a minimum of four (4) hours pay at his regular rate except in cases of major mechanical breakdown, fire, flood, or similar conditions beyond the control of the Company. . . .

Article XXII, Section 4.   It is mutually agreed that this contract supersedes and negates any previous agreements, either written or oral, established by negotiation, contracts, force of law, mediation, or arbitration or otherwise, including but not limited to precedence and past practices, and incorporates all conditions of employment applicable to employees covered by this Agreement.

QUESTIONS

1. Did the company act discriminatorially against the union warehouse workers by not paying them for the full eight hours? Why, or why not?
2. Evaluate the union argument that the "men were available and ready to work and that they were deprived of the opportunity to work through no fault of their own."
3. Was a telephone bomb threat a condition "beyond the control of the company" as specified in Article IX of the agreement? If so, how can this be reconciled with the union argument that the company had "voluntarily closed the plant"?
4. Should blue-collar employees covered by a union agreement be treated any differently than white-collar personnel who are not represented by a labor union? Is there a difference between what a company is obligated to do under an agreement as compared to what it may wish to do from some other point of view? Discuss.

55. THE RELUCTANT RETIREE

COMPANY: Honneggers & Company, Inc., Indianola, Iowa

UNION: International Brotherhood of Teamsters, Chauffeurs, Warehousemen and Helpers of America, Local 90

BACKGROUND

The company raises, processes, and sells livestock and poultry, and retails livestock feed at its Indianola, Iowa plant. The production and maintenance employees and truck drivers were represented by the union since November, 1968.

Ralph Winkle[1] had been hired on March 31, 1960 as a truck driver, a position he held at the time of this case. Winkle reached his 65th birthday on June 17, 1970. At the end of May he was informed by the Operations Manager, Carl Souci, that the company had a policy of compulsory retirement at age 65 and that he would be retired as of June 30. However, Mr. Winkle did not wish to retire, and he filed a grievance, charging that his employment had been terminated without just cause. The union carried the grievance to arbitration. The union contended that there was no clause in the collective agreement requiring retirement at age 65, and it requested that Winkle be reinstated with full back pay and with full restoration of all rights and privileges, including seniority.

The history of the company's compulsory retirement policy dated back to 1958 when the company established its "Employees' Profit Sharing Plan", which was since amended on several occasions. This plan provided that a participant would retire upon attaining age 65, but he could remain in active service beyond that age if he was requested to do so by the company. The company's employees were not unionized at the time the plan was established. At the time of unionization in 1968, the agreement signed by the parties in that year was silent on the question of compulsory retirement.

In 1965, the company had issued a revised edition of its

---

[1] All names have been disguised.

"Employee Manual," which originally was issued in 1962. The 1965 edition stated that the normal retirement age was age 65, but it did not mention compulsory retirement. Late in 1968, the company requested that employees return the 1965 Employee Manual, because several policy matters outlined in it conflicted in part with various clauses of the new union negotiated agreement.

Ralph Winkle had participated in the Employees' Profit Sharing Plan, and upon his compulsory retirement he received a lump sum payment of $383.11 from the profit sharing trust. He received no further payments, since the company did not maintain a pension plan.

POSITION OF THE UNION

The union contended that Mr. Winkle was improperly terminated in violation of Articles V and XVI of the agreement.[2] The union claimed that at no time had anyone ever informed Winkle that there was a compulsory retirement age of 65 until shortly before he was terminated in June, 1970.

The union argued that Mr. Winkle had never received a copy of the original "Employee Manual" published in 1962. Winkle testified that he received only the revised 1965 version which referred only to a "normal" retirement at age 65 and which did not mention compulsory retirement. The union thus argued that Honneggers & Company did not have a formally established retirement policy which required employees to retire at age 65.

The union further pointed out that the collective bargaining agreement did not contain a "Management Rights Clause," and that Articles V and XVI referred only to "discharge for cause." The union argued that the company had made no claim that Mr. Winkle was either physically or mentally unfit to perform satisfactorily his duties as a truck driver. By forcing Winkle to retire even though Winkle was a healthy and capable employee, the company in effect had discharged him without sufficient cause. This violated the agreement.

Finally, the union contended that neither Winkle nor any other employee was aware that the company had a policy concerning a compulsory retirement age. At no time during the 1968 negotiations did the company inform the union that such a policy was in effect. In order to substantiate this point, Mr. John Coleman, the union president and business representative who represented the union in

---

[2] See Appendix to case.

negotiating the agreement, testified that he had never seen the "Employees' Profit Sharing Plan" until it was submitted by the company as an exhibit at the arbitration hearing. Mr. Horace Troutman, who participated in the negotiations on behalf of the company, corroborated Mr. Coleman's testimony. Coleman also testified that the question of compulsory retirement at age 65 was not discussed during negotiations.

The union submitted in evidence an affidavit, dated August 17, 1970, and signed by 15 active or former bargaining unit employees and the former plant manager of the Indianola plant, in which they stated that they "were not aware of any company policy which required retirement at age 65 by employees."

In summary, the union argued that the company had no cause for terminating the employment of Mr. Winkle under the provisions of the agreement, and that the company presented insufficient evidence to support its contention that there existed a long-established company policy of compulsory retirement understood and agreed to by employees.

POSITION OF THE COMPANY

The company contended that, in the absence of any provision in the collective agreement to the contrary, it had the right to follow its normal compulsory retirement policy. The company emphasized that the collective agreement placed no restrictions upon the company, and that the profit sharing plan in which Winkle participated prescribed a compulsory retirement at the age of 65 unless an employee was specifically requested to defer his retirement and consented to such request.

The company argued that, although the collective bargaining agreement did not say anything about compulsory retirement, this did not mean that management did not have the right to exercise its normal policy of retiring employees at age 65. Further, the company pointed out that, during negotiations with the union, compulsory retirement was not even brought up for discussion by the union. Since the union did not submit compulsory retirement as an important issue for discussion, the company asserted that it retained the right to terminate Mr. Winkle when he reached his 65th birthday.

The company pointed out that many years before the employees became unionized, the company had always distributed employee manuals which included information concerning its normal retirement policy to the employees. To further substantiate the fact that the company was following a consistent policy, the company pointed out that another employee, Mr. Philip Moreland, was also retired by the company at the Indianola plant upon his reaching age 65.

In concluding, the company argued that since compulsory retirement was not brought up for discussion during negotiations with the union, plus the fact that the agreement was silent on the issue of compulsory retirement, the company was justified in retiring Ralph Winkle as part of its consistent policy of compulsorily retiring employees at age 65. The grievance should be dismissed.

APPENDIX

Pertinent Provisions of the Agreement

Article V—Seniority

In case of layoff, if employee does not return to work when called back by registered letter to his last known address within one (1) week after the letter has been received by him, or within one (1) week after the letter has been sent, he shall lose his seniority rights. Seniority rights shall be lost by discharge for cause, transferring out of the unit without an express leave of absence, or voluntary quit.

Article XVI—Discharge

The employer shall not discharge any employee, except new employees during the first thirty (30) working days trial period, without just cause, and shall give at least one (1) warning notice of any complaint against such employee to the employee, in writing, and a copy of same to the Union, except that no warning notice needs to be given to an employee before he is discharged if the cause of such discharge is dishonesty, drunkenness, including the drinking of alcoholic beverages on the job . . . .

QUESTIONS

1. Did the company have the right to force employee Ralph Winkle to retire at age 65? Discuss.
2. Evaluate the union's argument that the agreement provided only for discharge for cause, and that by forcing Winkle to retire the company in effect had discharged him without sufficient cause.
3. If the agreement is silent on the issue of compulsory retirement, does the company retain the right to exercise its own policy forcing employees to retire at a specified age level? Why is this a very controversial area which preferably should be covered in a collective agreement?
4. What are the precedent implications of this case which go beyond the immediate problem of employee Ralph Winkle?

56. MUST THE COMPANY SELECT A FEMALE CREDIT TRAINEE?

COMPANY: Phillips Petroleum Company, Kansas City Sales Department

UNION: Phillips Petroleum Company Employees Union

BACKGROUND

Ms. Marian McPhee,[1] 24 years old, was hired by the Phillips Petroleum Company in its Kansas City office on January 17, 1967, as a "typist-transcriber," a salary grade-four position. She applied on six different occasions for higher grade jobs between that date and May 27, 1967. She was turned down the first five times because of lack of seniority; however, by May 27 she became the senior qualified bidder for the job of "steno-transcriber" in salary-grade five, and she was awarded the promotion.

Early in June, Ms. McPhee reenrolled on a part-time basis at the Metropolitan Junior College in Kansas City to continue her studies in a prebusiness curriculum.

On July 7, 1967, McPhee applied for an assignment to the training program in the position of "credit trainee." The company reviewed her application and denied her petition "for lack of qualifications." She again requested on August 14, 1967, that she be considered for assignment to the training position. The company again refused her request, and on August 24 she filed the following grievance.

August 24, 1967

"When I had my appraisal interview with my Supervisor Mr. Kay, he told me that I would start in the Typing Section, but that I could go as far as I wanted with Phillips Petroleum Company. Taking this into consideration, I started back to college.

Early in July, I requested by letter to Personnel Director Morton consideration for the Credit Training Program, which is necessary to be a Collection Analyst. On July 12, 1967, I was called to Mr. Morton's office, at which time I was informed I had been turned down for the following reasons:

---
[1] All names have been disguised.

1. I was on probation at Metropolitan Junior College and considered a sophomore at this time.

2. I was also told, by Mr. Morton, that I needed 60 hours and to raise my grade point average.

3. Mr. Morton went on to say that Phillips did not always hire men right off campus with only a "C" grade average.

4. Mr. Morton said that my low grades were all in business courses and not my art and science courses, which, I pointed out to him, was incorrect.

I explained to him that a "C" is known to be a decent grade from Metropolitan Junior College; it is often comparable to a "B" at other colleges. I thanked Mr. Morton for the interview and left. However, I decided I would like to have a written explanation of the reasons I was "turned down at this time", so I went back to Mr. Morton's office and requested one. I was advised by him that no one anywhere in the office receives such a letter.

After completing two hours credit this summer and receiving my grades on August 14, 1967, I once again requested permission to take this program.

On August 23, 1967, I was called to Mr. Terry Wilton's office (Mr. Wilton is doing Mr. Morton's work while he is on vacation). As I walked in I saw Mr. Bill Majill, who is directly over my immediate supervisor. Mr. Wilton told me again that I had been turned down because my grade points were too low and said that I was still on probation as far as Phillips was concerned. I showed him a letter from Mr. W. D. Hartley, Administrative Dean of Metropolitan Junior College, stating that I was not on probation. Then, finding that they could not disqualify me through college, Mr. Majill spoke up and said my production is low in Steno and I talk too much. He went on to say that my work is unsatisfactory and very poor. On several occasions I have been told that my production is low and that I talk too much, but so does everyone else. They want fifty letters a day and do not care about quality, – all they want is quantity. I am used to doing things right the first time they leave my desk. Mr. Majill said he wants only one thing, and this is fifty letters a day.

I feel that Phillips Petroleum Company is discriminating against me because of my sex, and they are using everything they can throw at me to keep me from qualifying for this training program.

Mr. Wilton on August 24, 1967 called me to his office. I asked the President of our Union, Mr. George Lang, to go with me, which he did. Mr. Wilton had a copy of our meeting between himself, Mr. Majill, and me, and wanted me to read it and initial it. Mr. Lang read it and asked Mr. Wilton if there was a copy of the first meeting between Mr. Morton and myself. He said there was and Mr. Lang requested to see it; but Mr. Wilton did not know where this copy was.

Mr. Lang advised me not to sign or initial this copy until I had read the first one. I also told Mr. Lang I did not like the way this copy was worded.

As you can see by the above paragraphs, I get one story from one person and another from the other person. I feel like they are playing "Merry-go-round" with me, because I am a girl. I am qualified for the Credit Trainee Program and am being discriminated against because of my sex and because I am at present an employee of the Phillips Petroleum Company.

I am filing this grievance because the employer refused to appoint me to the position of Credit Trainee.

Marian McPhee
First Floor Steno
Credit Card Division

The grievance eventually was carried to arbitration.

POSITION OF THE UNION

The union argued that since the company refused to appoint Marian McPhee to the position of credit trainee, even though she met the requirements for this position, the company had discriminated against her due to her sex and because she was at present an employee of the company.

The union pointed out that, in Spring of 1967, the company posted a notice to the effect that employees who had completed at least two years (60 units) of college courses in a prebusiness program would be eligible for consideration for the position credit trainee. Ms. McPhee had already satisfied this requirement by completing 61 unit hours of prebusiness study at Metropolitan Junior College in Kansas City. In fact, the company had encouraged her to complete this work by financing 75 per cent of her tuition costs. The 61 units had been completed prior to her filing the final application on August 14.

The union pointed out that Ms. McPhee had almost two years of successful work experience prior to her employment by Phillips. She had worked for ten months in the accounting section of a securities company; subsequently she was promoted from that position into the accounts receivable section of the securities firm where she worked for one year handling customer accounts and insurance claims.

The union objected to the introduction into the case by the company of two reports written by Ms. McPhee's immediate supervisor Mr. Kay. These appraisals claimed that her work performance was less than satisfactory; that she did not adapt well to the various duties assigned her; that she was a low volume producer; that she talked excessively; and that at least on one occasion she had used obscene language especially inappropriate for a woman in an office. The union pointed out that both reports had been written subject to McPhee's request for promotion on August 14. The union claimed that the appraisals were deliberately constructed and slanted to "build a case" against her appointment to the training program.

The union further alleged that since the company continually recruited candidates for the credit trainee program from universities, it was discriminating against Ms. McPhee because she was presently a Phillips employee and not a graduate of a four-year college or university.

The union charged that the company had shown a consistent pattern of sex discrimination by the fact that no woman had ever been appointed to the position of credit trainee in the Kansas City office since the program began there in 1961. This pattern of sexual discrimination directly was in violation of the Federal Civil Rights Act of 1964 and the Fair Employment Practices Act of the State of Missouri as well as being in direct violation of Article XIV, Paragraph 4 of the agreement.[2] The union cited testimony of Mr. Robert Mount, manager of the credit card division, who reported that 115 men—no women—had completed the credit trainee program since its inception. Of these 115, 45 occupied supervisory positions and 70 worked as credit card analysts, collection analysts, or assistants. The union argued that these latter positions were particularly suited for women employees and that there could be no reason to deny these positions to women other than that the company was reserving the position to train men for future higher level supervisory positions. The union asserted that the effect of the company's discriminatory practices was to place a barrier in the promotional path of women who wished to advance, since satisfactory completion of the credit trainee program was a prerequisite to any salary grade level beyond grade seven.

For all these reasons, the union urged that the arbitrator should order the company to offer the credit trainee position to Ms. Marian McPhee, and that the company should be ordered to cease its sexual discrimination against female employees in future selection from among credit trainee applicants.

POSITION OF THE COMPANY

The company argued that Ms. McPhee did not meet the company's standards for the credit trainee position.

The company stated that the sole purpose of the credit trainee position was to groom employees who possess considerable potential for advancement to more responsible positions in the finance and credit departments of the company, both in the Kansas City office and in various locations throughout the country. The company

[2] See Appendix to case.

argued that since the training program was such an important source of supervisory talent, it must retain exclusive control over the selection and appointment of persons to the program.

The company cited Article II, Management Functions, and Article X, Sections 2 and 7, to support its right to exercise exclusive control over appointment to the program. Article II, it contended, clearly states that all rights held by the company prior to the time that the union became the bargaining representative were retained by the company except in those matters expressly limited by the collective agreement. The company had never bargained away or restricted its right to assign whomever it wished to the position of credit trainee.

The company further claimed exclusive jurisdiction over the Credit Trainee program by referring to Article X, Section 7. It argued that the language is clear and to the point-that is, jobs specifically designed for training purposes, including credit trainee, are not regular full-time vacancies and shall be filled by assignment. The selection of candidates was left to the sole discretion of management.

The company also cited Article X, Section 2, to support its right to maintain unilateral control over the credit trainee position. This provision outlines the job-bidding procedure for positions, except for jobs specifically excluded in Section 7. Management claimed that the union here was attempting to gain through arbitration something it was unable to obtain through negotiation.

According to the company, the educational requirements indicated in the posted notice of Spring, 1967, were only the minimum acceptable educational requirements for acceptance into the credit trainee program. These minimum educational requirements could in no way be construed to mean that all persons who possess them automatically would be taken into a training position. These minimum requirements were posted to inform present employees that workers with less than a college degree would be considered for acceptance if they were qualified in other ways. However, the minimum requirements listed in the notice dealt only with education; they did not include the many other factors which are considered. In fact, the notice stated that these were "minimum requirements".

The company denied that it had acted discriminatorily towards Ms. McPhee or any other employee because of their sex or present employee status. In the past, women had been considered for the credit trainee position, but none of the female applicants was found acceptable. Management representatives pointed out that, in their opinion, many features of the job made it unattractive to women: extensive travel, frequent geographical relocations, long hours, and occasional abusive language from customers. As a consequence, few women applied for the position. If, however, a female with genuine interest in the position, and with qualifications to succeed in this and related higher-level jobs, should apply, she would be given an opportunity to enter the program. However, this decision must remain with management.

The company stressed that past experiences indicated that college graduates with a specialization in finance or accounting had been the most successful trainees. However, the company wanted to leave "the door open" to outstanding employees who, through personal development, experience, and desire, could substitute other qualities for the college degree.

The company responded to the union's charge that 70 graduates from the program were engaged essentially in clerical work especially suited to women by stating that not all graduates were promoted immediately to managerial positions. The jobs of assistant collection analyst, collection analyst and credit analyst were excellent training positions for promotion into management jobs.

Finally, the company argued that Ms. McPhee was not appointed to the credit trainee position because she simply was not qualified. Mr. Mount testified that the areas considered by him in selecting credit trainees included education, past work performance, ability to work with peers and superiors, quality and quantity of output, maturity in accepting responsibility, ability to handle more responsible assignments, willingness to travel and ability to meet people, including dealers, jobbers and the public. In his opinion, Ms. McPhee was found lacking in certain respects in most of these areas.

For all of the above reasons, the company urged that the grievance be denied.

APPENDIX

Provisions of the Collective Agreement between the Phillips Petroleum Company and the Phillips Petroleum Company Employees Union

Article II—Management Functions

All the rights, power and authority had by the Company prior to the time the Union became the bargaining agent, are specifically retained hereunder by the Company except to the extent that they are expressly limited by specific provision of this Agreement.

Article X – Promotions, Demotions, Transfers, Layoffs, Terminations and Re-employment

Section 2. Promotions. Job vacancies, as determined by the Company, which are to be filled on a regular full-time basis by promotion, shall be posted for bids for three full working days. Employees desiring to bid on such jobs shall file a written request with the Personnel Office within said three-day period. Promotions will be based on seniority and qualifications, the senior employee that is qualified being given preference. Until a successful bidder is determined and assigned to such a job vacancy, it may be filled by assignment. Where there are no qualified eligible employees bidding on job vacancies, such job vacancies may be filled by hiring from the outside or from any other source. Regularity of attendance shall be a factor in determining qualifications. Where it is not known how long a temporary vacancy will exist, it may be filled temporarily up to sixty (60) calendar days. If the vacancy is still filled on a temporary basis at the expiration of sixty (60) days, it will be posted as specified above.

In the event of promotion as provided in this section, there will be a probationary period of thirty (30) days. If at any time during said period the employee shall be determined to be unsatisfactory, he will be notified accordingly and may be returned to his previous classification at any time during the probation period.

Section 7. It is understood and agreed that jobs specifically for training purposes and carrying the title of Credit Trainee, Graduate Business Trainee, and Division Office Trainee, are not regular full-time job vacancies and shall be filled by assignment. Any employee desiring to be considered for one of these training positions shall notify the Personnel Office in writing. The Company agrees to give every consideration to anyone who so applies. A notice stating that employees may apply for these positions and outlining how they can apply, will be permanently posted on bulletin boards.

Article XIV–Miscellaneous

Section 4. There shall be no discrimination because of race, sex, national origin, creed or color or because of membership or non-membership in the Union.

Relevant Sections of the Civil Rights Act of 1964

Section 703 (a) of the Civil Rights Act of 1964, 42 U.S.C. 2000e-2(a) provides:

(a) It shall be an unlawful employment practice for an employer—

(1) to fail or refuse to hire or to discharge any individual or otherwise to discriminate against any individual with respect to his compensation, terms, conditions or privileges of employment, because of such individual's race, color, religion, sex, or national origin; or

(2) to limit, segregate, or classify his employees in any way which would deprive

or tend to deprive any individual of employment opportunities or otherwise adversely affect his status as an employee, because of such individual's race, color, religion, sex, or national origin.

Relevant Sections of the Missouri Revised Statutes, entitled the Missouri Fair Employment Practices Act, Sections 297.010 - 296.070

It shall be an unlawful employment practice:

(1) For an employer, because of the race, creed, color, religion, national origin, sex, or ancestry of any individual:

. . . .

(b) To limit, segregate, or classify his employees in any way which would deprive or tend to deprive any individual of employment opportunities or otherwise adversely affect his status as an employee, because of such individual's race, creed, color, religion, national origin, sex, or ancestry.

QUESTIONS

1. Evaluate each of the arguments presented by the union on behalf of Marian McPhee. Could the union have filed sexual discrimination charges against the company under the Equal Employment Opportunity Act? Discuss.
2. Evaluate each of the company arguments in denying Marian McPhee's petition for the credit training program.
3. Under the agreement, did the company have sole discretion to select candidates for the credit training position? Why, or why not?
4. Under the affirmative action program of the Equal Employment Opportunity Commission, how might the company be considered in violation of the Civil Rights Act in this type of situation even though an arbitrator might uphold management in this specific case? Discuss.

57. CAN THE COMPANY ELIMINATE THE QUATROPULPER HELPER'S JOB?

COMPANY: Ethyl Corporation, Oxford Paper Company Division, West Carrollton, Ohio

UNION: United Papermakers and Paperworkers, Local 19.

BACKGROUND

On August 5, 1970, the company notified the union that it was putting into effect a new "quatropulper operator" job description. In its notice to the union, the company expressed a desire "to continue our discussions regarding the job description," but the company also stated in its notice that meetings had been held on August 3 and August 4 without the parties making "any significant progress regarding the listing of duties for this job."

As a result of the company action, the various duties defined in the job description of the "quatropulper helper" were combined with that of the quatropulper operator, and the lesser job was eliminated. The two former job classifications appeared in a section on "Job Classifications & Rates" in the labor agreement. A comparison of these two job descriptions indicated that a new number 7 was added to the duties of the quatropulper operator: "Brings dry stock from storage room to Quatropupler by means of a hand or power truck as required by order specifications." This was item No. 1 in the description of the helper's duties, and his other requirements were mainly to "assist" the operator in each category of their overlapping duties.[1]

The union filed a grievance protesting management's action in eliminating the quatropulper helper's job. The grievance ultimately was carried to arbitration.

---

[1] See Appendix for various job descriptions.

POSITION OF THE UNION

The union contended that the jobs of the quatropulper operator and quatropulper helper had not changed to the degree that the company could load one man, the operator, with two jobs. The union insisted that during the last 13 years there had not been any significant changes in these jobs.

The union introduced two witnesses with respectively 24 years' seniority and 13 years' seniority working on the quatropulper.[2] These witnesses stated that no significant job changes had been made in the last 13 years, that there was no physical relocation of equipment, and no introduction of automation. The only change which they noted over the years was that currently production of some 600 feet per minute was achieved, whereas ten years ago it was 400 feet per minute.

It was the union's position that the company completely abolished a job of 13 years' duration solely on the basis of its view of the economics involved. Yet, under Article XI, Section A of the agreement,[3] the company could not unilaterally change or abolish a job unless there was a significant change in job content. This was not the case with the operator's and helper's jobs.

Further, according to the union, the requirements of Article XI offset Article VI, the Management Rights Clause, and negotiation was required before a job could be abolished. If the company could abolish this job of helper, said the union, it could nullify any job and any job description in the agreement. According to the union, this would have the effect of undermining all jobs.

In summary, the union claimed that the arbitrator should uphold the union grievance by ordering reinstatement of the quatropulper helper's job classification and ordering the company to negotiate any proposed changes with the union. The union emphasized that this was exactly what the contract required. However, counsel for the union also stated as follows: "If by any miracle the award goes to the Company, the Union wishes the Arbitrator to retain jurisdiction for the determination of an equitable rate for the new combined job decription of Quatropulper Operator."

---

[2] The quatropulper is a large machine which is used to make paper pulp. It contains a tile tank with dimensions of a 12 foot diameter and 15 foot depth; several impellers churn and beat sheets of pulpwood and chemical additives such as clay, alum and titanium. The quatropulper mixes these raw materials into a slush with a proper consistency which then is pumped to the machines which actually manufacture the paper.

[3] See Appendix for applicable provisions.

POSITION OF THE COMPANY

The company basically argued that it was justified under the agreement in eliminating the quatropulper's helper's job because of: (1) significant changes in job requirements, and (2) economic necessities.

Company witnesses insisted that "substantial" changes had been made in the job of quatropulper operator by the elimination of the necessity for putting shavings into the quatropulper, a reduction in bag size for ingredients from 100 to 50 pounds so that they could be handled easily by one man, and by the installation of a so-called "probe" which senses the approach of the pulp mixture to the full point so that it was not necessary any longer for the operator to maintain constant surveillance to avoid an overflow.

According to company testimony, the change followed a thorough job study of the two old jobs indicating that the "incumbents of each" spent approximately 85 percent "waiting time" and only 15 percent "actual physical activity." Job studies since the change indicated 70 percent "waiting time" and only 30 percent "physical activity" for the remaining operator. The combined job was in no way too much work for one man to handle.

The company introduced considerable testimony indicating that the change was necessary in the interest of the plant maintaining a "competitive position in the market." Company witnesses expressed concern that it might be necessary to close this plant in the manner that the company's very old operation, in Lawrence, Massachusetts, recently was shut down. According to the company, the Management Rights Clause (Article VI) and the Declaration of Principles Clause (Article I) vested in management the responsibility to make those decisions which were required by economic necessity to promote efficient operation.

In support of its position, the company cited a number of decisions by other arbitrators for their persuasive effect in stating the principles which the company said should govern the case here. In a case at Edition Book Binders of N.Y., Inc., the arbitrator found that there was no contract provision fixing the crew compliment of any machine; that, said the company, was the situation here. An arbitrator held in a Georgia-Pacific Corporation case that under a broad management rights clause, such as that which existed in this instance, the company had the right to eliminate lower rated jobs and to reassign them for reasons of economy and protection of its economic position. The company further cited the award of an arbitrator at International Salt Company. The arbitrator held that, where there is no provision in the contract forbidding it, an employer may unilaterally eliminate employees or vary crew size, provided that it is not capricious or arbitrary but is based on legitimate operation requirements. Finally, the company cited a case at the Lone Star Brewing Co. where the arbitrator ruled to the effect that the reduction of a two-man crew did not result in an "unreasonable" increase in the burden of other employees' job duties and therefore the reduction was sustained.

The company argued that all of these cases and other similar rulings of arbitrators supported the company's position in this case. The company claimed that the union's grievance was therefore without merit, and it should be denied.

APPENDIX

Pertinent Job Descriptions

1. Quatropulper Operator (prior to August 5, 1970).

Duties

Under the supervision of the Beater Department Foreman, Night Superintendent and Colorman, is responsible for the operation of a Quatropulper, pumps, and auxiliary equipment in the preparation of furnish for making paper.

Specific Duties:
1. Mixes, beats and hydrates pulp, broke, and other ingredients in Quatropulper to prepare furnish.
2. Charges Quatropulper with pulp, broke, book stock, mill bleach, fillers, size, alum, special chemical, and other ingredients as may be required by order specifications.
3. Operates pumps, valves, etc., to insure proper hydration and stock consistency.
4. Pumps furnish to storage chests and regulates agitators to maintain consistency.
5. Keeps record of all material used in accordance with instructions.
6. Cleans Quatropulper and other operating equipment as needed.
7. Cooperates to promote good housekeeping and safety within the department.
8. Performs, when assigned by his foreman or by the superintendent under whose jurisdiction the department falls, such temporary duties that are related to the job covered by this description, and such other temporary duties that are necessary for orderly operation of the mill when such work results from an emergency or an unusual temporary situation.

2. Quatropulper Helper (prior to August 5, 1970).

Duties

Under the supervision of the Beater Department Foreman, Night Superintendent and Colorman, assists the Quatropulper Operator in the preparation of furnish for making paper.

Specific Duties:
1. Brings dry stock from storage room to Quatropulper by means of a hand or power truck as required by order specifications.
2. Assists in charging Quatropulper with stock and broke according to order specifications.
3. Assists Operator in handling bagged material from storage and into Quatropulper.
4. Assists Operator in washing up on shut downs.
5. Assists Operator in cleaning up Quatropulper and other operating equipment as needed.
6. Assists Operator in addition of mill bleach and book stock as necessary.
7. Cooperates to promote good housekeeping and safety within the department.
8. Performs, when assigned by his foreman or by the superintendent under whose jurisdiction the department falls, such temporary duties that are necessary for orderly operation of the mill when such work results from an emergency or an unusual temporary situation.

3. Quatropulper Operator (after August 5, 1970).

Duties

Under the supervision of the Beater Department Foreman, Night Superintendent and Colorman, is responsible for the operation of a Quatropulper, pumps, and auxiliary equipment in the preparation of furnish for making paper.

Specific Duties:
1. Mixes, beats and hydrates pulp, broke and other ingredients in Quatropulper to prepare furnish.
2. Charges Quatropulper with pulp, broke, book stock, mill bleach, fillers, size, alum, special chemicals and other ingredients as may be required by order specifications.
3. Operates pumps, valves, etc., to insure proper hydration and stock consistency.
4. Pumps furnish to storage chests and regulates agitators to maintain consistency.
5. Keeps record of all material used in accordance with instructions.

6. Cleans Quatropulper and other operating equipment as needed.
7. Brings dry stock from storage room to Quatropulper by means of a hand or power truck as required by order specifications.
8. Cooperates to promote good housekeeping and safety within the department.
9. Performs, when assigned by his foreman or by the superintendent under whose jurisdiction the department falls, such temporary duties that are related to the job covered by this description, and such other temporary duties that are necessary for orderly operation of the mill when such work results from an emergency or an unusual temporary situation.

Pertinent Contract Provisions

Article I—Declaration of Principles
Section A. It is in the mutual interest of the employer and employee to provide for the operation of the Plant hereinafter mentioned, under methods which will further, to the fullest extent possible, the economic welfare of the Company and its employees, . . . economy of operation, quality and quantity of output, . . .

Section B. It is recognized by the Agreement to be the duty of the Company and the Union and the employees to cooperate fully for the advancement of said conditions.

Article VI—Management
Section A. The management of the work and the direction of the working forces including the right to hire, promote, suspend or discharge for proper cause, or transfer, and the rights to relieve employees from duty because of lack of work or for other legitimate reasons, is vested exclusively in the Company. . . .

Article XI—Wages
Section A. The Job Evaluation and Job Descriptions agreed upon in writing between the parties on August 27, 1953, and amended through October 4, 1970, shall remain the basis of Job Evaluations and Job Descriptions for all present and any new jobs in this Plant. It is understood and agreed that future claims of job inequalities will not be made unless there has been a permanent change in job content sufficient to warrant a re-evaluation of the job.

QUESTIONS

1. Based upon the information in the case, had there been significant changes in job content of such a type and magnitude which required bargaining with the union over this issue? Discuss.

2. Evaluate the argument of the union that if the company could abolish the job of helper, it could "nullify any job description in the agreement." Why is this a very sensitive issue to a labor union?
3. Does company management have the right to eliminate a job because of economic necessities under the provisions in this contract?
4. Why did the company cite a number of parallel decisions in support of its position? Is an arbitrator obligated to consider parallel cases in reaching his decision in this case? Discuss.